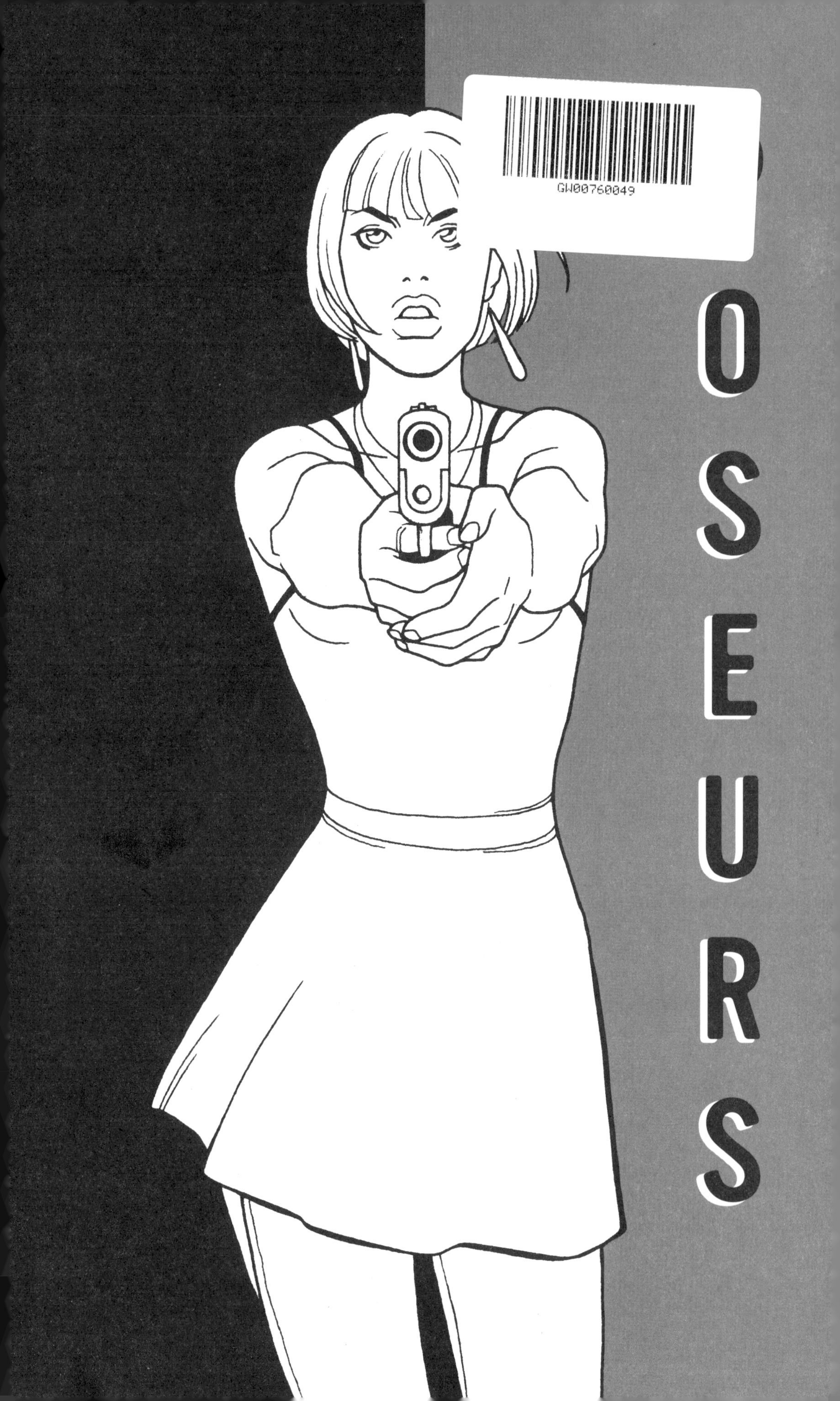
OSEURS

Written and Art Directed by
Deborah Vankin

Illustrated by
Rick Mays

Lettering by
Robert Clark, Jr.
Clem Robins
and **Drew Gill**

Cover art by
Rick Mays

Cover design by
Laila Derakhshanian

Production and additional
editing/design by **Drew Gill**

IMAGE COMICS, INC.
Robert Kirkman - chief operating officer
Erik Larsen - chief financial officer
Todd McFarlane - president
Marc Silvestri - chief executive officer
Jim Valentino - vice-president

Eric Stephenson - publisher
Todd Martinez - sales & licensing coordinator
Sarah deLaine - pr & marketing coordinator
Branwyn Bigglestone - accounts manager
Emily Miller - administrative assistant
Tyler Shainline - production manager
Drew Gill - art director
Jonathan Chan - senior production artist
Monica Howard - production artist
Vincent Kukua - production artist
Kevin Yuen - production artist
Jana Cook - production artist
www.imagecomics.com

ISBN: 978-1-60706-358-2

POSEURS
First printing
April 2011

Published by Image Comics, Inc. Office of publication:
2134 Allston Way, 2nd Floor, Berkeley, CA 94704

Printed in South Korea

International Rights Representative:
Christine Meyer – christine@gfloystudio.com

PROLOGUE

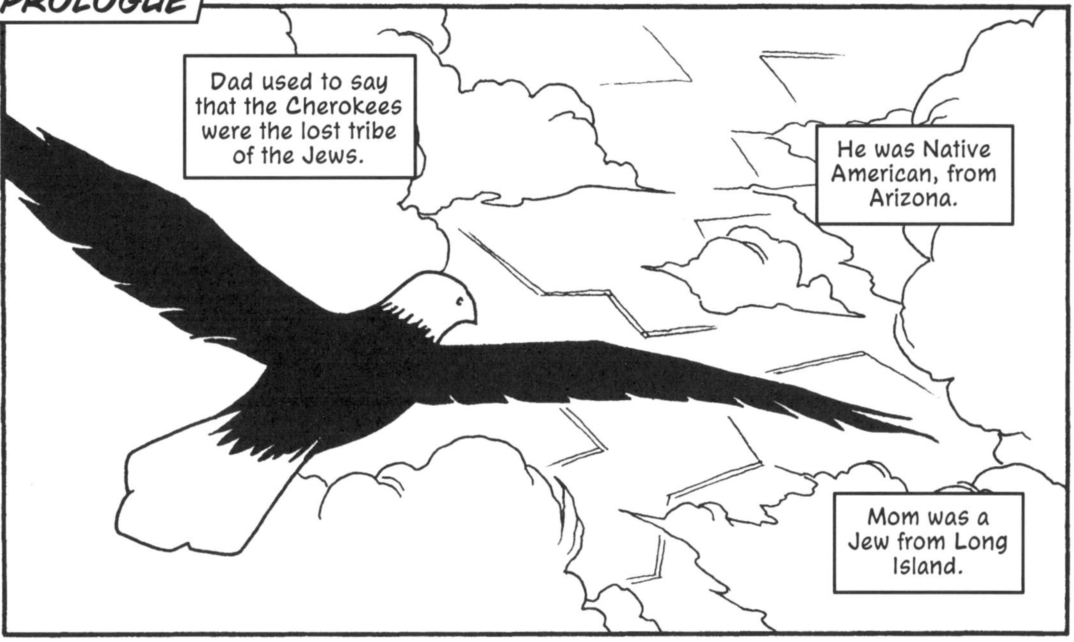
Dad used to say that the Cherokees were the lost tribe of the Jews.
He was Native American, from Arizona.
Mom was a Jew from Long Island.

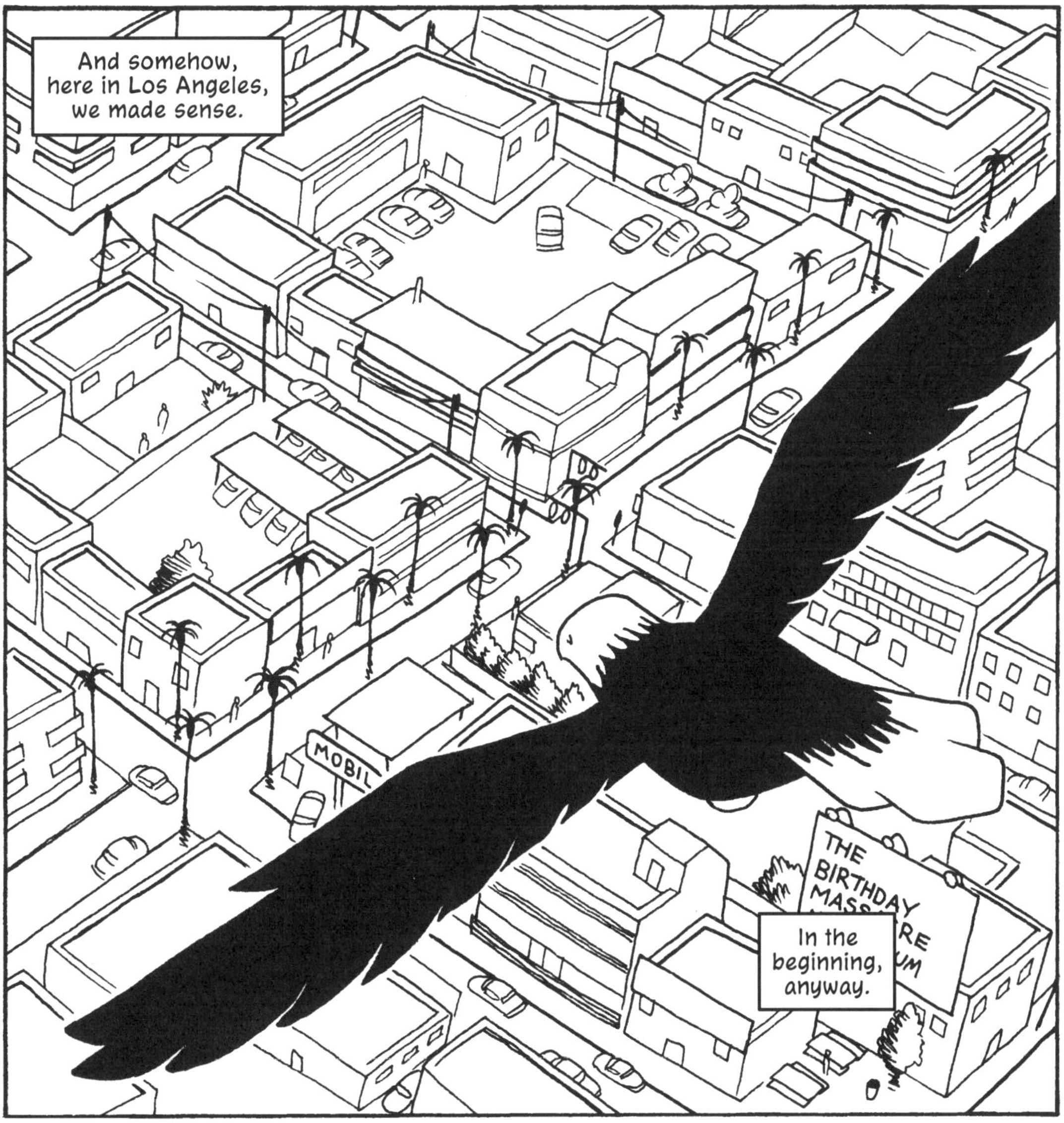
And somehow, here in Los Angeles, we made sense.
MOBIL
THE BIRTHDAY
In the beginning, anyway.

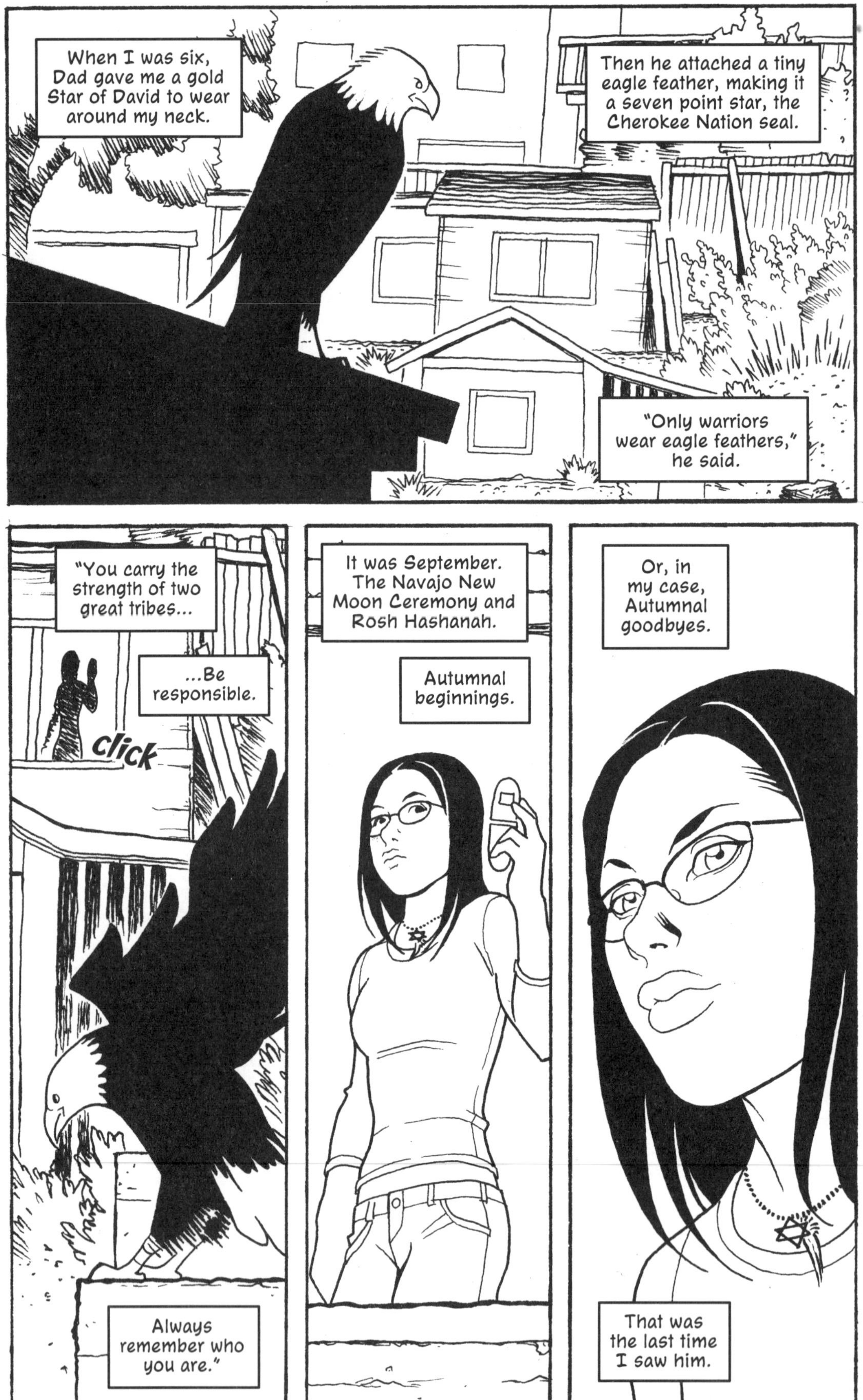
When I was six, Dad gave me a gold Star of David to wear around my neck.
Then he attached a tiny eagle feather, making it a seven point star, the Cherokee Nation seal.
"Only warriors wear eagle feathers," he said.
"You carry the strength of two great tribes...
...Be responsible.
CLICK
Always remember who you are."
It was September. The Navajo New Moon Ceremony and Rosh Hashanah.
Autumnal beginnings.
Or, in my case, Autumnal goodbyes.
That was the last time I saw him.

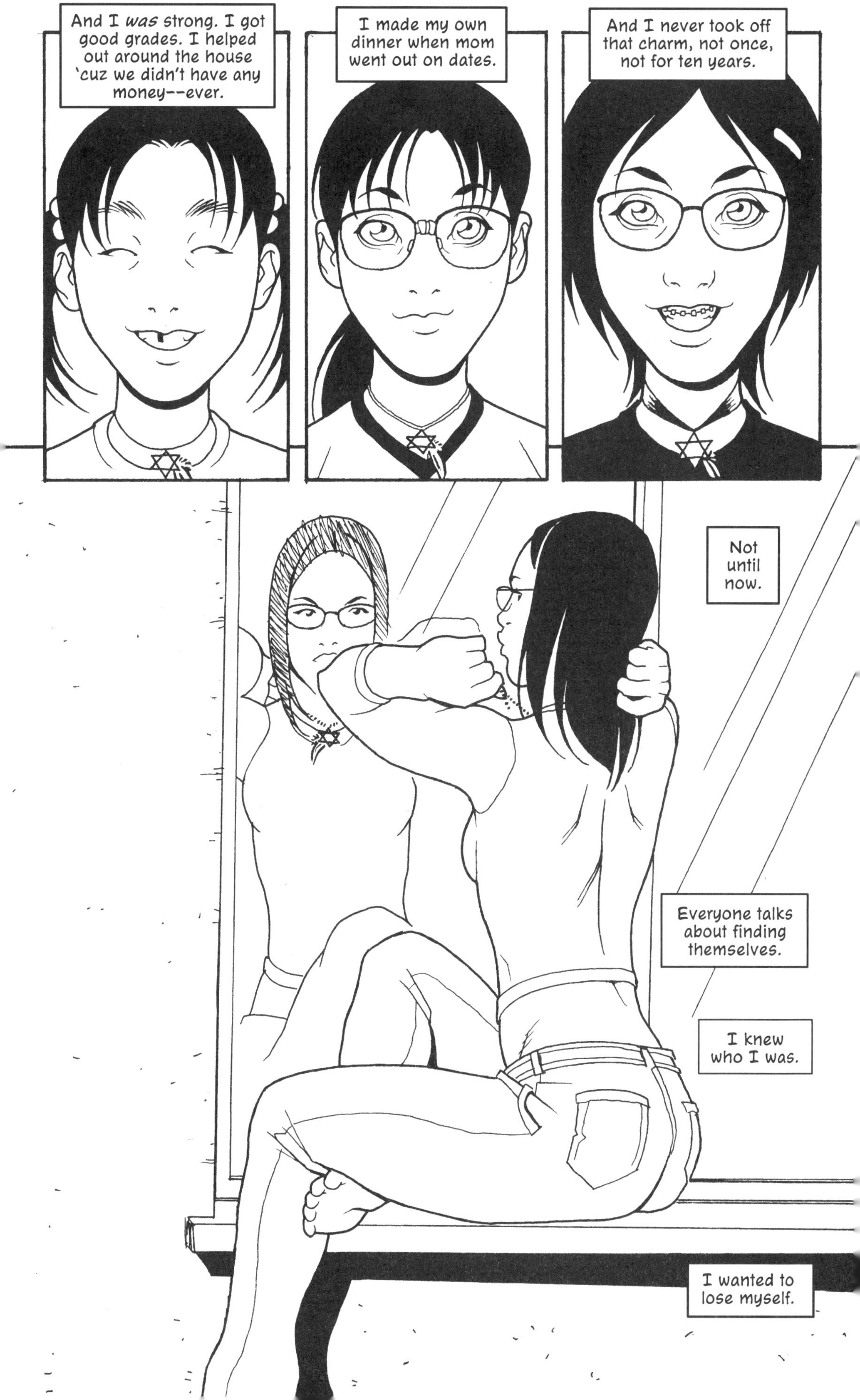

And I *was* strong. I got good grades. I helped out around the house 'cuz we didn't have any money--ever.
I made my own dinner when mom went out on dates.
And I never took off that charm, not once, not for ten years.
Not until now.
Everyone talks about finding themselves.
I knew who I was.
I wanted to lose myself.

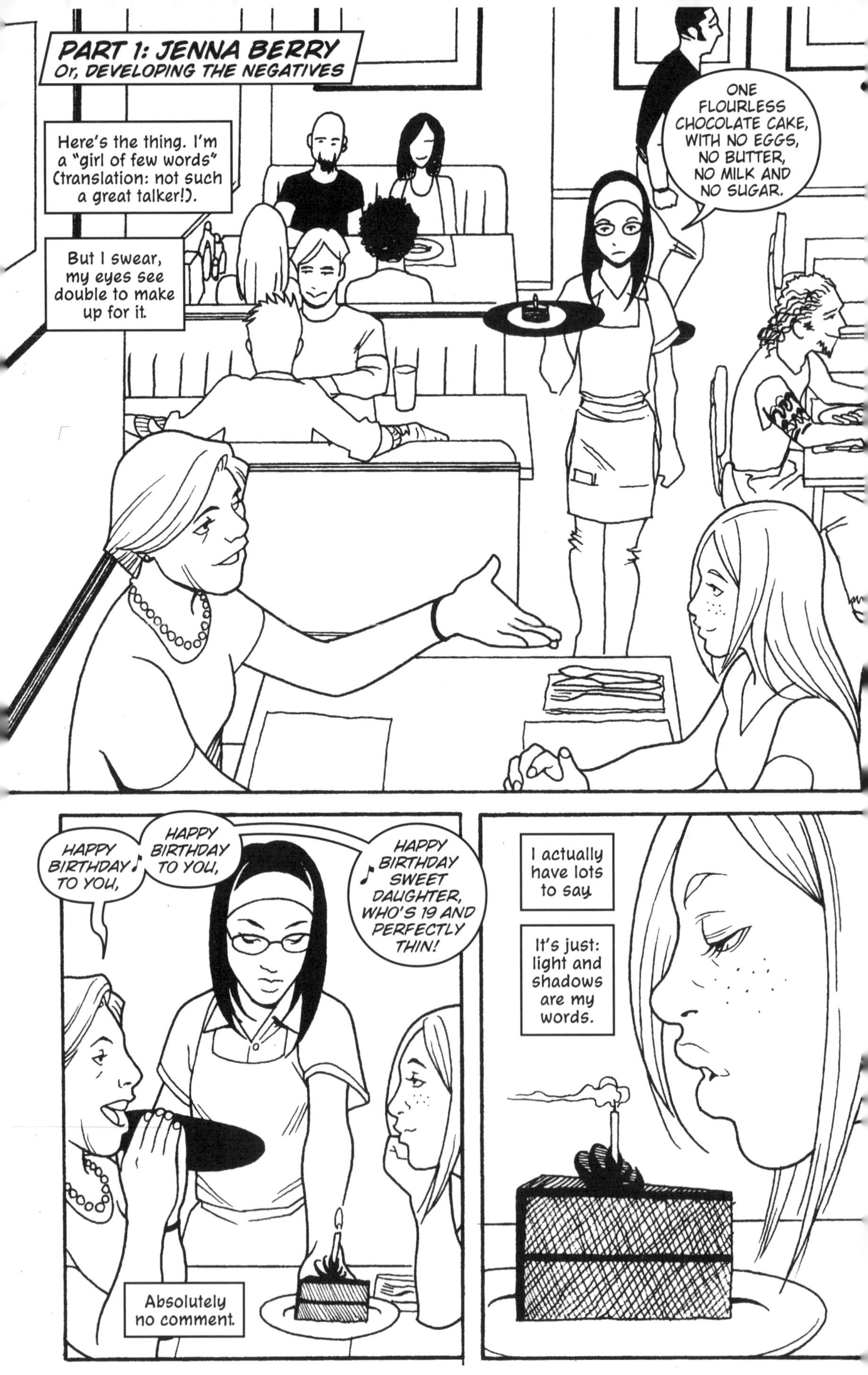
PART 1: JENNA BERRY
Or, DEVELOPING THE NEGATIVES
Here's the thing. I'm a "girl of few words" (translation: not such a great talker!).
But I swear, my eyes see double to make up for it.
ONE FLOURLESS CHOCOLATE CAKE, WITH NO EGGS, NO BUTTER, NO MILK AND NO SUGAR.
HAPPY BIRTHDAY TO YOU,
HAPPY BIRTHDAY TO YOU,
HAPPY BIRTHDAY SWEET DAUGHTER, WHO'S 19 AND PERFECTLY THIN!
Absolutely no comment.
I actually have lots to say.
It's just: light and shadows are my words.

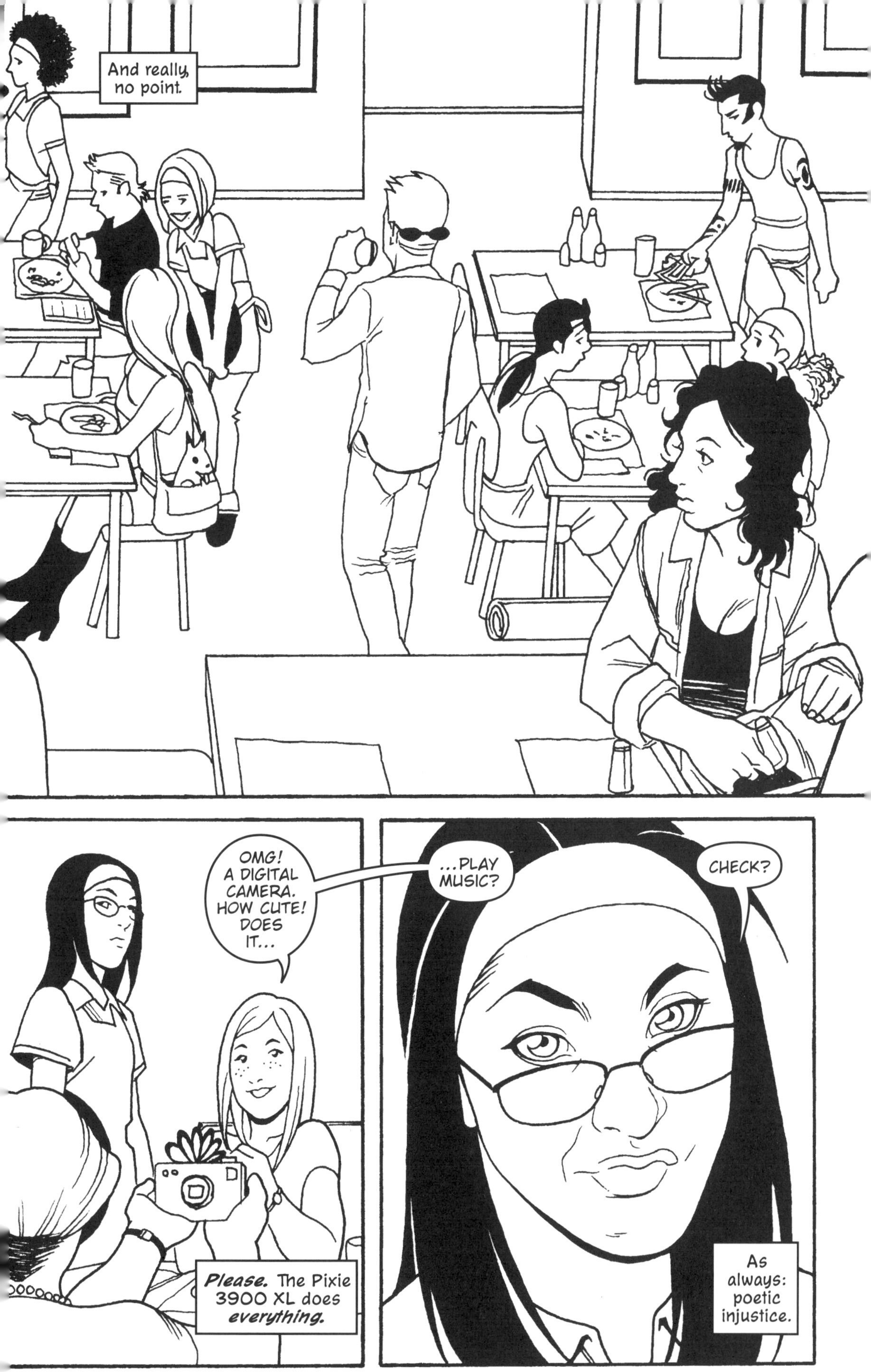
And really, no point.
OMG! A DIGITAL CAMERA. HOW CUTE! DOES IT...
...PLAY MUSIC?
Please. The Pixie 3900 XL does everything.
CHECK?
As always: poetic injustice.

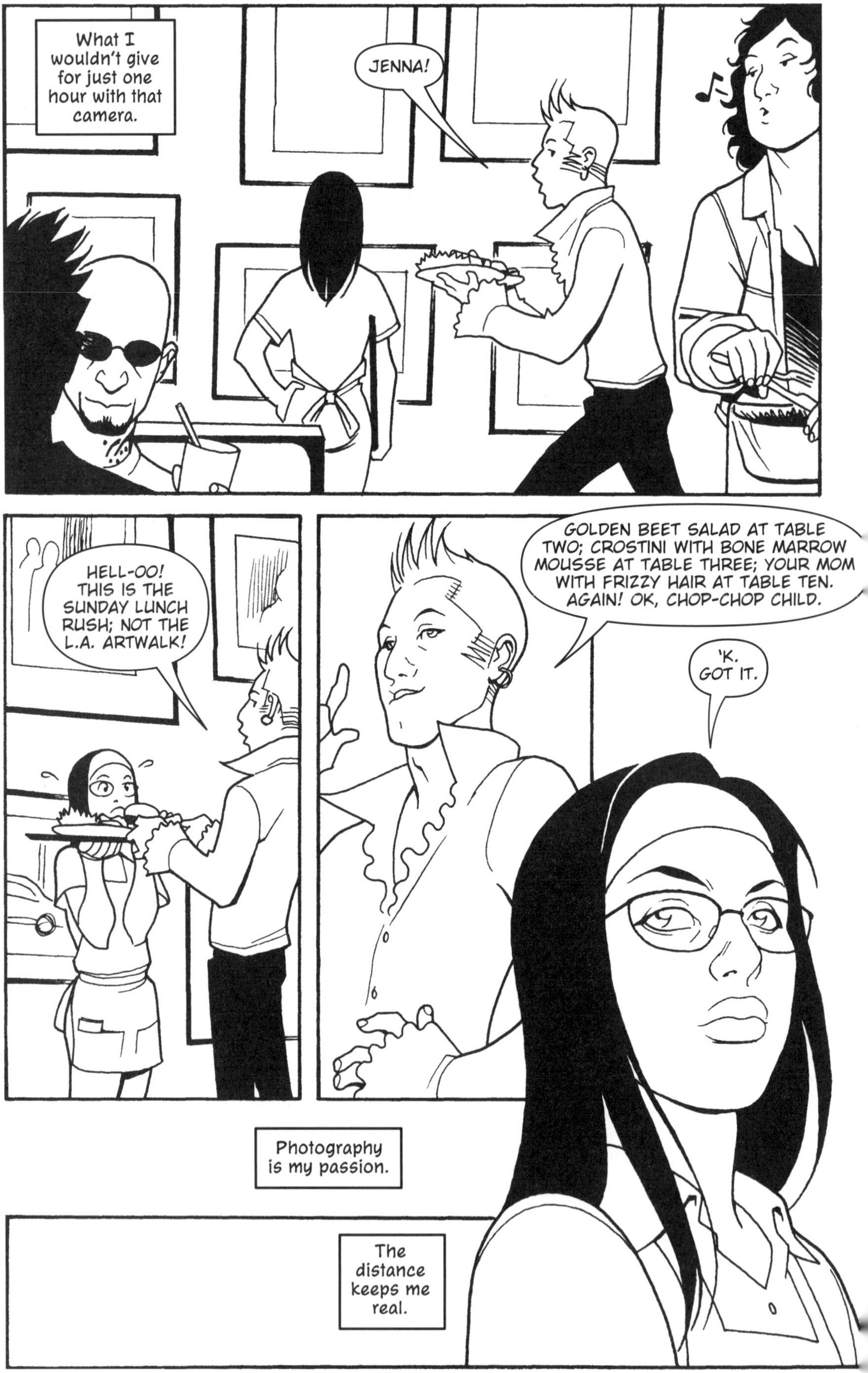

What I wouldn't give for just one hour with that camera.
JENNA!
HELL-OO! THIS IS THE SUNDAY LUNCH RUSH; NOT THE L.A. ARTWALK!
GOLDEN BEET SALAD AT TABLE TWO; CROSTINI WITH BONE MARROW MOUSSE AT TABLE THREE; YOUR MOM WITH FRIZZY HAIR AT TABLE TEN. AGAIN! OK, CHOP-CHOP CHILD.
'K. GOT IT.
Photography is my passion.
The distance keeps me real.

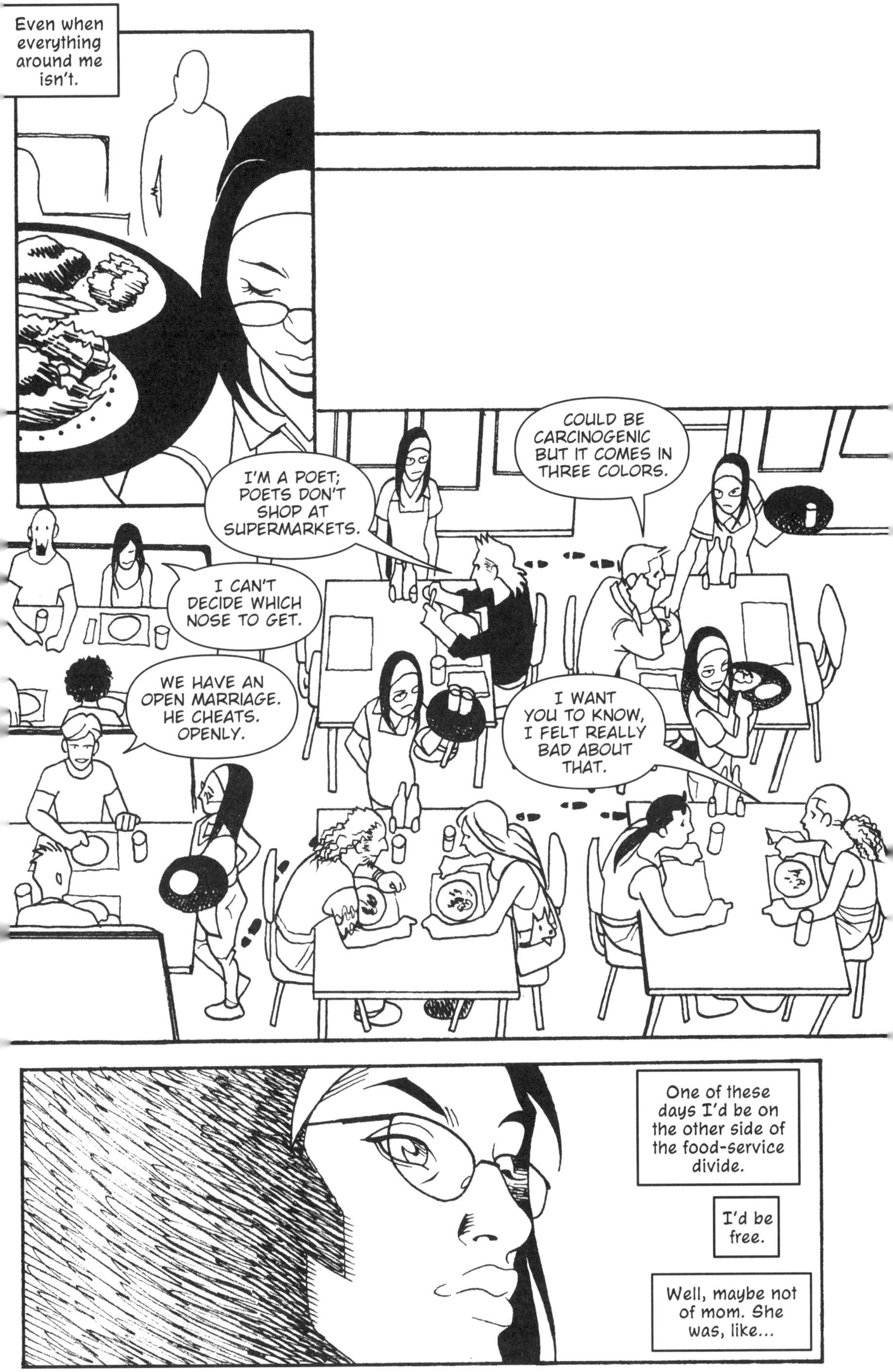
Even when everything around me isn't.
I'M A POET; POETS DON'T SHOP AT SUPERMARKETS.
COULD BE CARCINOGENIC BUT IT COMES IN THREE COLORS.
I CAN'T DECIDE WHICH NOSE TO GET.
WE HAVE AN OPEN MARRIAGE. HE CHEATS. OPENLY.
I WANT YOU TO KNOW, I FELT REALLY BAD ABOUT THAT.
One of these days I'd be on the other side of the food-service divide.
I'd be free.
Well, maybe not of mom. She was, like...

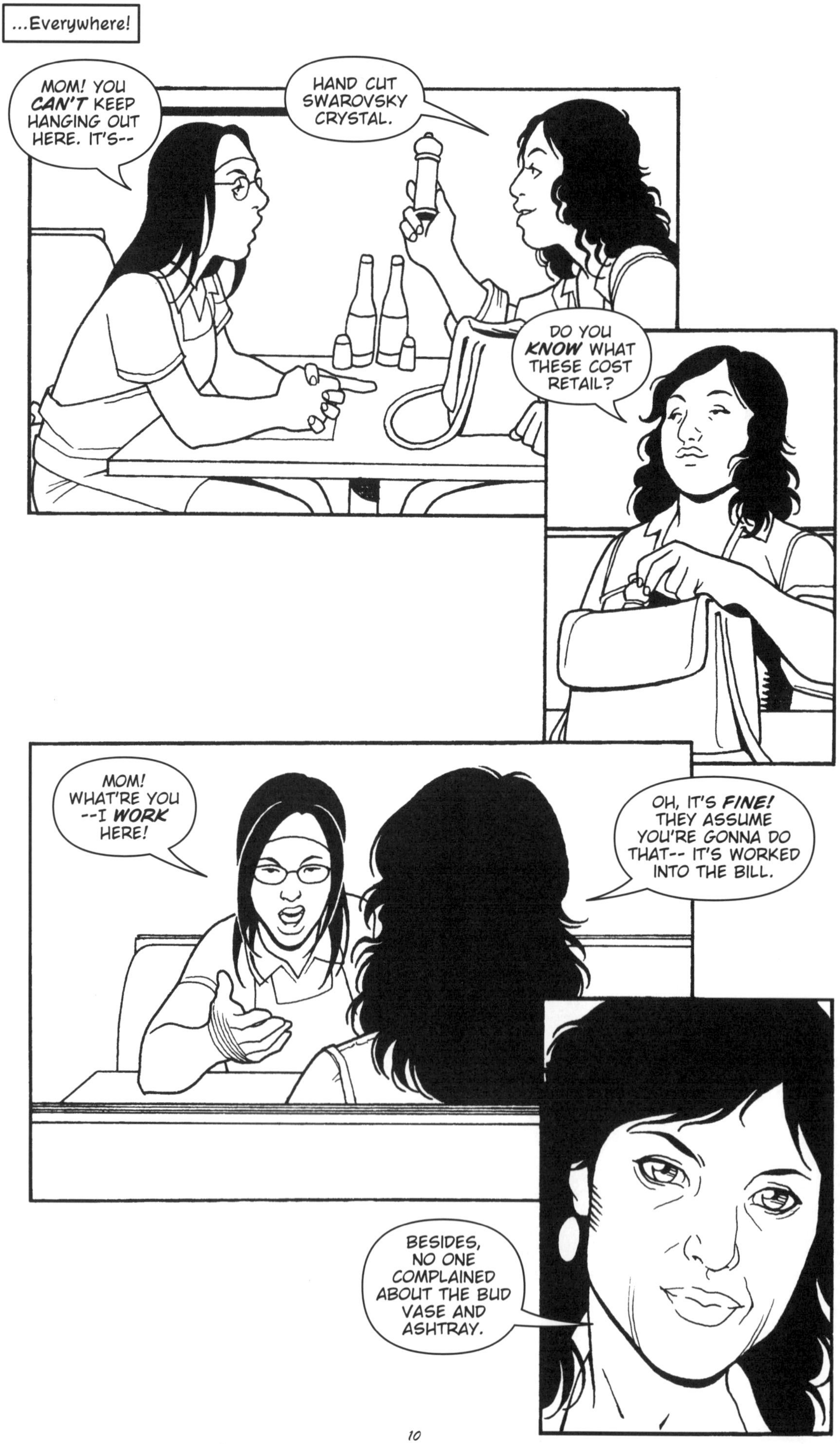
...Everywhere!
MOM! YOU CAN'T KEEP HANGING OUT HERE. IT'S--
HAND CUT SWAROVSKY CRYSTAL.
DO YOU KNOW WHAT THESE COST RETAIL?
MOM! WHAT'RE YOU --I WORK HERE!
OH, IT'S FINE! THEY ASSUME YOU'RE GONNA DO THAT-- IT'S WORKED INTO THE BILL.
BESIDES, NO ONE COMPLAINED ABOUT THE BUD VASE AND ASHTRAY.

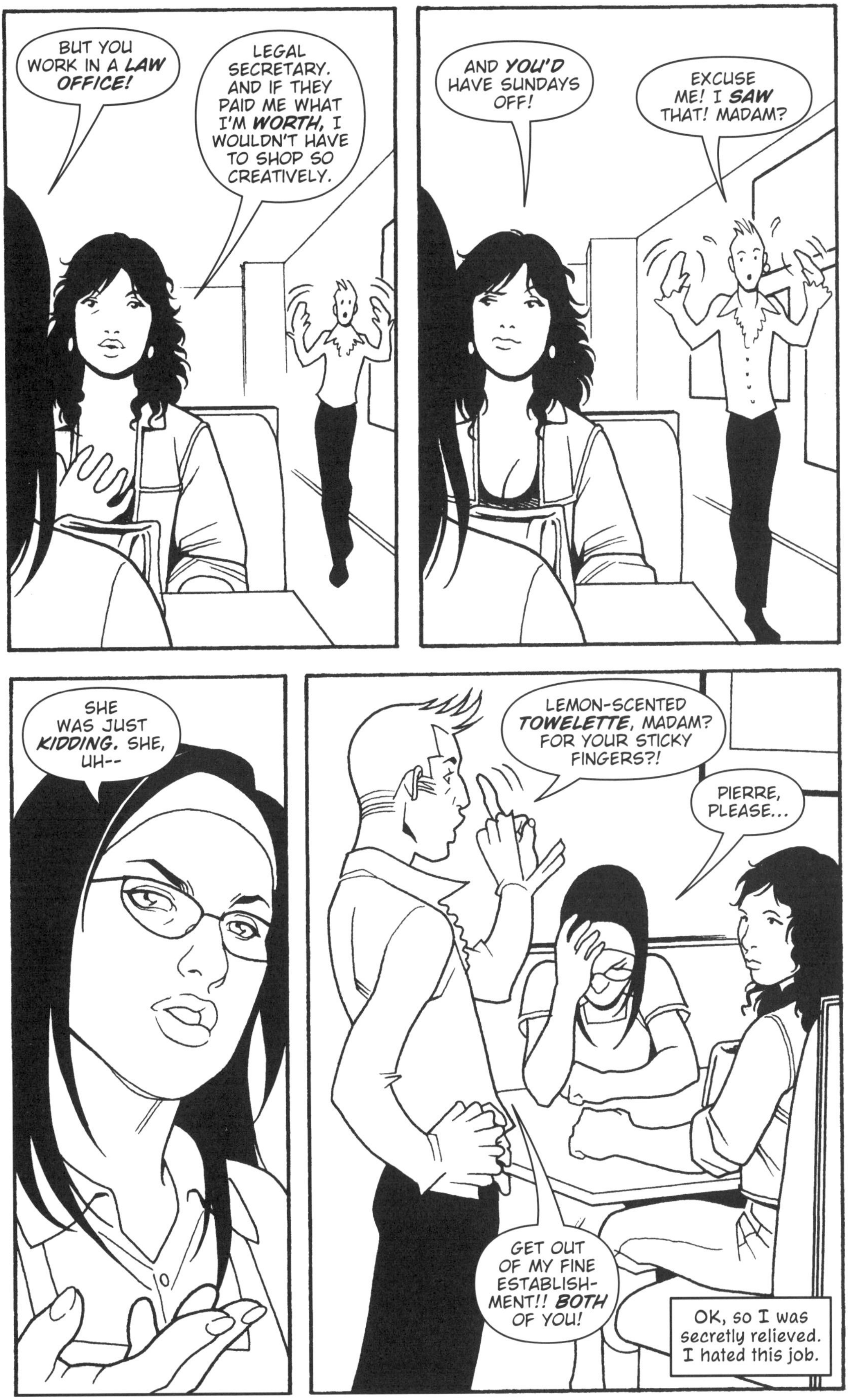

BUT YOU WORK IN A LAW OFFICE!
LEGAL SECRETARY. AND IF THEY PAID ME WHAT I'M WORTH, I WOULDN'T HAVE TO SHOP SO CREATIVELY.
AND YOU'D HAVE SUNDAYS OFF!
EXCUSE ME! I SAW THAT! MADAM?
SHE WAS JUST KIDDING. SHE, UH--
LEMON-SCENTED TOWELETTE, MADAM? FOR YOUR STICKY FINGERS?!
PIERRE, PLEASE...
GET OUT OF MY FINE ESTABLISH-MENT!! BOTH OF YOU!
OK, so I was secretly relieved. I hated this job.

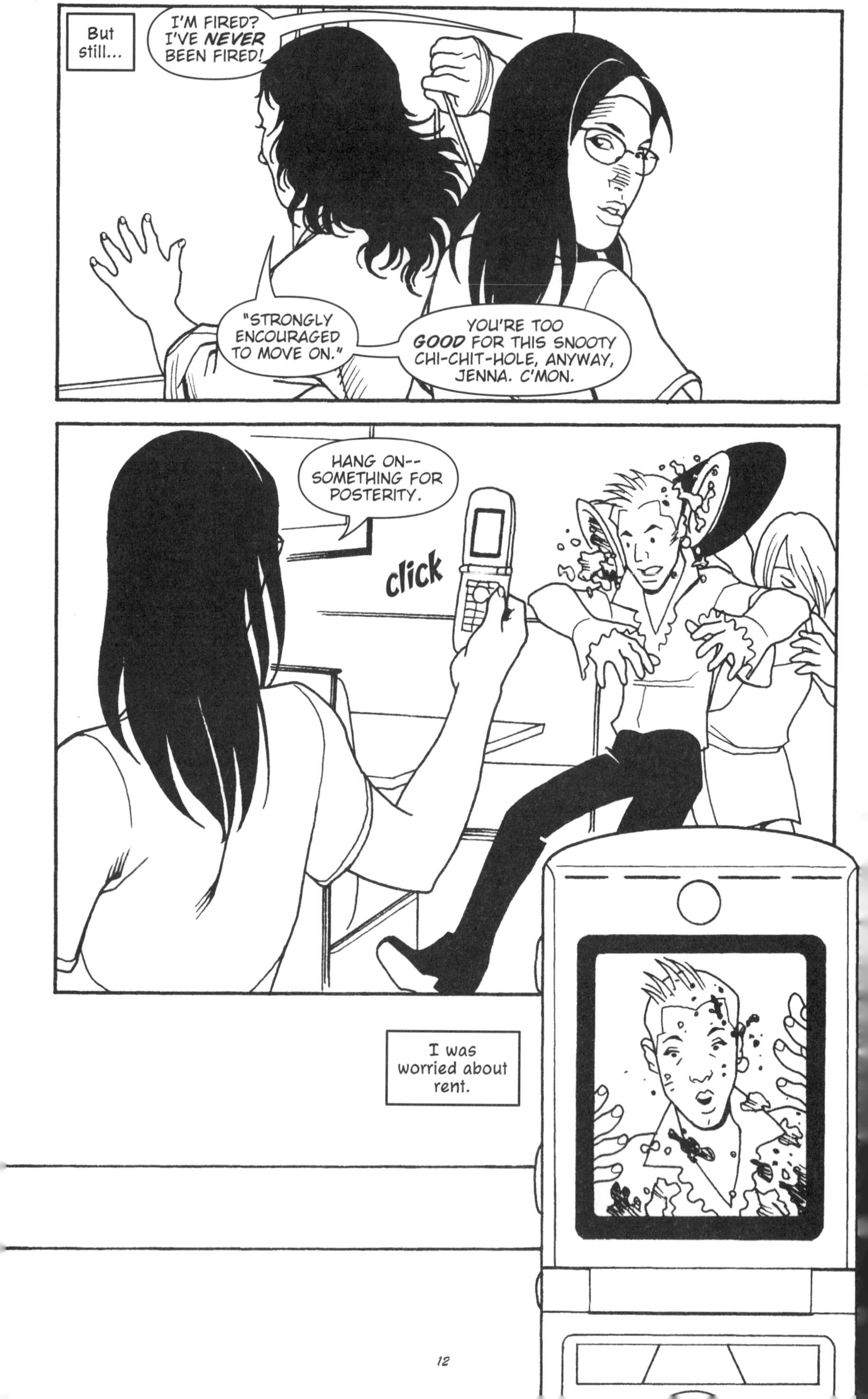
But still...
I'M FIRED? I'VE NEVER BEEN FIRED!
"STRONGLY ENCOURAGED TO MOVE ON."
YOU'RE TOO GOOD FOR THIS SNOOTY CHI-CHIT-HOLE, ANYWAY, JENNA. C'MON.
HANG ON-- SOMETHING FOR POSTERITY.
click
I was worried about rent.

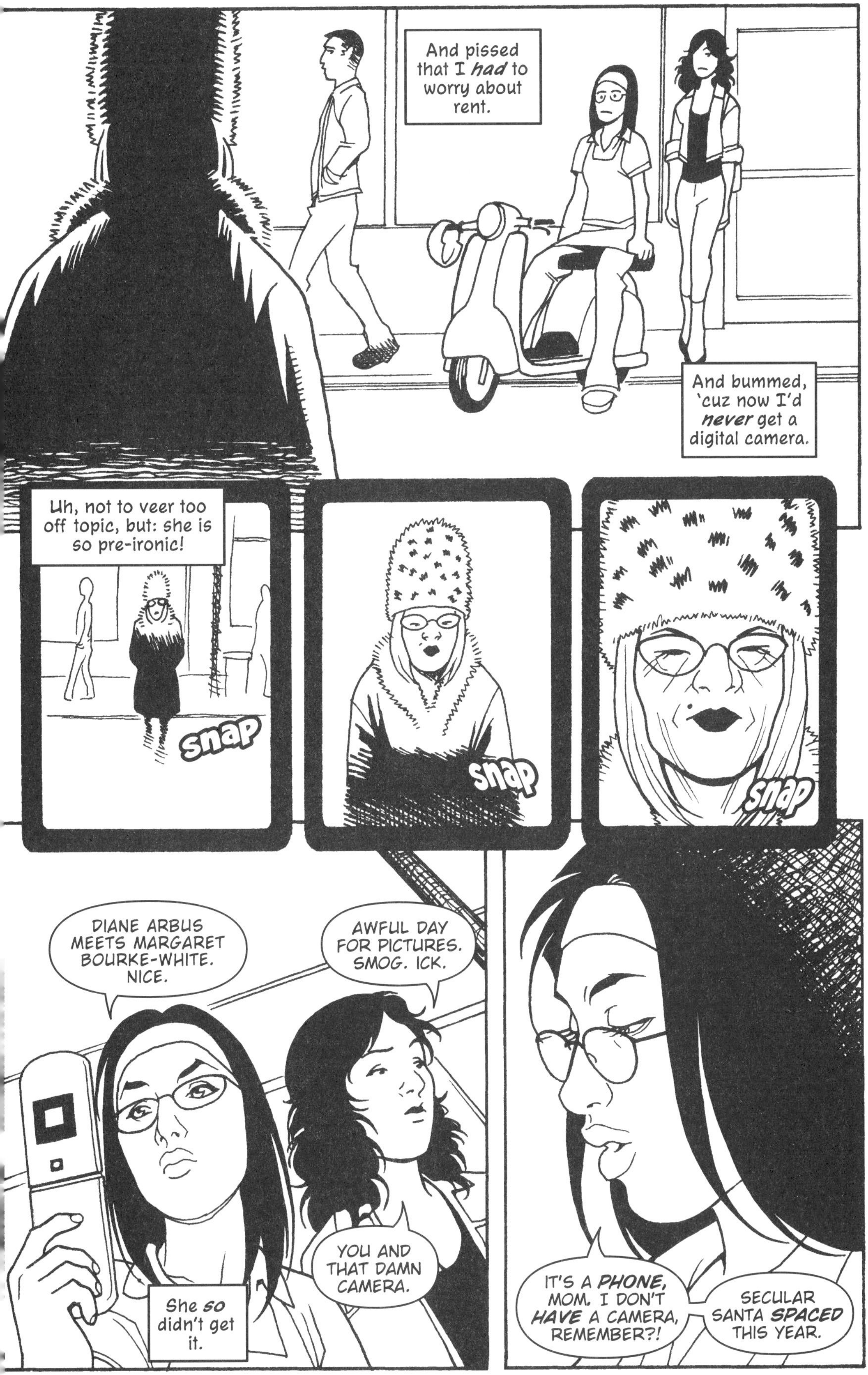
And pissed that I *had* to worry about rent.
And bummed, 'cuz now I'd *never* get a digital camera.
Uh, not to veer too off topic, but: she is so pre-ironic!
snap
snap
snap
DIANE ARBUS MEETS MARGARET BOURKE-WHITE. NICE.
AWFUL DAY FOR PICTURES. SMOG. ICK.
YOU AND THAT DAMN CAMERA.
She *so* didn't get it.
IT'S A *PHONE,* MOM. I DON'T *HAVE* A CAMERA, REMEMBER?!
SECULAR SANTA *SPACED* THIS YEAR.

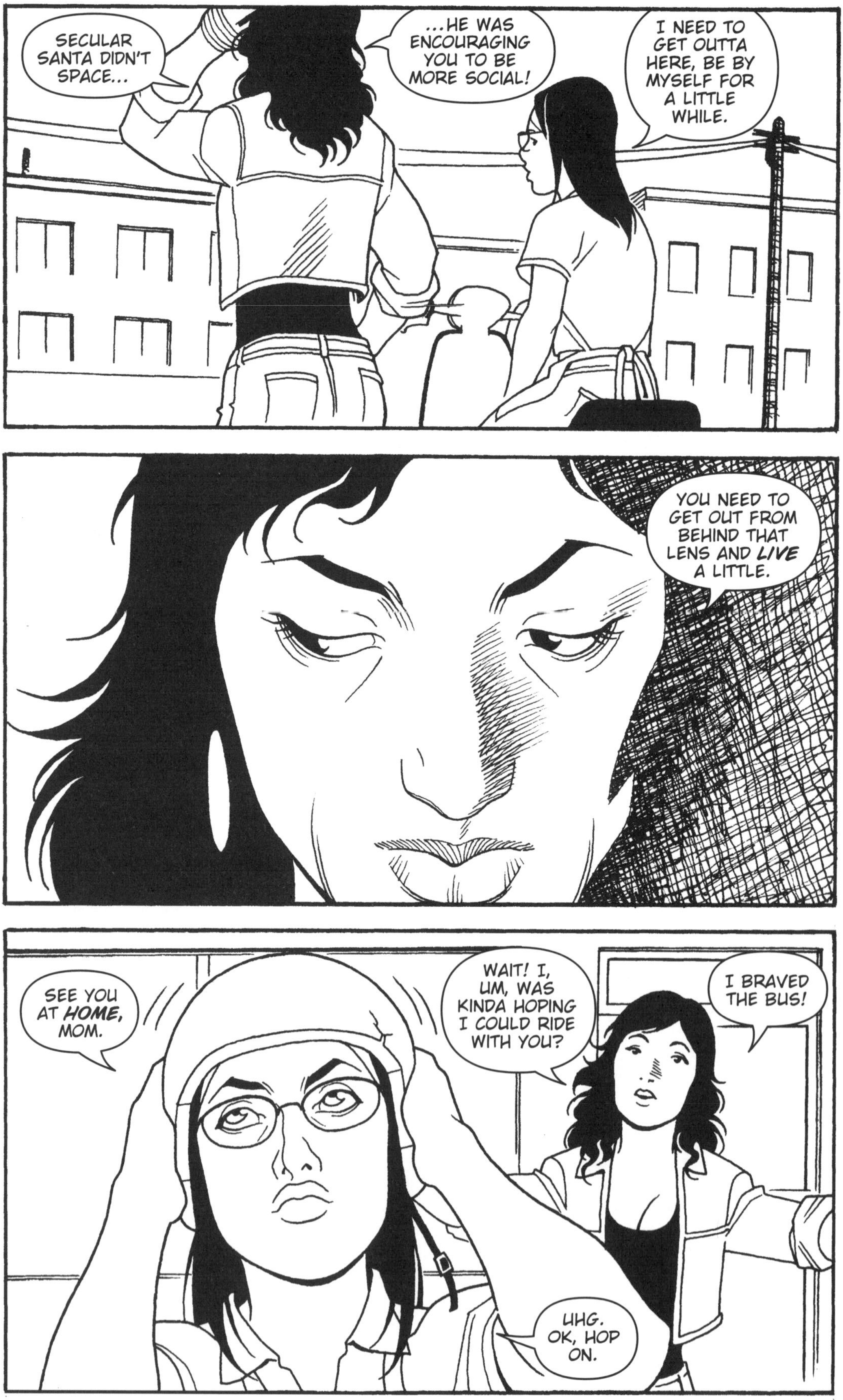
SECULAR SANTA DIDN'T SPACE...
...HE WAS ENCOURAGING YOU TO BE MORE SOCIAL!
I NEED TO GET OUTTA HERE, BE BY MYSELF FOR A LITTLE WHILE.
YOU NEED TO GET OUT FROM BEHIND THAT LENS AND *LIVE* A LITTLE.
SEE YOU AT *HOME,* MOM.
WAIT! I, UM, WAS KINDA HOPING I COULD RIDE WITH YOU?
I BRAVED THE BUS!
UHG. OK, HOP ON.

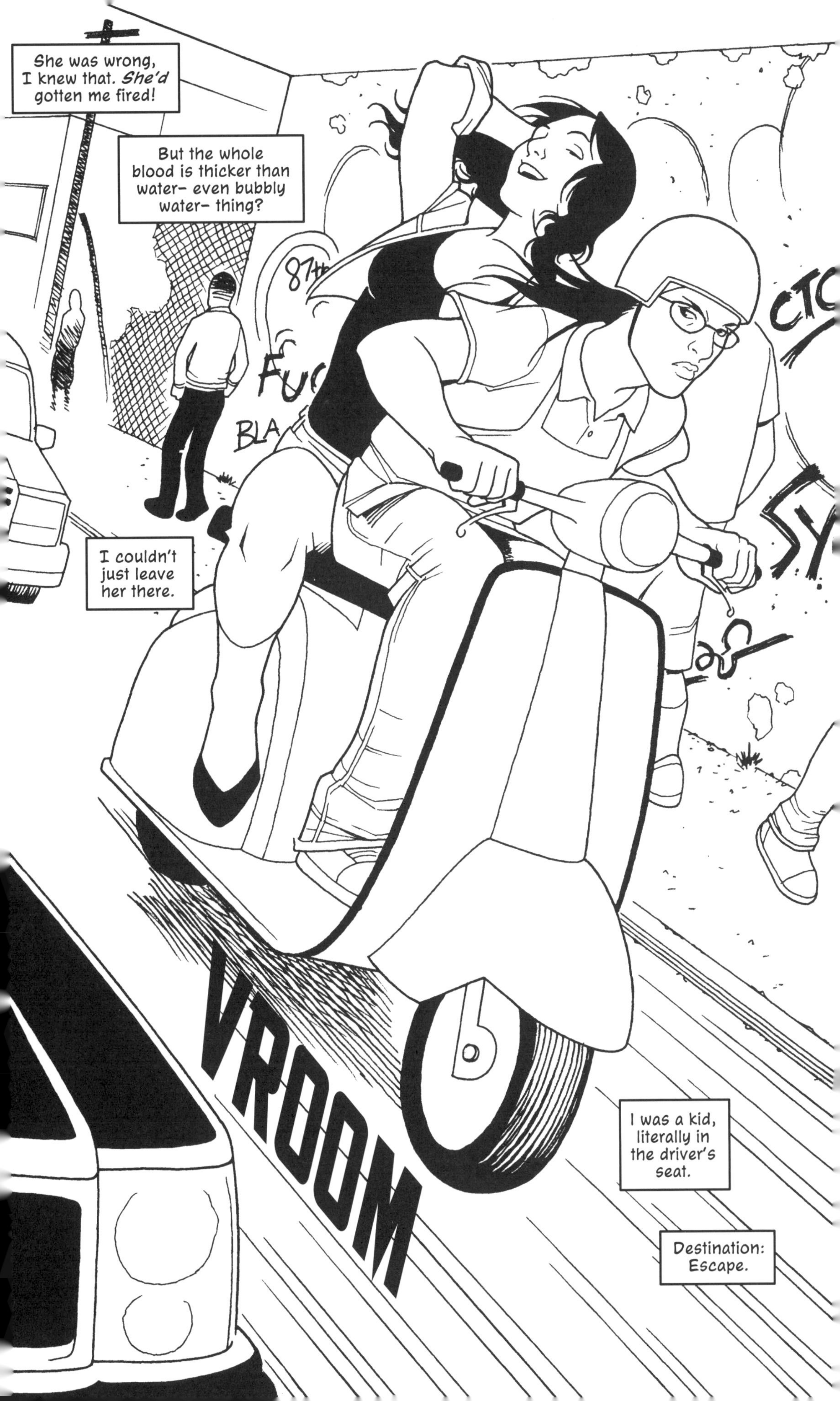
She was wrong, I knew that. *She'd* gotten me fired!
But the whole blood is thicker than water– even bubbly water– thing?
I couldn't just leave her there.
VROOM
I was a kid, literally in the driver's seat.
Destination: Escape.

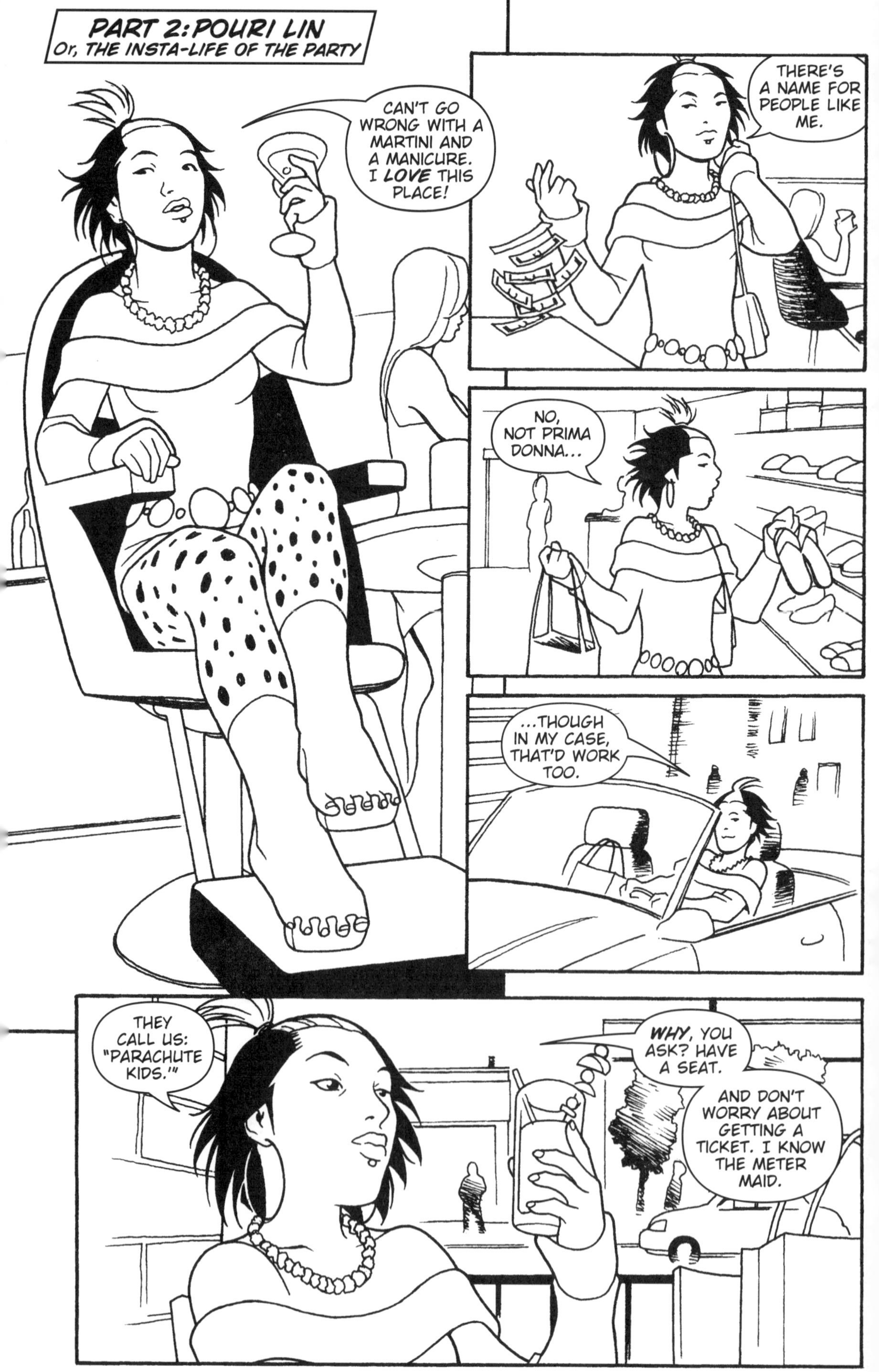
PART 2: POURI LIN
Or, THE INSTA-LIFE OF THE PARTY
CAN'T GO WRONG WITH A MARTINI AND A MANICURE. I LOVE THIS PLACE!
THERE'S A NAME FOR PEOPLE LIKE ME.
NO, NOT PRIMA DONNA...
...THOUGH IN MY CASE, THAT'D WORK TOO.
THEY CALL US: "PARACHUTE KIDS."
WHY, YOU ASK? HAVE A SEAT.
AND DON'T WORRY ABOUT GETTING A TICKET. I KNOW THE METER MAID.

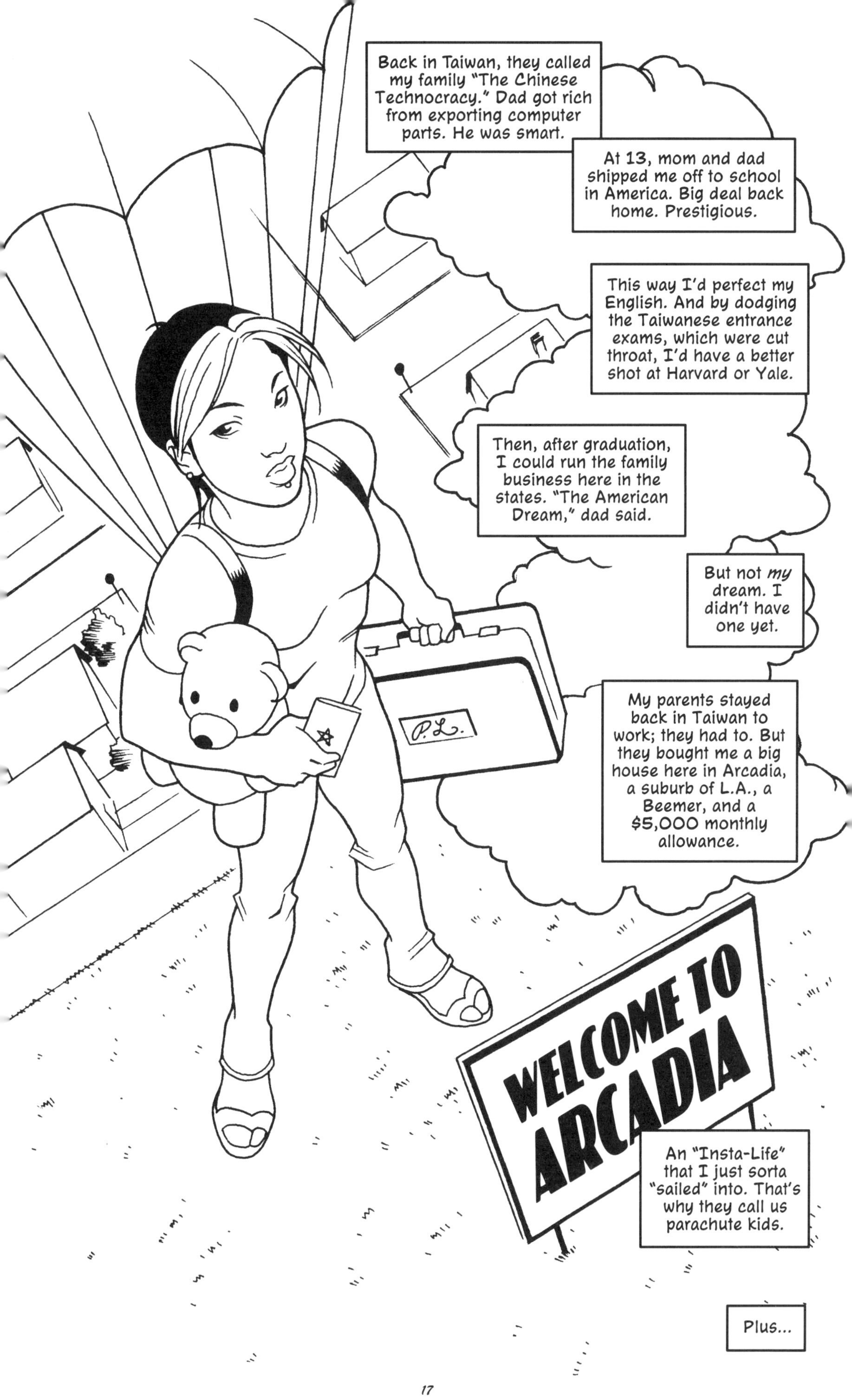
Back in Taiwan, they called my family "The Chinese Technocracy." Dad got rich from exporting computer parts. He was smart.
At 13, mom and dad shipped me off to school in America. Big deal back home. Prestigious.
This way I'd perfect my English. And by dodging the Taiwanese entrance exams, which were cut throat, I'd have a better shot at Harvard or Yale.
Then, after graduation, I could run the family business here in the states. "The American Dream," dad said.
But not *my* dream. I didn't have one yet.
My parents stayed back in Taiwan to work; they had to. But they bought me a big house here in Arcadia, a suburb of L.A., a Beemer, and a $5,000 monthly allowance.
P.L.
WELCOME TO ARCADIA
An "Insta-Life" that I just sorta "sailed" into. That's why they call us parachute kids.
Plus...

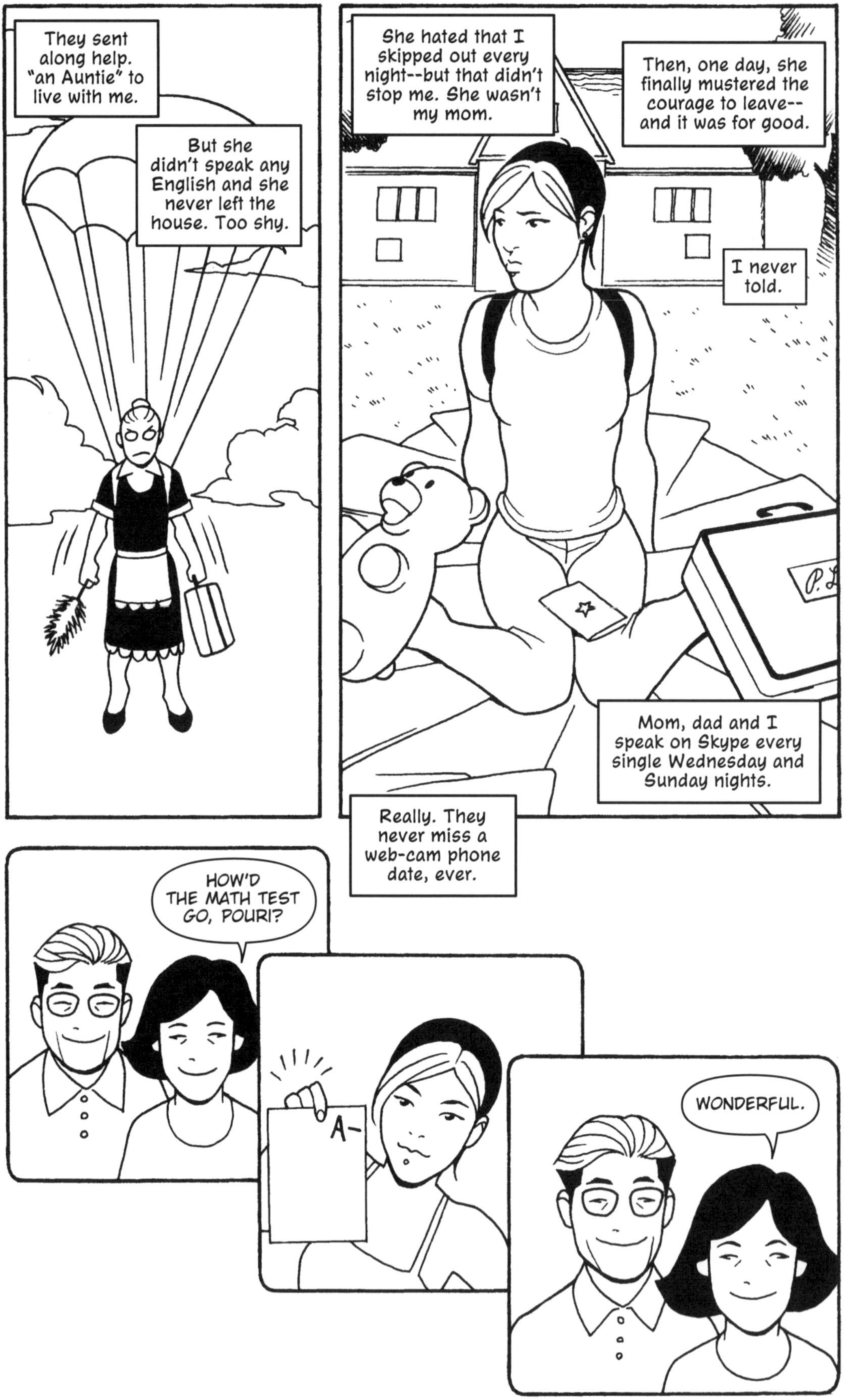
They sent along help. "an Auntie" to live with me.
But she didn't speak any English and she never left the house. Too shy.
She hated that I skipped out every night--but that didn't stop me. She wasn't my mom.
Then, one day, she finally mustered the courage to leave--and it was for good.
I never told.
P.L
Mom, dad and I speak on Skype every single Wednesday and Sunday nights.
Really. They never miss a web-cam phone date, ever.
HOW'D THE MATH TEST GO, POURI?
A-
WONDERFUL.

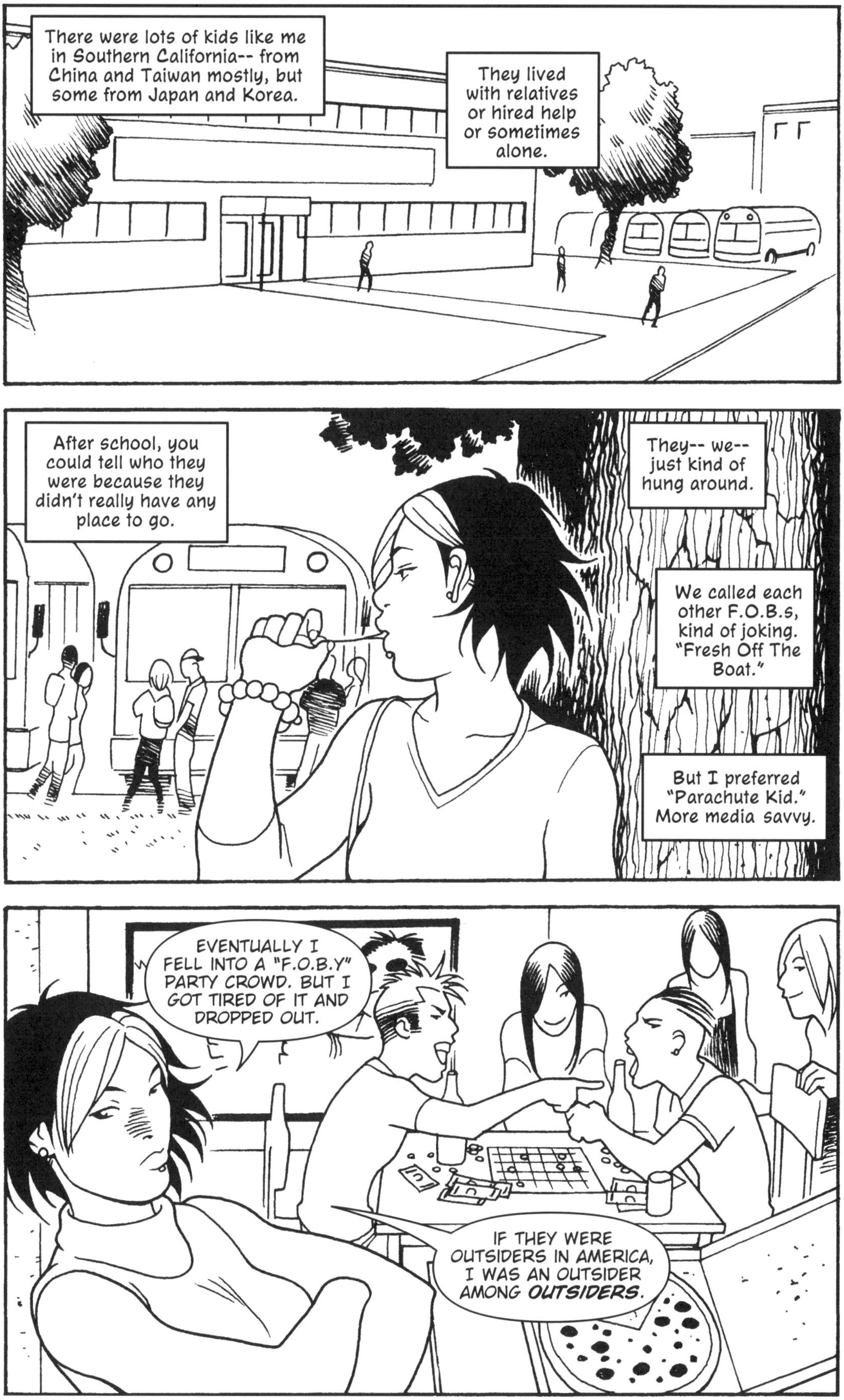

There were lots of kids like me in Southern California-- from China and Taiwan mostly, but some from Japan and Korea.
They lived with relatives or hired help or sometimes alone.
After school, you could tell who they were because they didn't really have any place to go.
They-- we-- just kind of hung around.
We called each other F.O.B.s, kind of joking. "Fresh Off The Boat."
But I preferred "Parachute Kid." More media savvy.
EVENTUALLY I FELL INTO A "F.O.B.Y" PARTY CROWD. BUT I GOT TIRED OF IT AND DROPPED OUT.
IF THEY WERE OUTSIDERS IN AMERICA, I WAS AN OUTSIDER AMONG ***OUTSIDERS***.

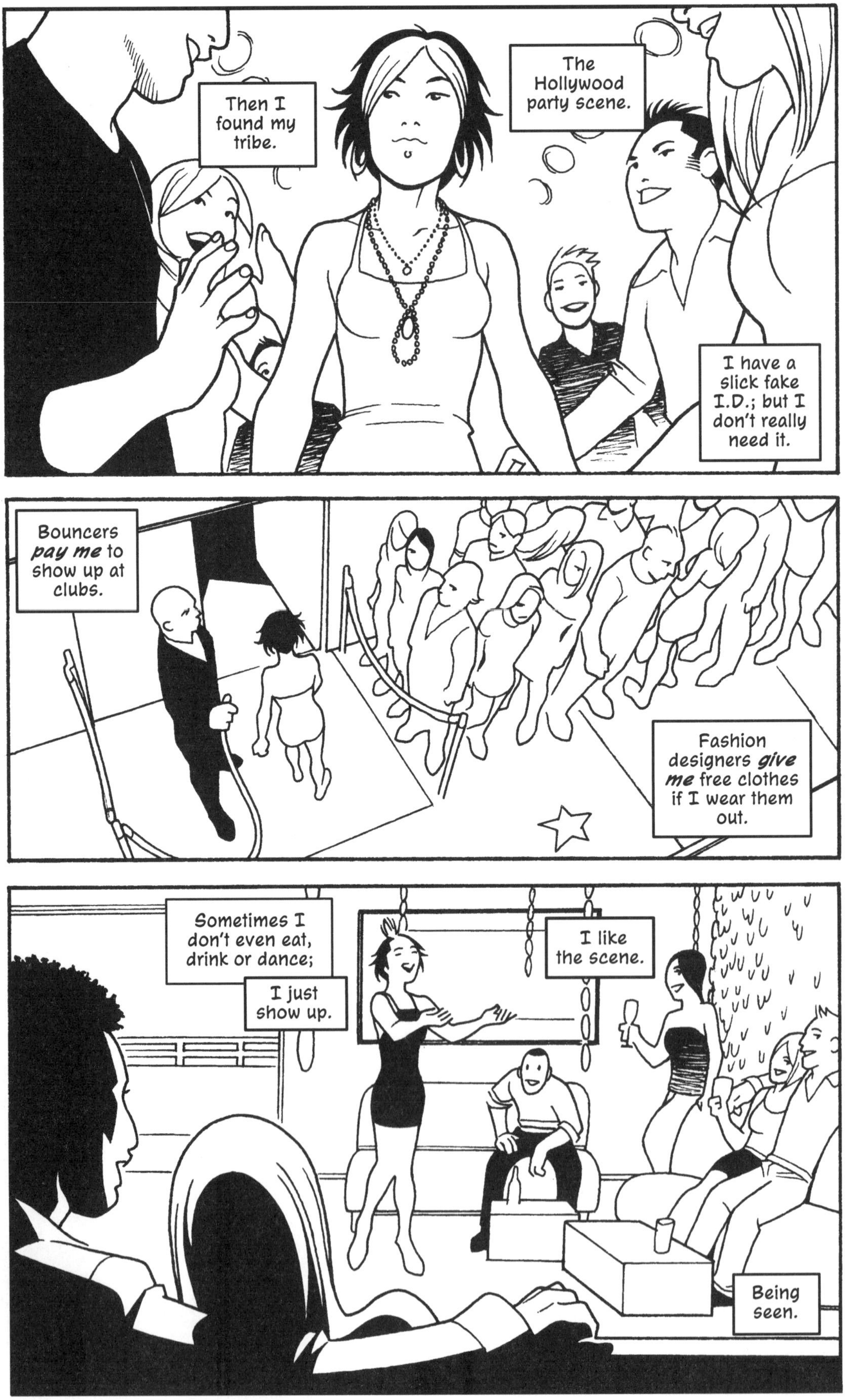
Then I found my tribe.
The Hollywood party scene.
I have a slick fake I.D.; but I don't really need it.
Bouncers *pay me* to show up at clubs.
Fashion designers *give me* free clothes if I wear them out.
Sometimes I don't even eat, drink or dance;
I just show up.
I like the scene.
Being seen.

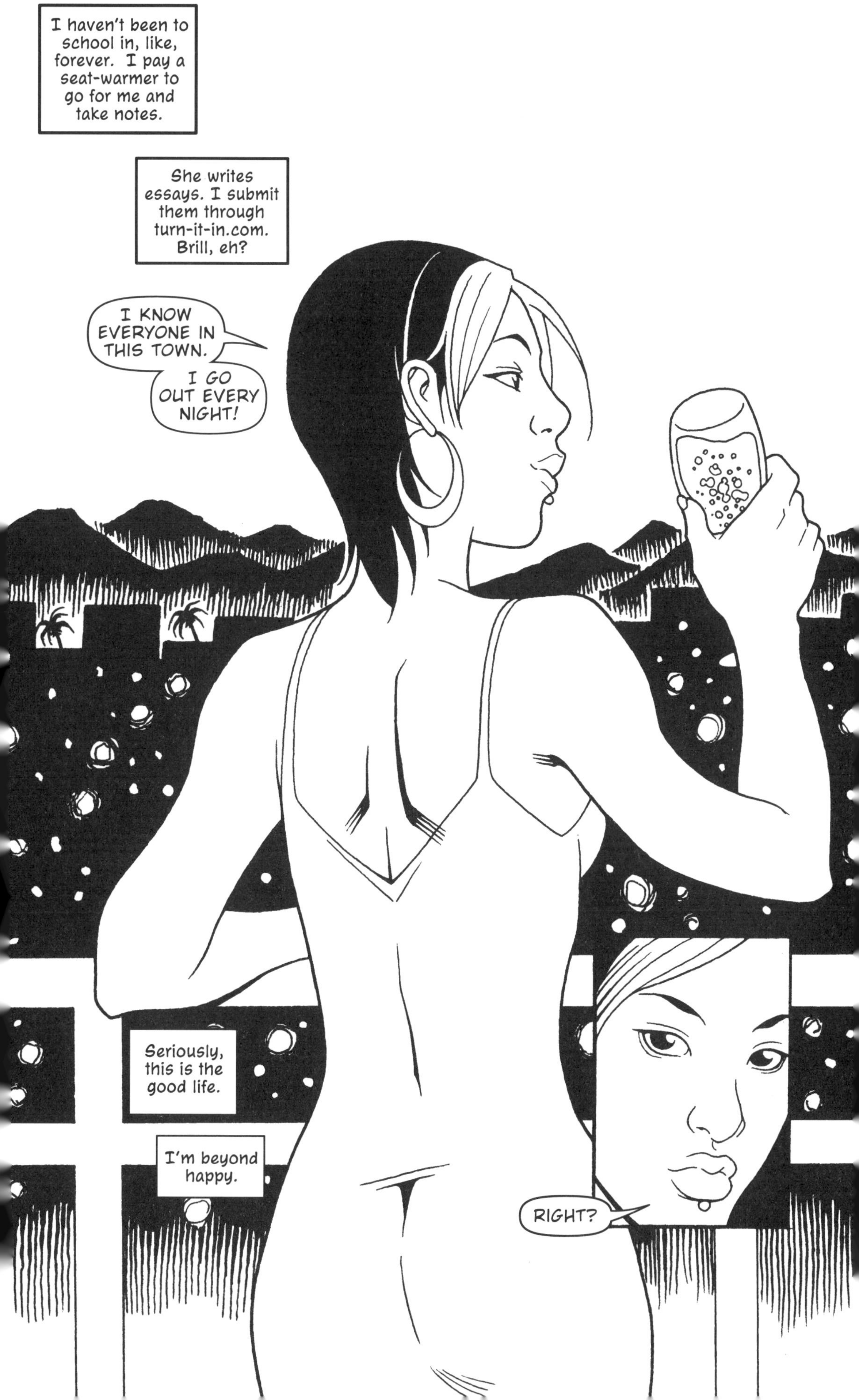
I haven't been to school in, like, forever. I pay a seat-warmer to go for me and take notes.
She writes essays. I submit them through turn-it-in.com. Brill, eh?
I KNOW EVERYONE IN THIS TOWN.
I GO OUT EVERY NIGHT!
Seriously, this is the good life.
I'm beyond happy.
RIGHT?

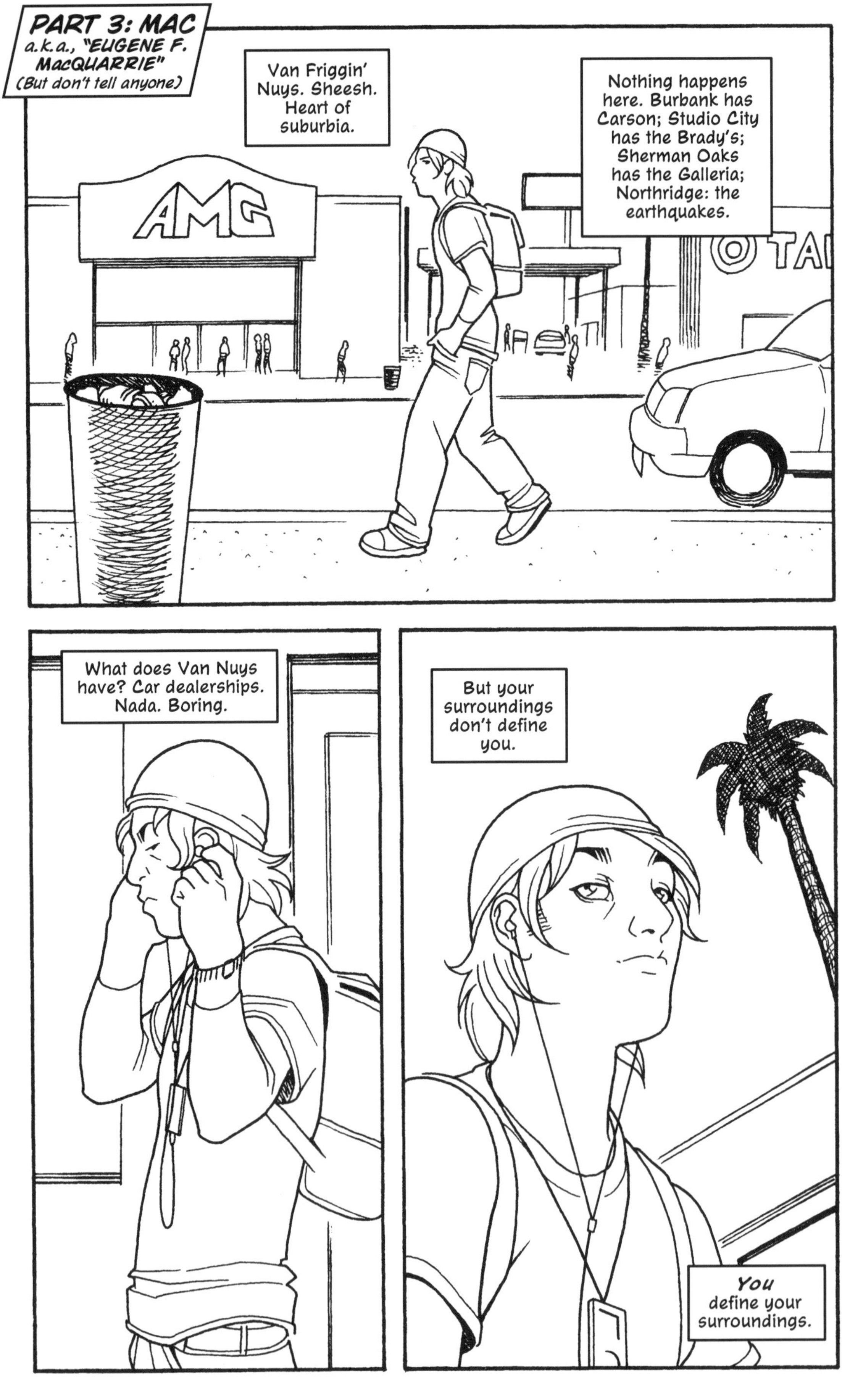

PART 3: MAC
a.k.a., "EUGENE F. MacQUARRIE"
(But don't tell anyone)
Van Friggin' Nuys. Sheesh. Heart of suburbia.
Nothing happens here. Burbank has Carson; Studio City has the Brady's; Sherman Oaks has the Galleria; Northridge: the earthquakes.
AMC
What does Van Nuys have? Car dealerships. Nada. Boring.
But your surroundings don't define you.
You define your surroundings.

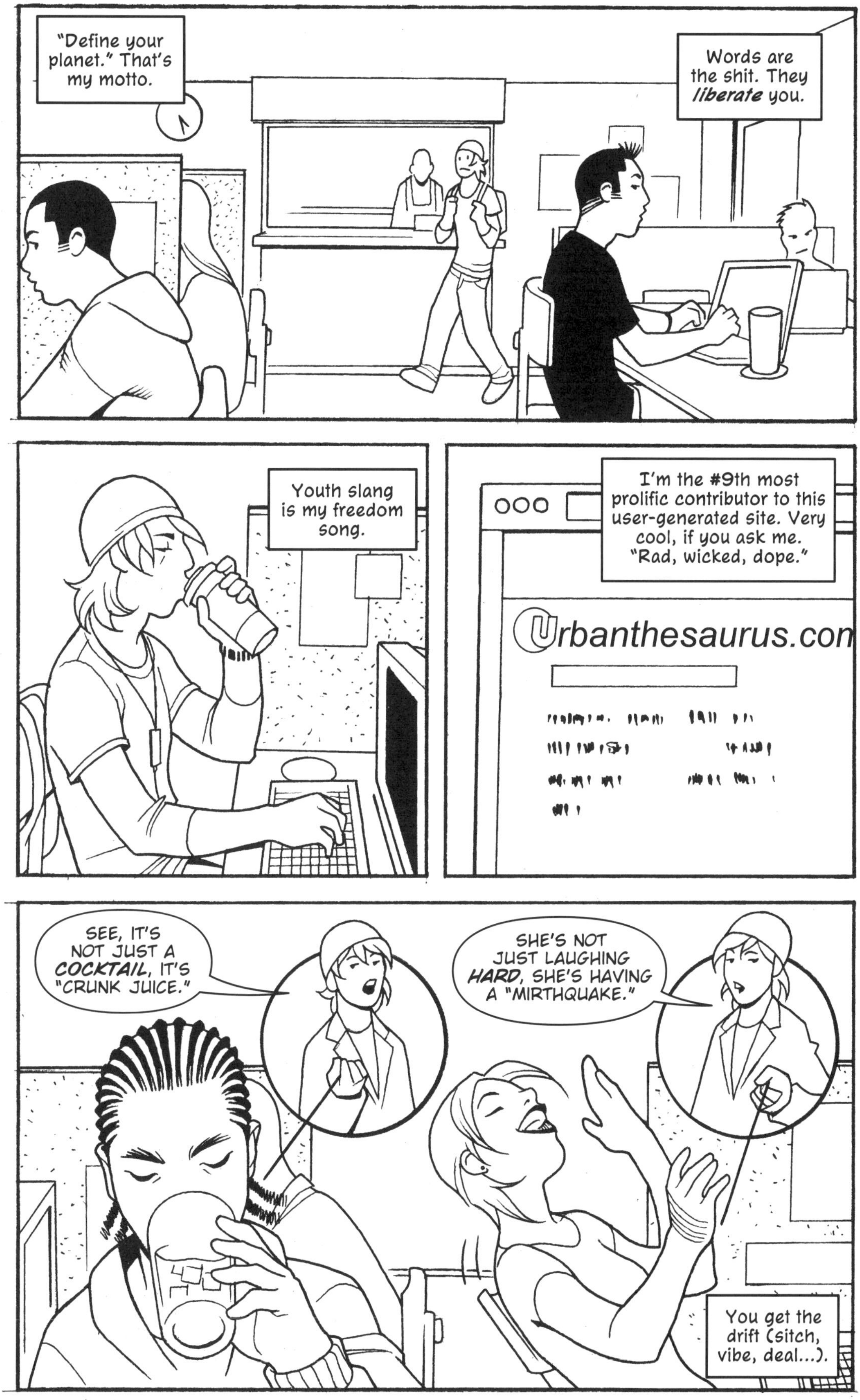

"Define your planet." That's my motto.
Words are the shit. They *liberate* you.
Youth slang is my freedom song.
I'm the #9th most prolific contributor to this user-generated site. Very cool, if you ask me. "Rad, wicked, dope."
Urbanthesaurus.com
SEE, IT'S NOT JUST A *COCKTAIL*, IT'S "CRUNK JUICE."
SHE'S NOT JUST LAUGHING *HARD*, SHE'S HAVING A "MIRTHQUAKE."
You get the drift (sitch, vibe, deal...).

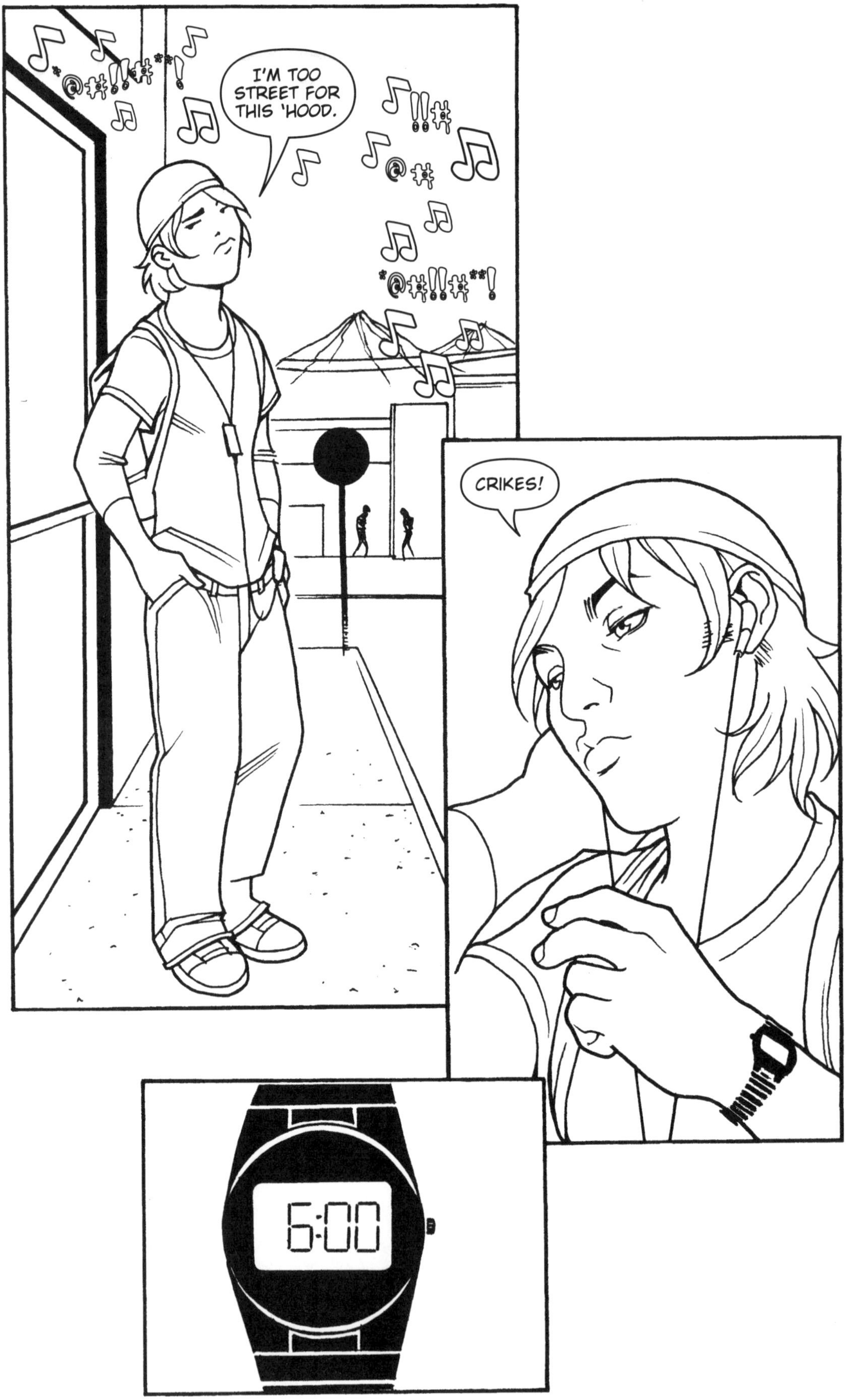
I'M TOO STREET FOR THIS 'HOOD.
CRIKES!
6:00

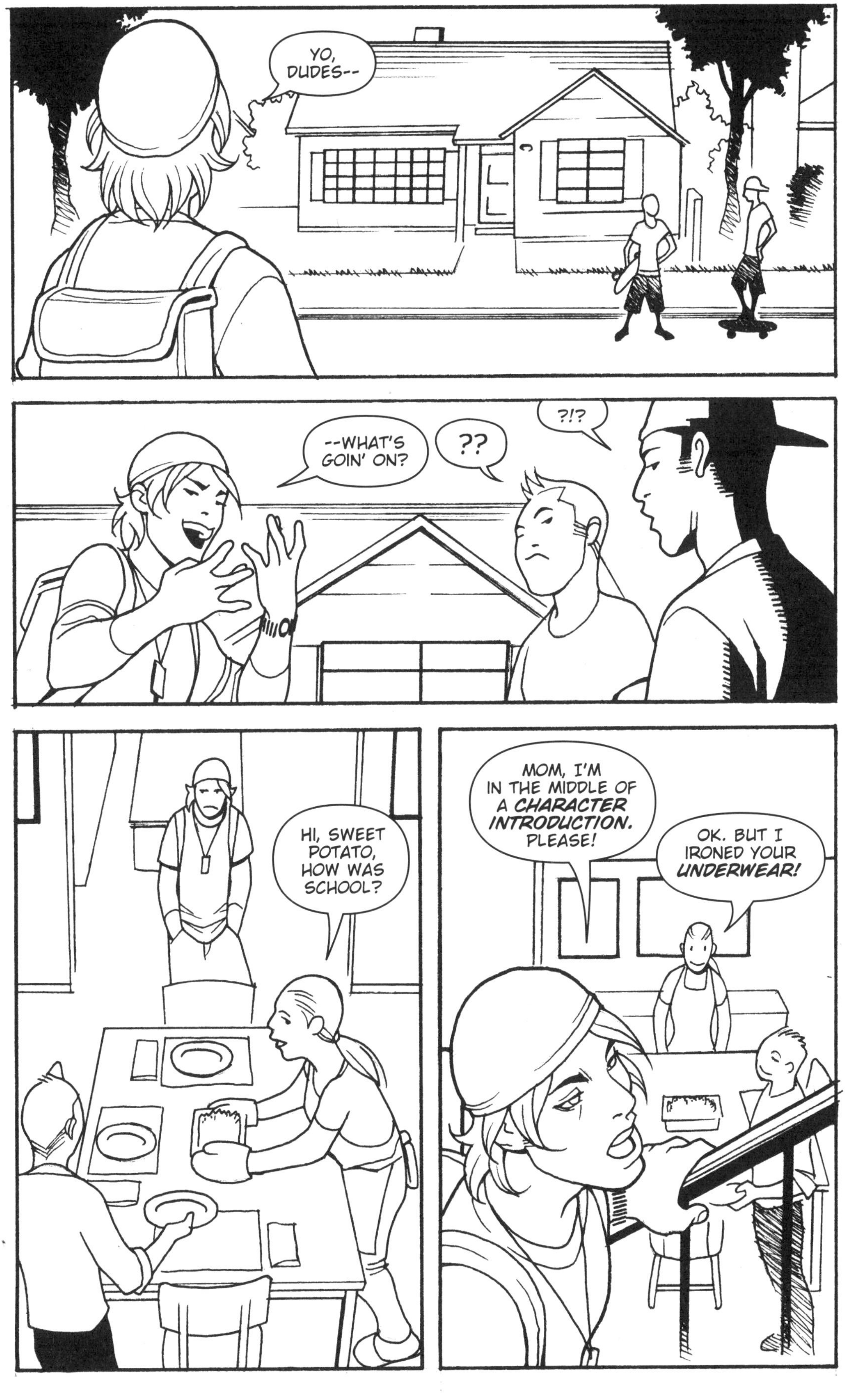
YO, DUDES--
--WHAT'S GOIN' ON?
??
?!?
HI, SWEET POTATO, HOW WAS SCHOOL?
MOM, I'M IN THE MIDDLE OF A ***CHARACTER INTRODUCTION.*** PLEASE!
OK. BUT I IRONED YOUR ***UNDERWEAR!***

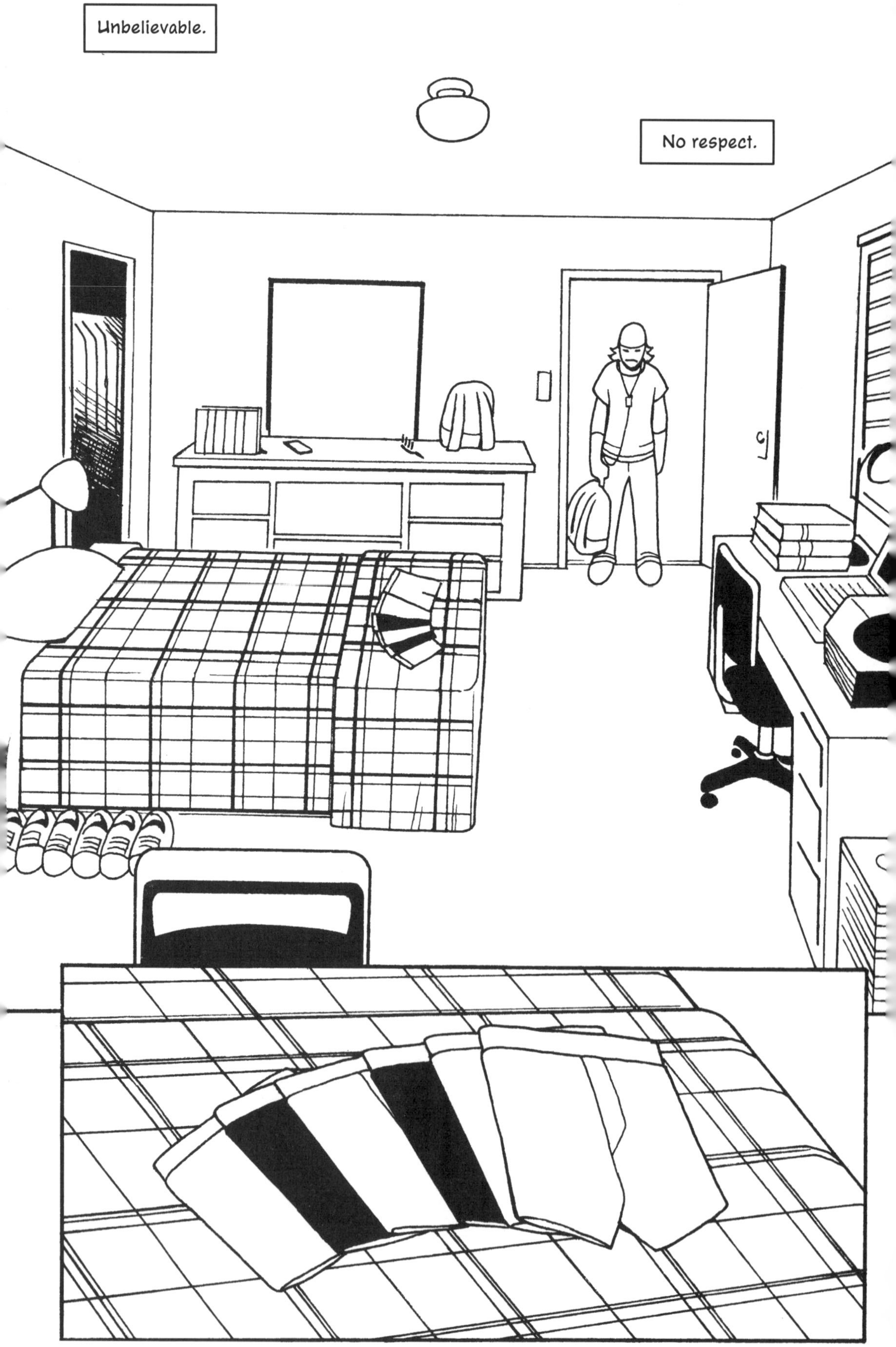
Unbelievable.
No respect.

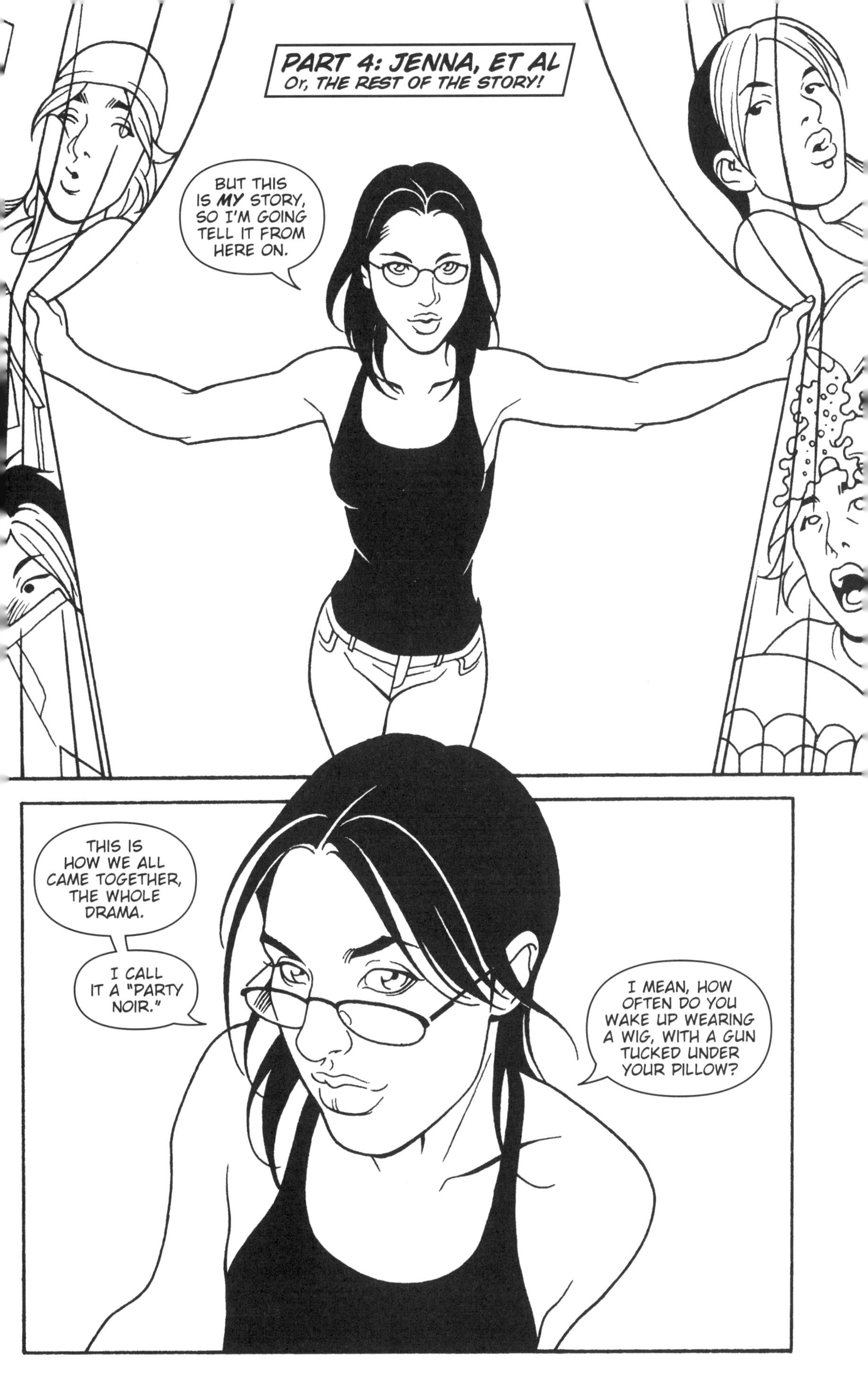
PART 4: JENNA, ET AL
Or, THE REST OF THE STORY!
BUT THIS IS *MY* STORY, SO I'M GOING TELL IT FROM HERE ON.
THIS IS HOW WE ALL CAME TOGETHER, THE WHOLE DRAMA.
I CALL IT A "PARTY NOIR."
I MEAN, HOW OFTEN DO YOU WAKE UP WEARING A WIG, WITH A GUN TUCKED UNDER YOUR PILLOW?

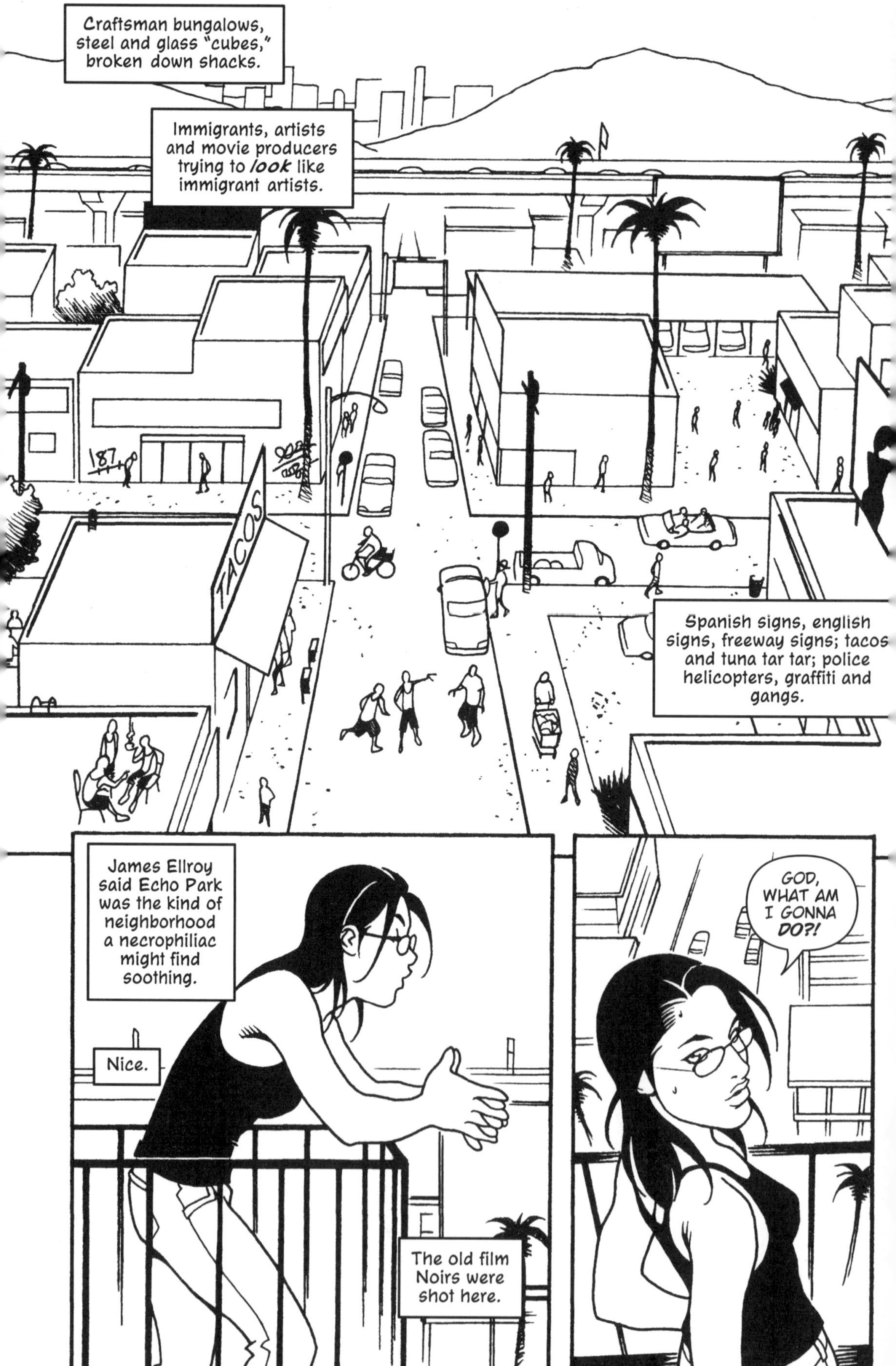
Craftsman bungalows, steel and glass "cubes," broken down shacks.
Immigrants, artists and movie producers trying to *look* like immigrant artists.
TACOS
Spanish signs, english signs, freeway signs; tacos and tuna tar tar; police helicopters, graffiti and gangs.
James Ellroy said Echo Park was the kind of neighborhood a necrophiliac might find soothing.
Nice.
The old film Noirs were shot here.
GOD, WHAT AM I GONNA *DO?!*

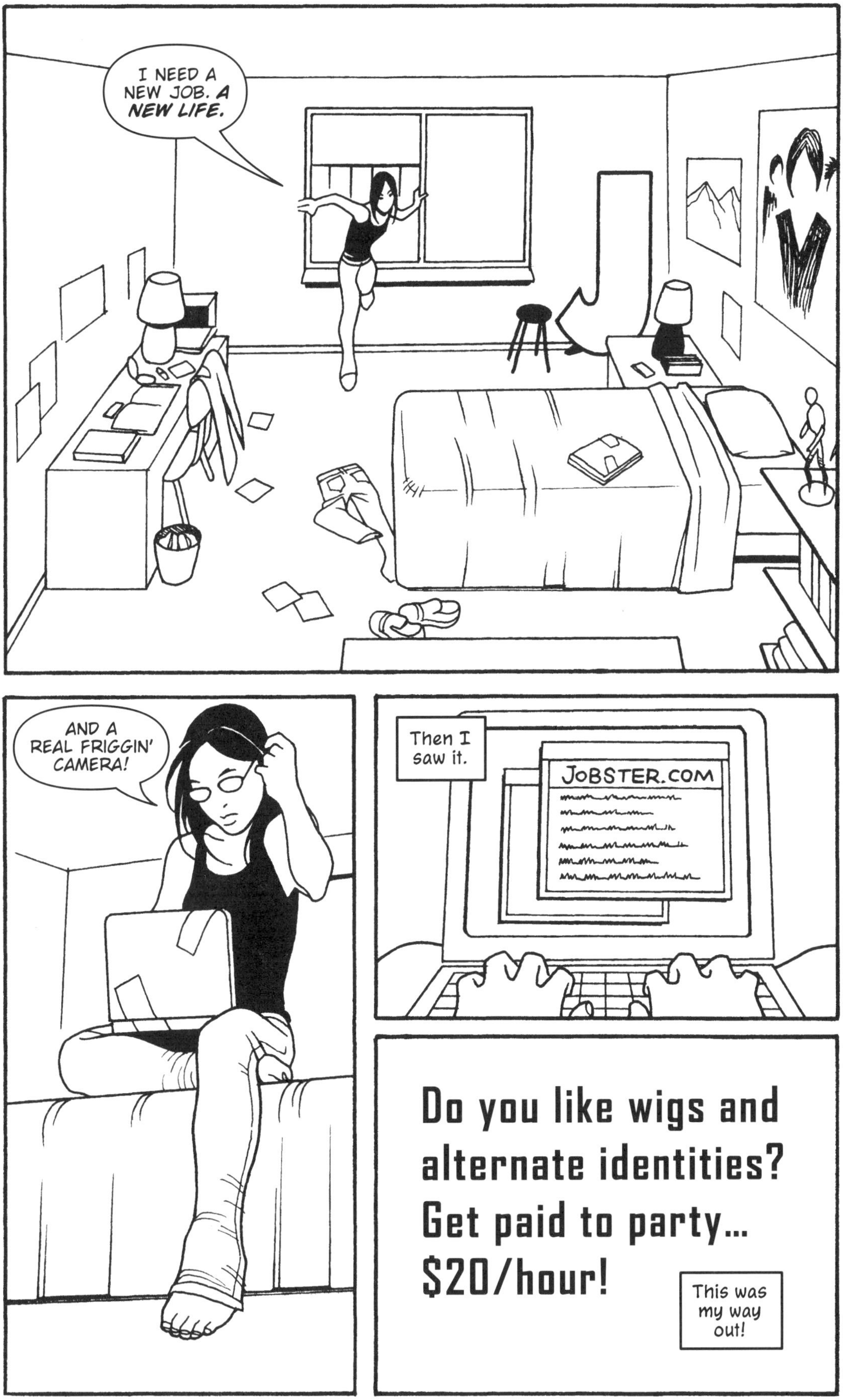

I NEED A NEW JOB. A NEW LIFE.
AND A REAL FRIGGIN' CAMERA!
Then I saw it.
JOBSTER.COM
Do you like wigs and alternate identities? Get paid to party... $20/hour!
This was my way out!

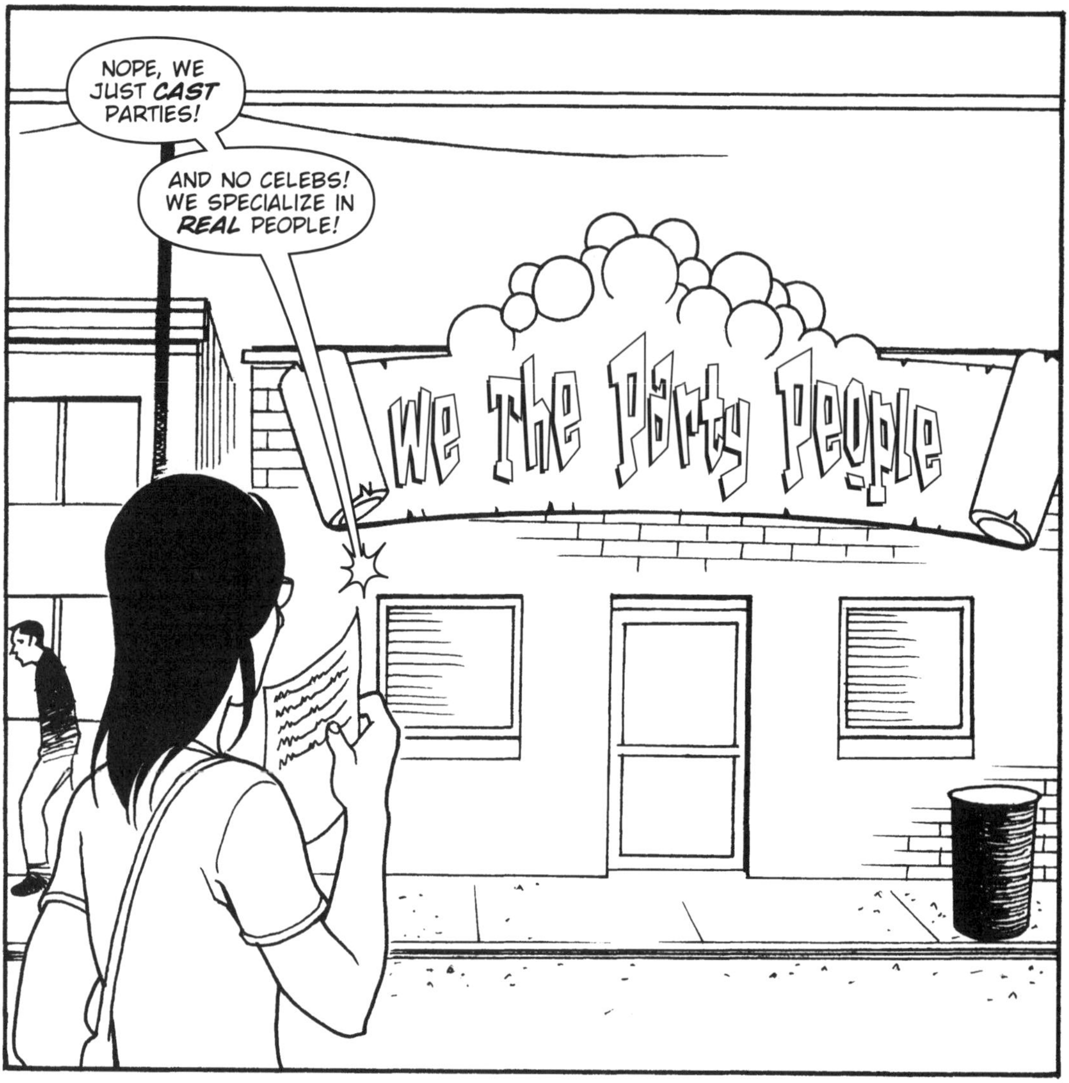
NOPE, WE JUST CAST PARTIES!
AND NO CELEBS! WE SPECIALIZE IN REAL PEOPLE!
We The Party People

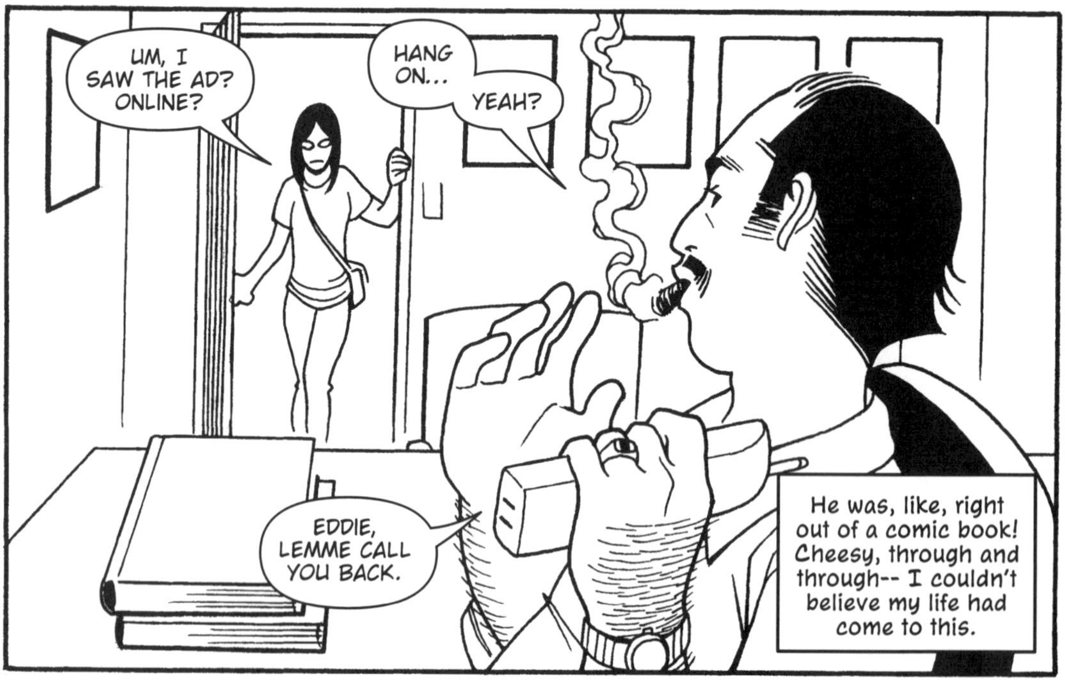
UM, I SAW THE AD? ONLINE?
HANG ON...
YEAH?
EDDIE, LEMME CALL YOU BACK.
He was, like, right out of a comic book! Cheesy, through and through-- I couldn't believe my life had come to this.

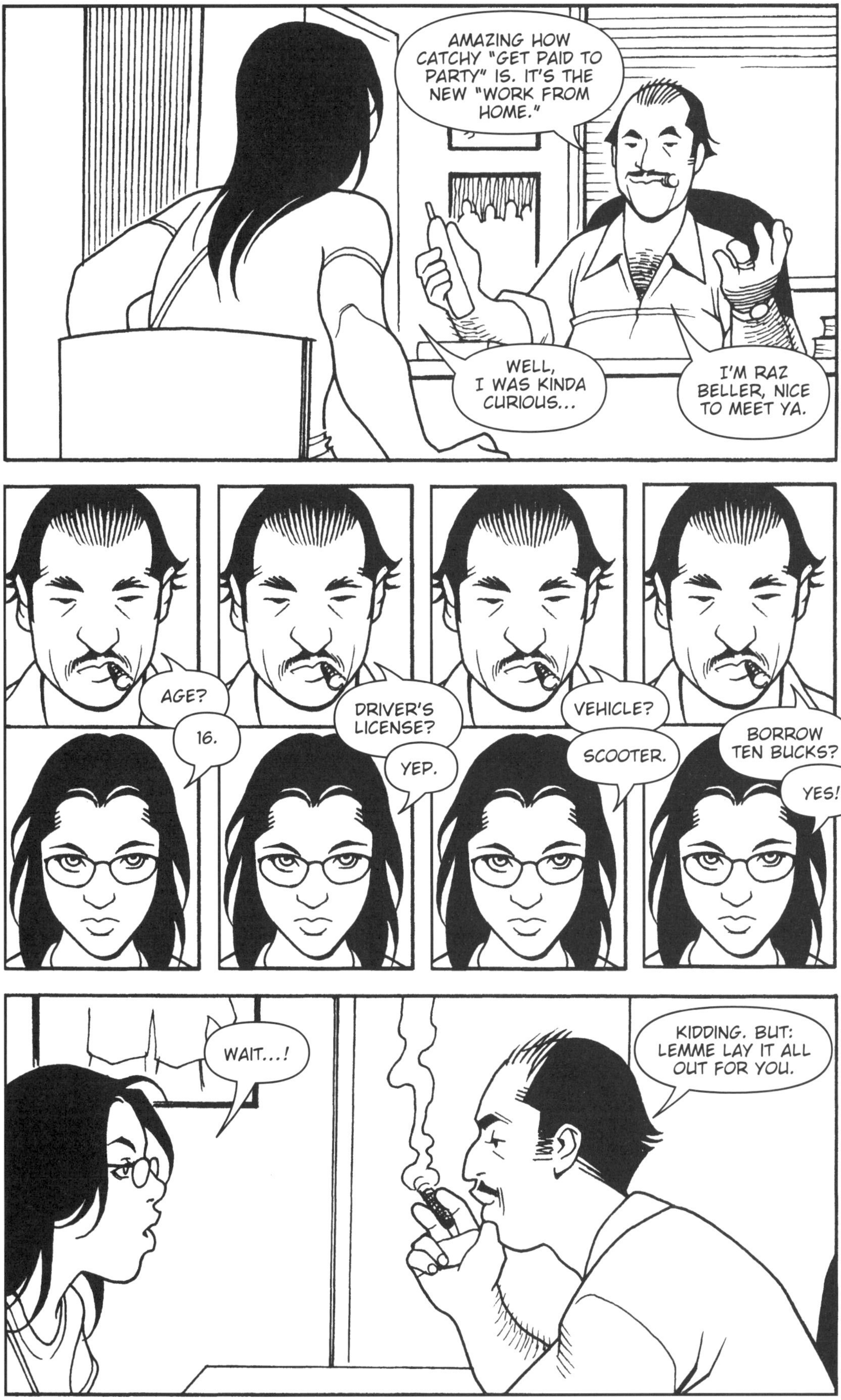
AMAZING HOW CATCHY "GET PAID TO PARTY" IS. IT'S THE NEW "WORK FROM HOME."
WELL, I WAS KINDA CURIOUS...
I'M RAZ BELLER, NICE TO MEET YA.
AGE?
16.
DRIVER'S LICENSE?
YEP.
VEHICLE?
SCOOTER.
BORROW TEN BUCKS?
YES!
WAIT...!
KIDDING. BUT: LEMME LAY IT ALL OUT FOR YOU.

"We used to cast TV commercials.

"Very low rent.

"Tap dancing citrus. Infommercials for cable.

"It was the '80s."

NEXT!

"Disaster.

"But our wrap parties *rocked.* Best parties of any frozen concentrate around."

"Why?"

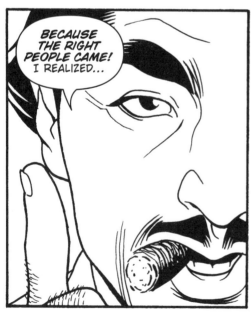

BECAUSE THE RIGHT PEOPLE CAME! I REALIZED...

...UNFORGETABLE FÊTÉS. IT ALL COMES DOWN TO THE GUEST LIST!

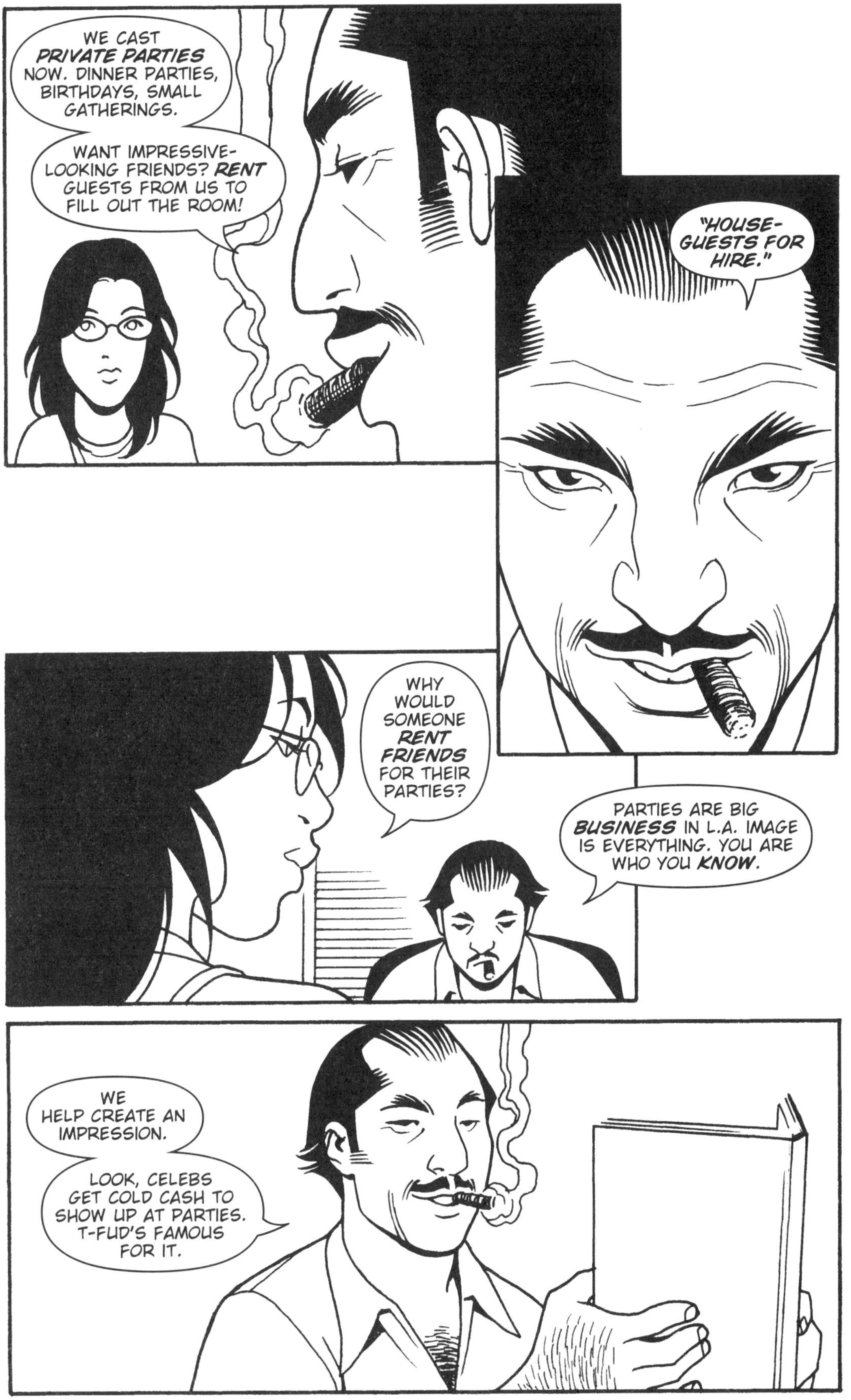
WE CAST PRIVATE PARTIES NOW. DINNER PARTIES, BIRTHDAYS, SMALL GATHERINGS.
WANT IMPRESSIVE-LOOKING FRIENDS? RENT GUESTS FROM US TO FILL OUT THE ROOM!
"HOUSE-GUESTS FOR HIRE."
WHY WOULD SOMEONE RENT FRIENDS FOR THEIR PARTIES?
PARTIES ARE BIG BUSINESS IN L.A. IMAGE IS EVERYTHING. YOU ARE WHO YOU KNOW.
WE HELP CREATE AN IMPRESSION.
LOOK, CELEBS GET COLD CASH TO SHOW UP AT PARTIES. T-FUD'S FAMOUS FOR IT.

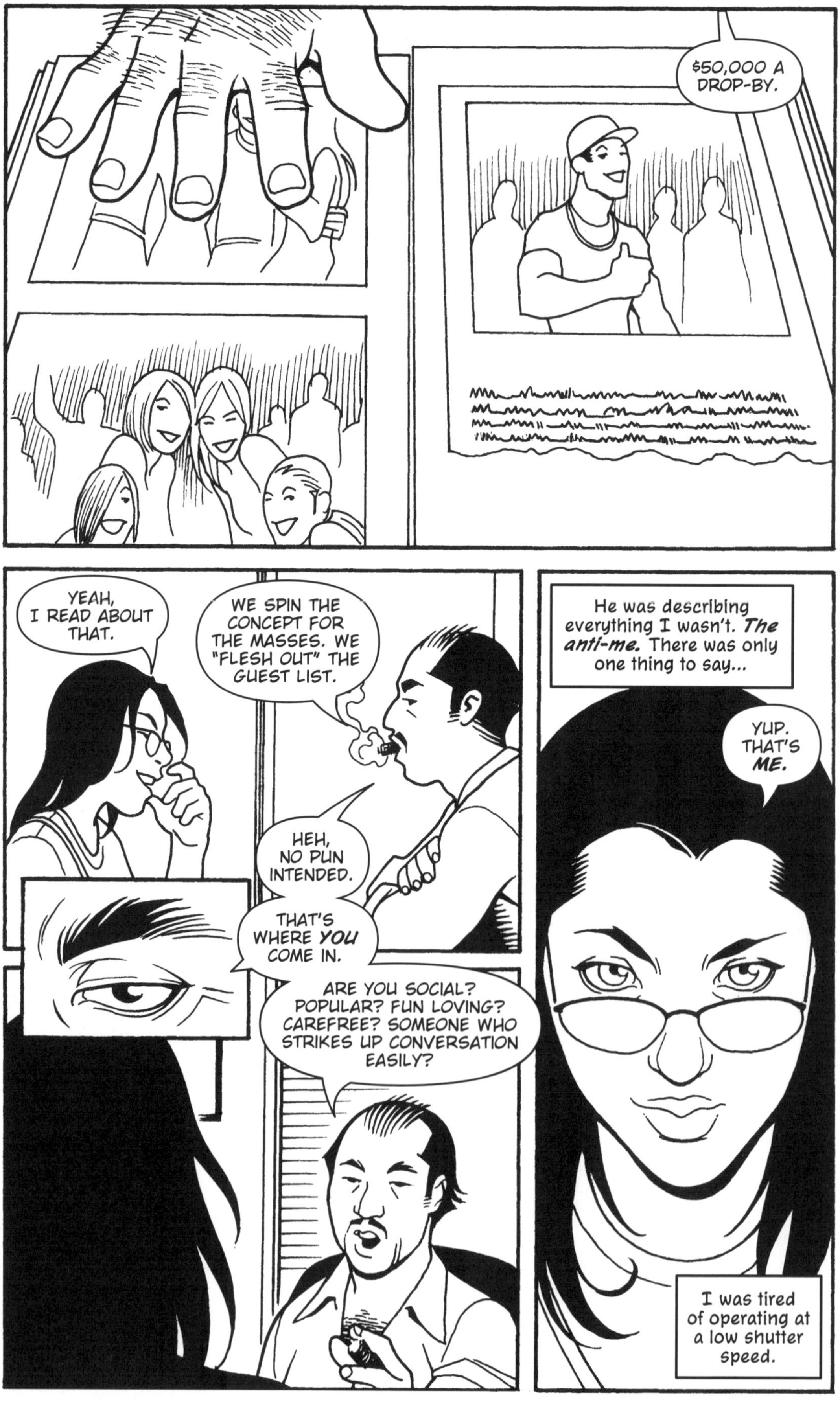
$50,000 A DROP-BY.
YEAH, I READ ABOUT THAT.
WE SPIN THE CONCEPT FOR THE MASSES. WE "FLESH OUT" THE GUEST LIST.
HEH, NO PUN INTENDED.
THAT'S WHERE *YOU* COME IN.
ARE YOU SOCIAL? POPULAR? FUN LOVING? CAREFREE? SOMEONE WHO STRIKES UP CONVERSATION EASILY?
He was describing everything I wasn't. ***The anti-me.*** There was only one thing to say...
YUP. THAT'S ***ME.***
I was tired of operating at a low shutter speed.

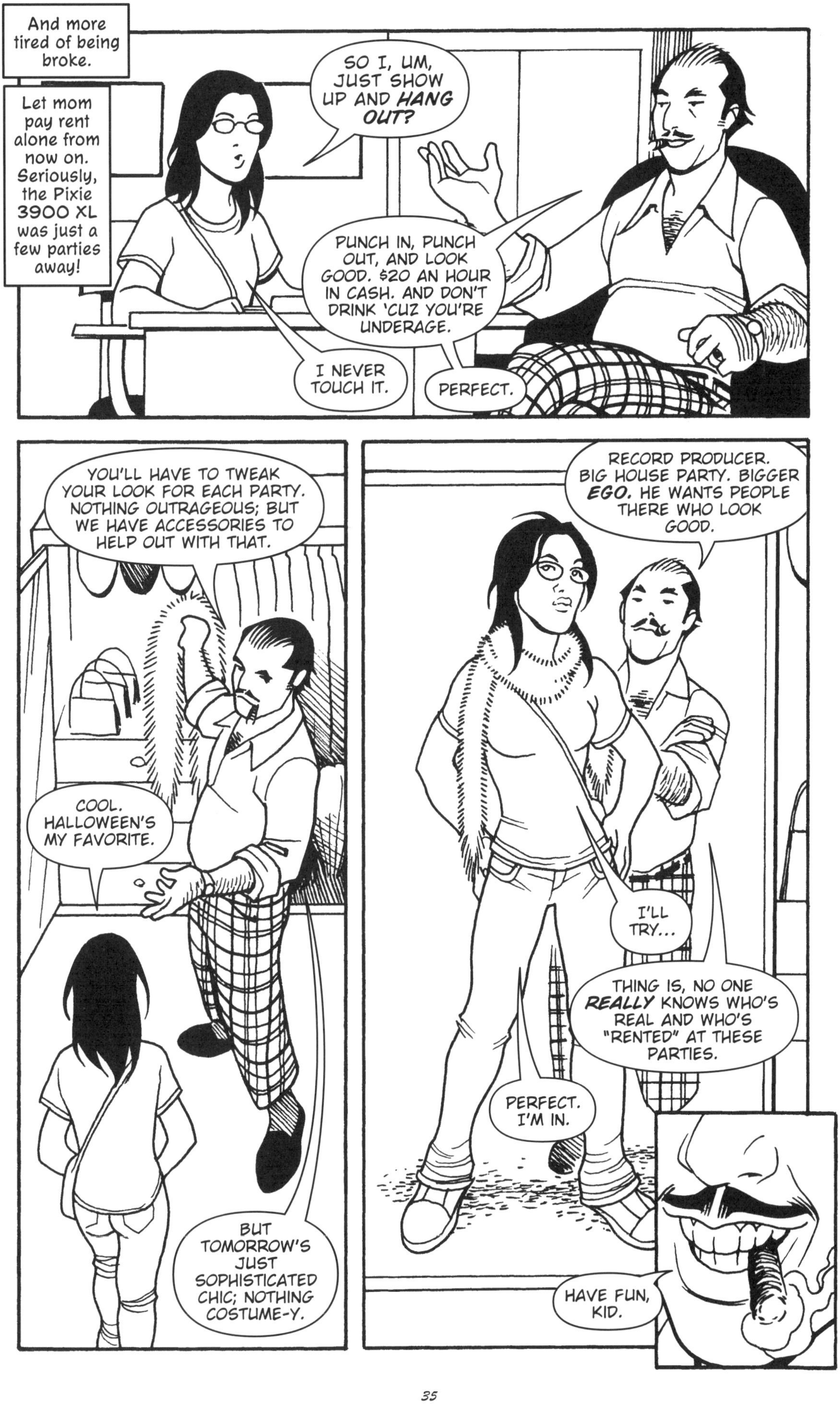
And more tired of being broke.
Let mom pay rent alone from now on. Seriously, the Pixie 3900 XL was just a few parties away!
SO I, UM, JUST SHOW UP AND HANG OUT?
PUNCH IN, PUNCH OUT, AND LOOK GOOD. $20 AN HOUR IN CASH. AND DON'T DRINK 'CUZ YOU'RE UNDERAGE.
I NEVER TOUCH IT.
PERFECT.
YOU'LL HAVE TO TWEAK YOUR LOOK FOR EACH PARTY. NOTHING OUTRAGEOUS; BUT WE HAVE ACCESSORIES TO HELP OUT WITH THAT.
COOL. HALLOWEEN'S MY FAVORITE.
BUT TOMORROW'S JUST SOPHISTICATED CHIC; NOTHING COSTUME-Y.
RECORD PRODUCER. BIG HOUSE PARTY. BIGGER EGO. HE WANTS PEOPLE THERE WHO LOOK GOOD.
I'LL TRY...
THING IS, NO ONE REALLY KNOWS WHO'S REAL AND WHO'S "RENTED" AT THESE PARTIES.
PERFECT. I'M IN.
HAVE FUN, KID.

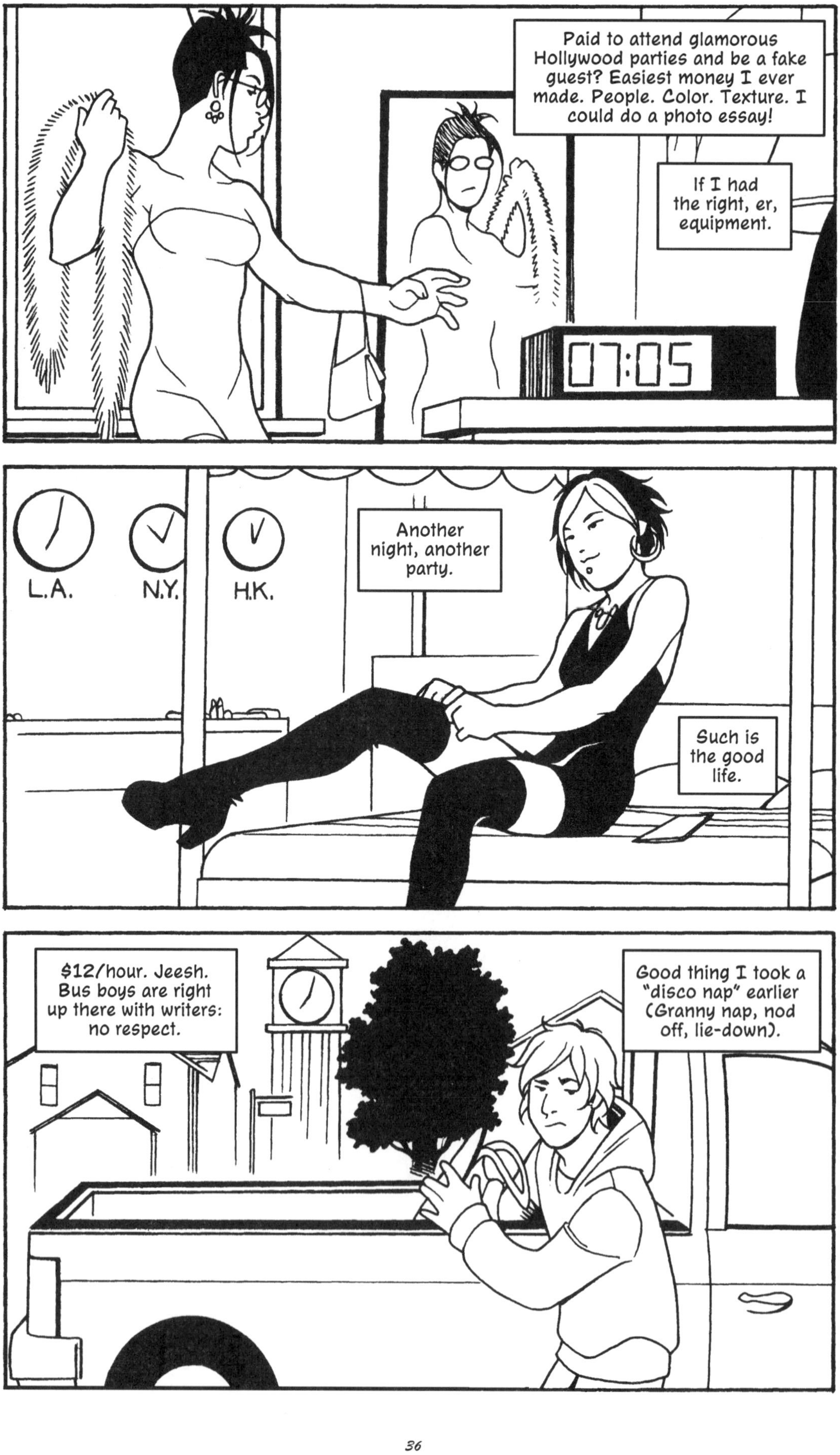
Paid to attend glamorous Hollywood parties and be a fake guest? Easiest money I ever made. People. Color. Texture. I could do a photo essay!
If I had the right, er, equipment.
07:05
L.A.
N.Y.
H.K.
Another night, another party.
Such is the good life.
$12/hour. Jeesh. Bus boys are right up there with writers: no respect.
Good thing I took a "disco nap" earlier (Granny nap, nod off, lie-down).

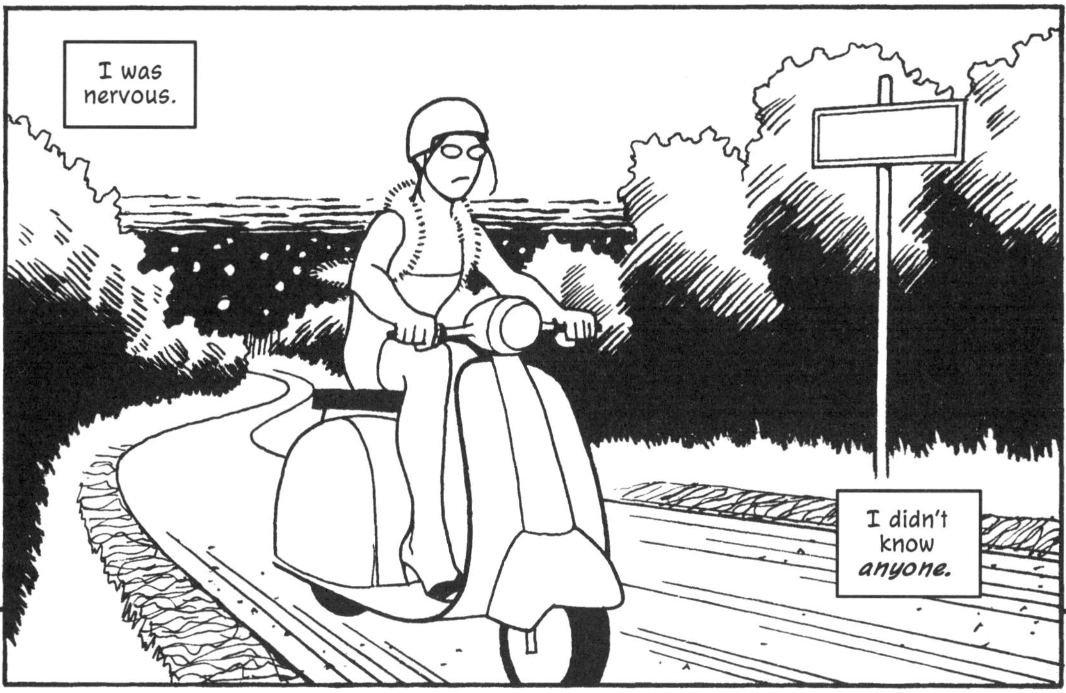
I was nervous.
I didn't know *anyone.*

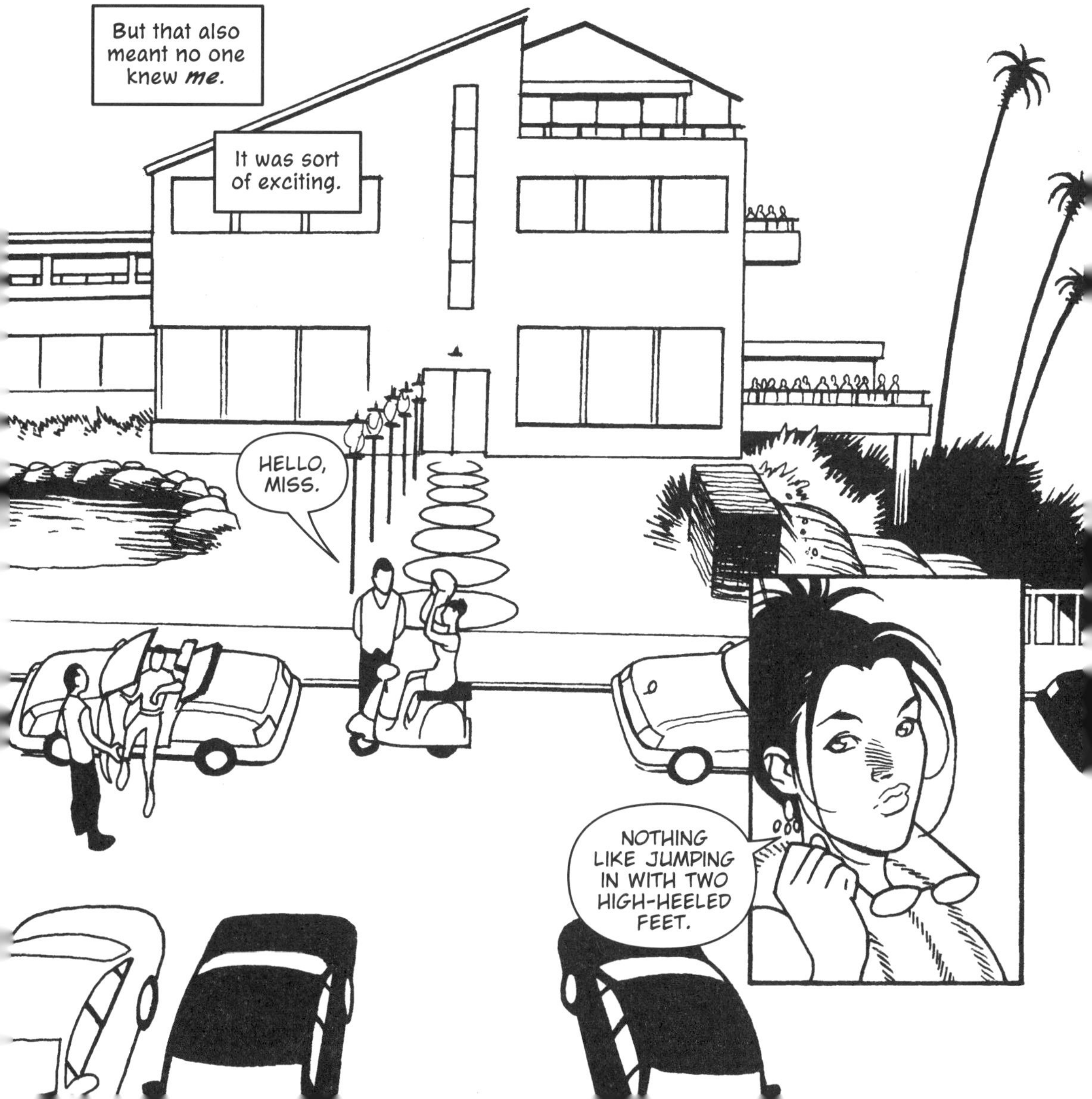
But that also meant no one knew *me.*
It was sort of exciting.
HELLO, MISS.
NOTHING LIKE JUMPING IN WITH TWO HIGH-HEELED FEET.

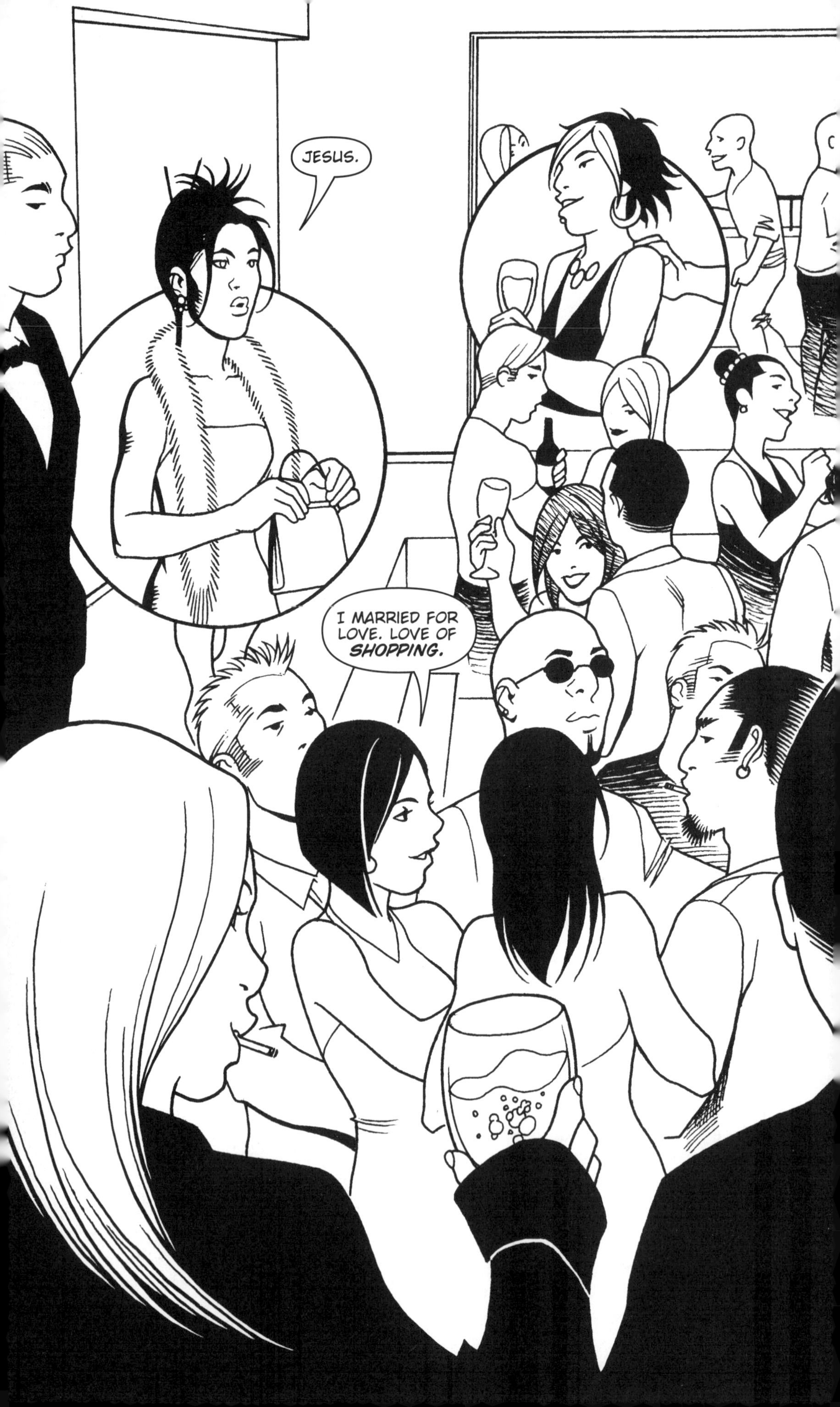
JESUS.
I MARRIED FOR LOVE. LOVE OF SHOPPING.

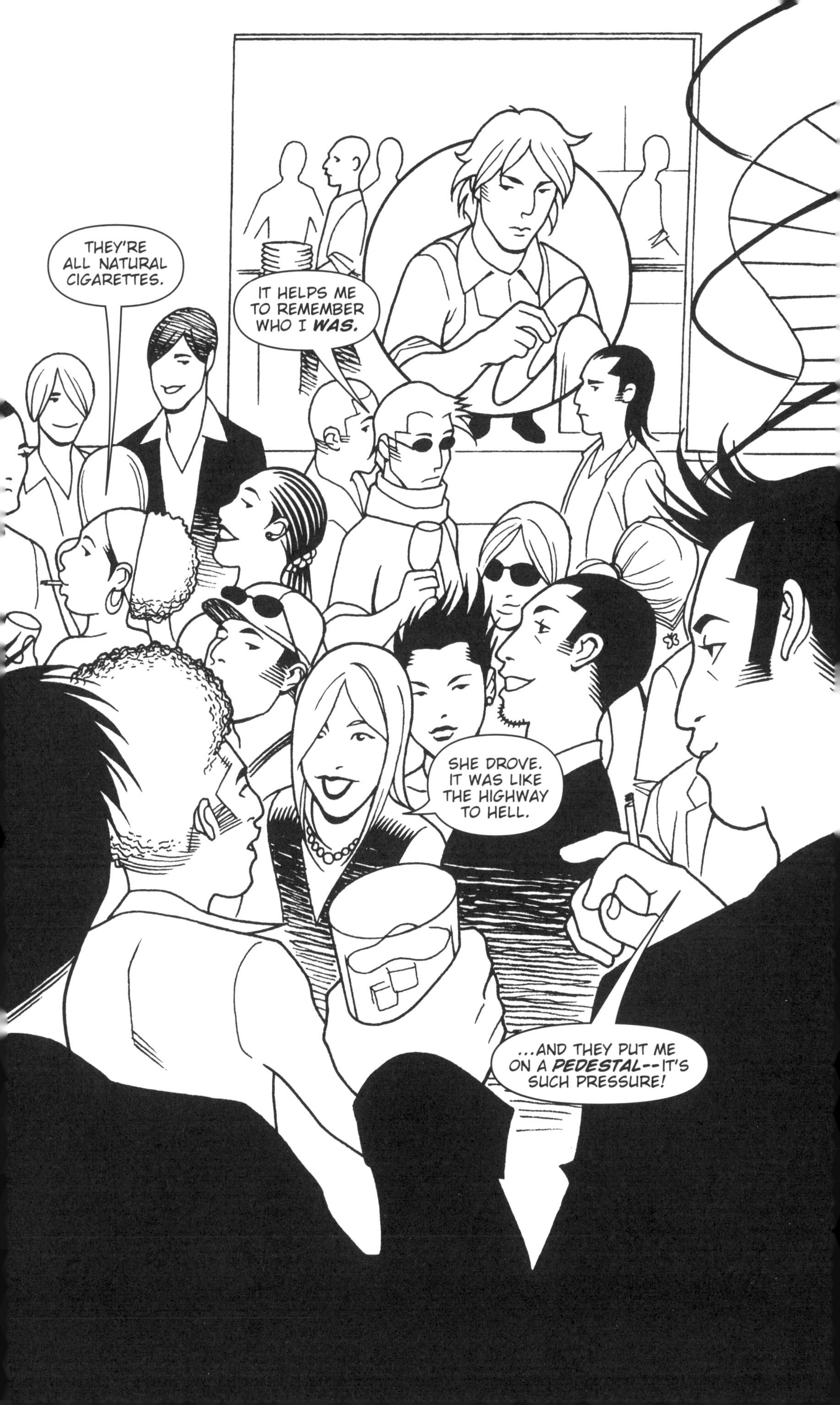

THEY'RE ALL NATURAL CIGARETTES.
IT HELPS ME TO REMEMBER WHO I WAS.
SHE DROVE. IT WAS LIKE THE HIGHWAY TO HELL.
...AND THEY PUT ME ON A PEDESTAL--IT'S SUCH PRESSURE!

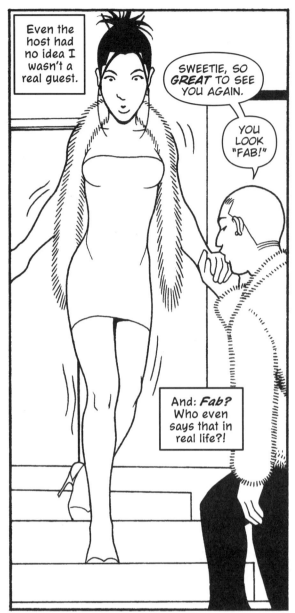

Even the host had no idea I wasn't a real guest.

SWEETIE, SO *GREAT* TO SEE YOU AGAIN.

YOU LOOK "*FAB!*"

And: *Fab?* Who even says that in real life?!

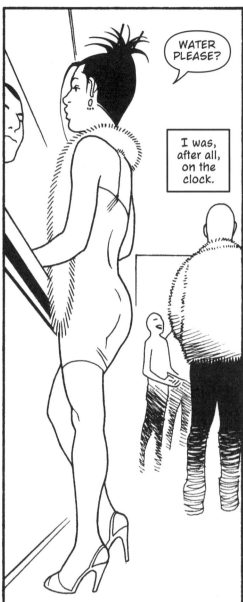

WATER PLEASE?

I was, after all, on the clock.

SPARKLING OR FLAT? IMPORTED OR DOMESTIC? FLAVORED, OXYGENIZED OR PLAIN? RECYCLED PLASTIC OR GLASS?

WHATEVER'S, UH, WETTEST?

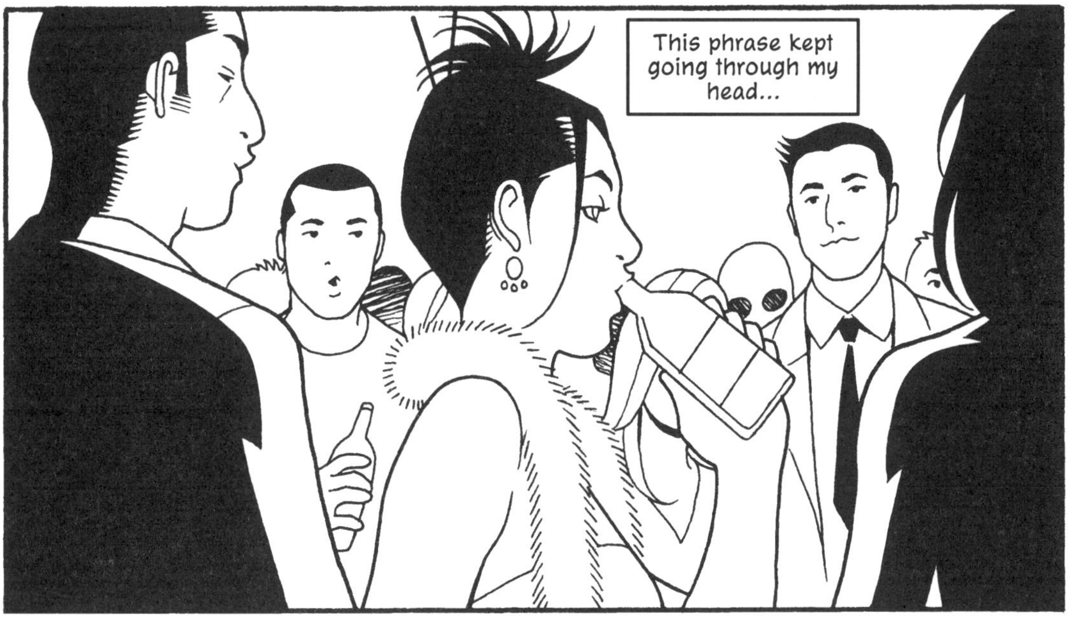
This phrase kept going through my head...

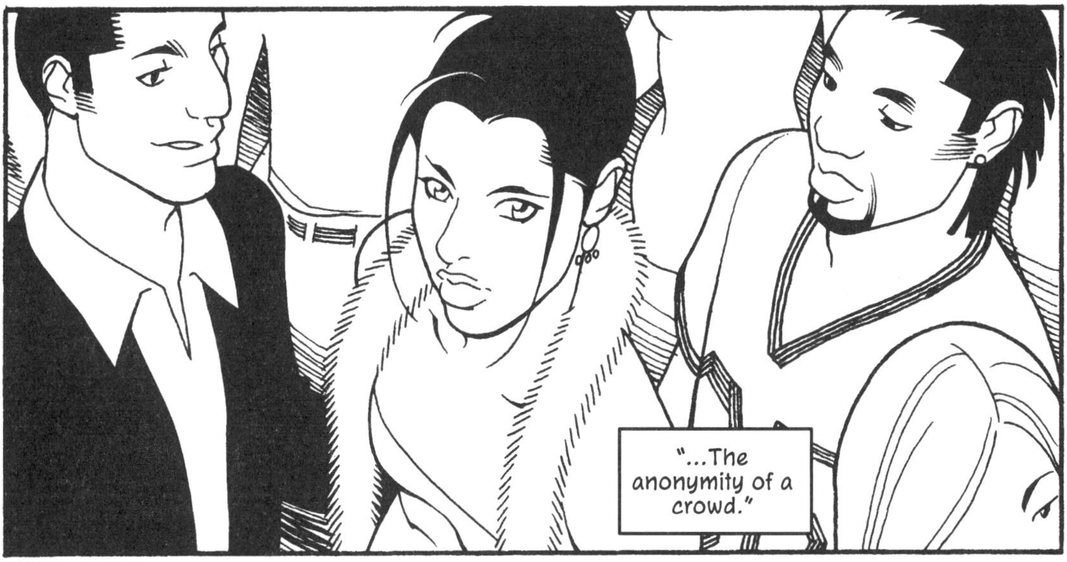
"...The anonymity of a crowd."

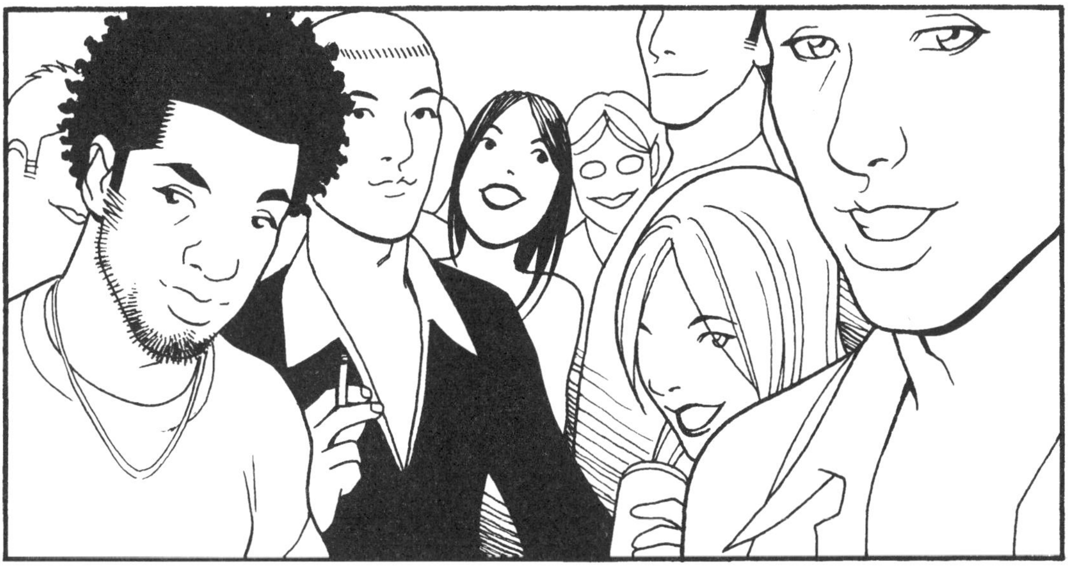

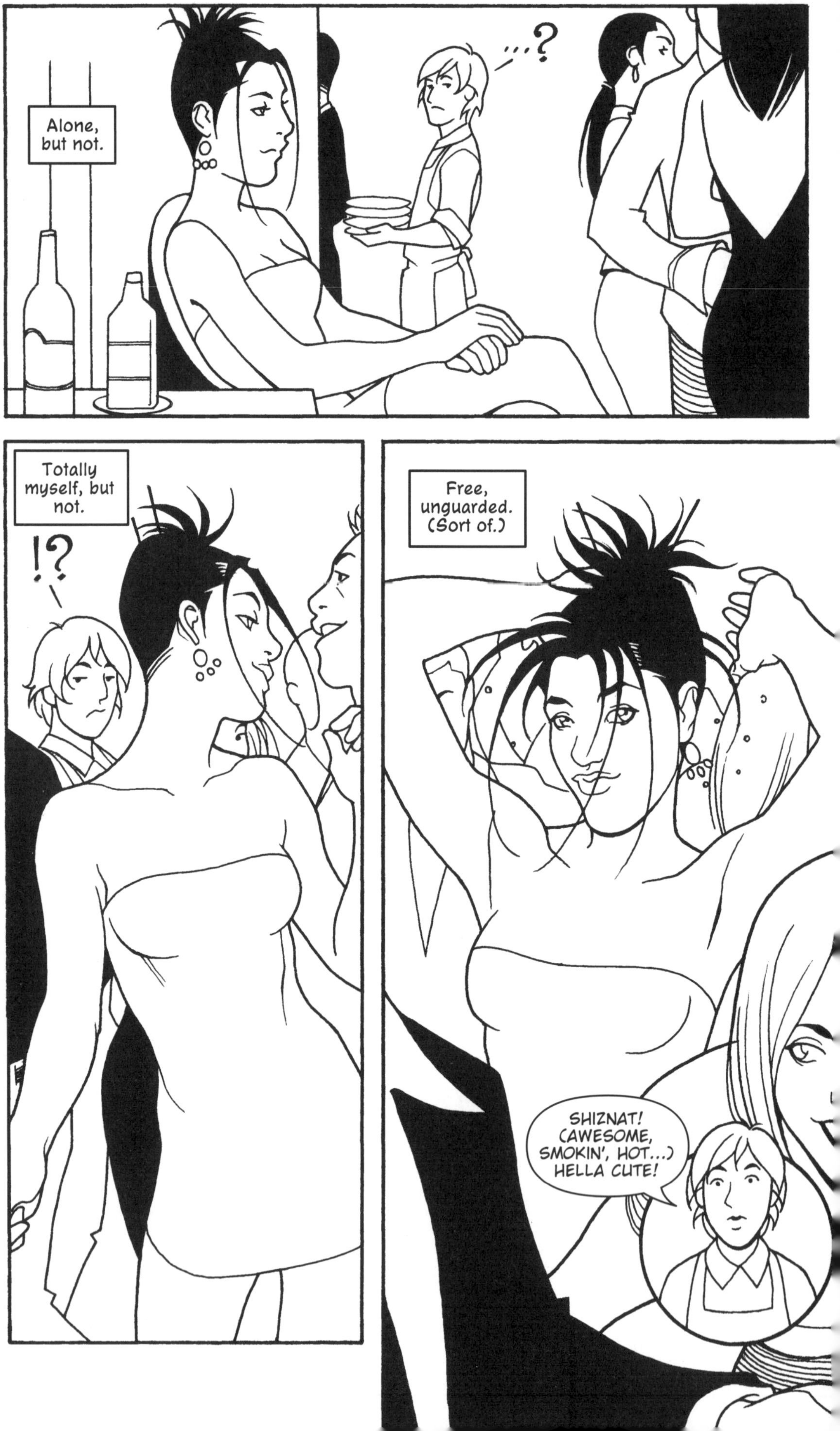
Alone, but not.
...?
Totally myself, but not.
!?
Free, unguarded. (Sort of.)
SHIZNAT! (AWESOME, SMOKIN', HOT...) HELLA CUTE!

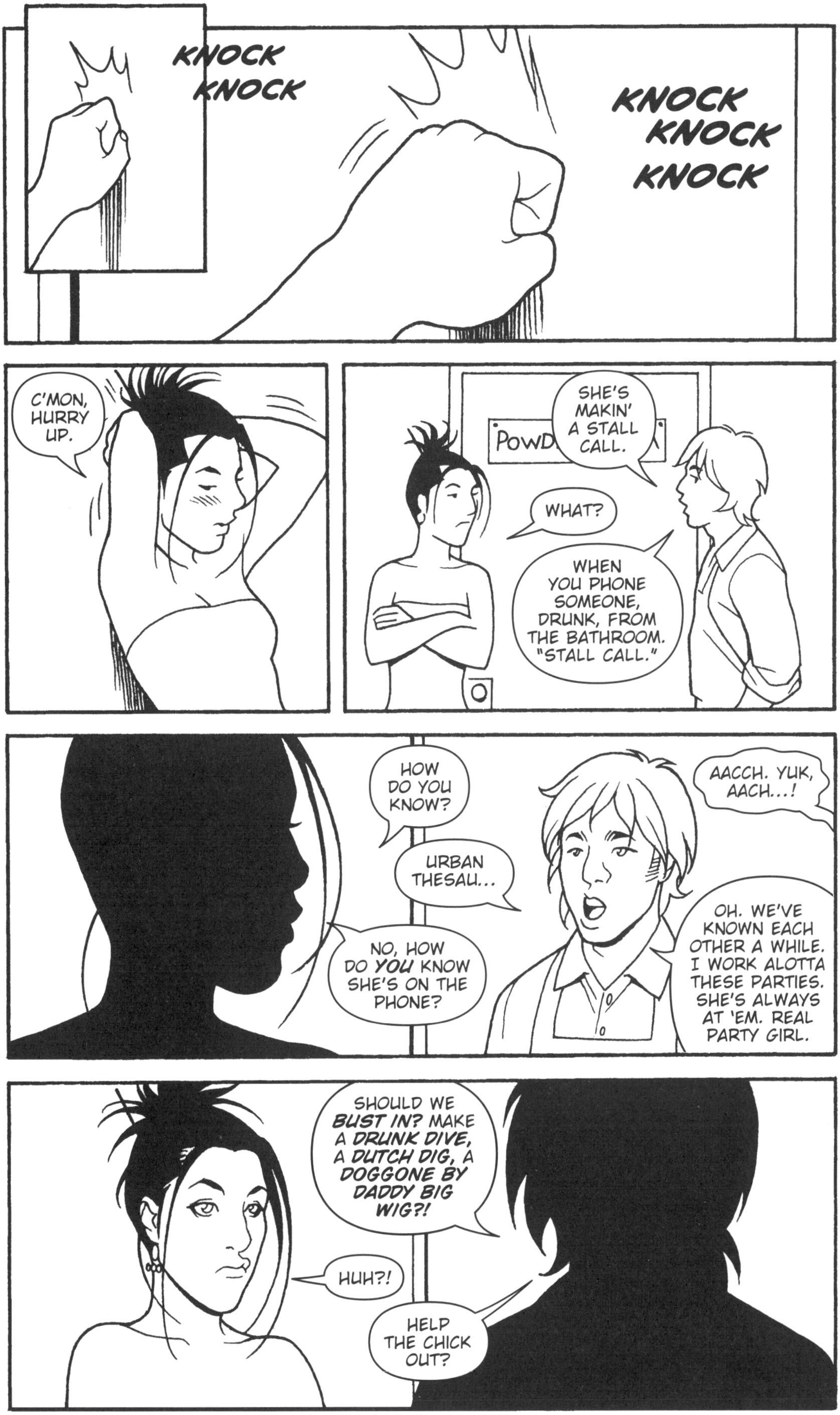
KNOCK KNOCK
KNOCK KNOCK KNOCK
C'MON, HURRY UP.
SHE'S MAKIN' A STALL CALL.
WHAT?
WHEN YOU PHONE SOMEONE, DRUNK, FROM THE BATHROOM. "STALL CALL."
HOW DO YOU KNOW?
URBAN THESAU...
AACCH. YUK, AACH...!
NO, HOW DO *YOU* KNOW SHE'S ON THE PHONE?
OH. WE'VE KNOWN EACH OTHER A WHILE. I WORK ALOTTA THESE PARTIES. SHE'S ALWAYS AT 'EM. REAL PARTY GIRL.
SHOULD WE *BUST IN?* MAKE A *DRUNK DIVE,* A *DUTCH DIG,* A *DOGGONE BY DADDY BIG WIG?!*
HUH?!
HELP THE CHICK OUT?

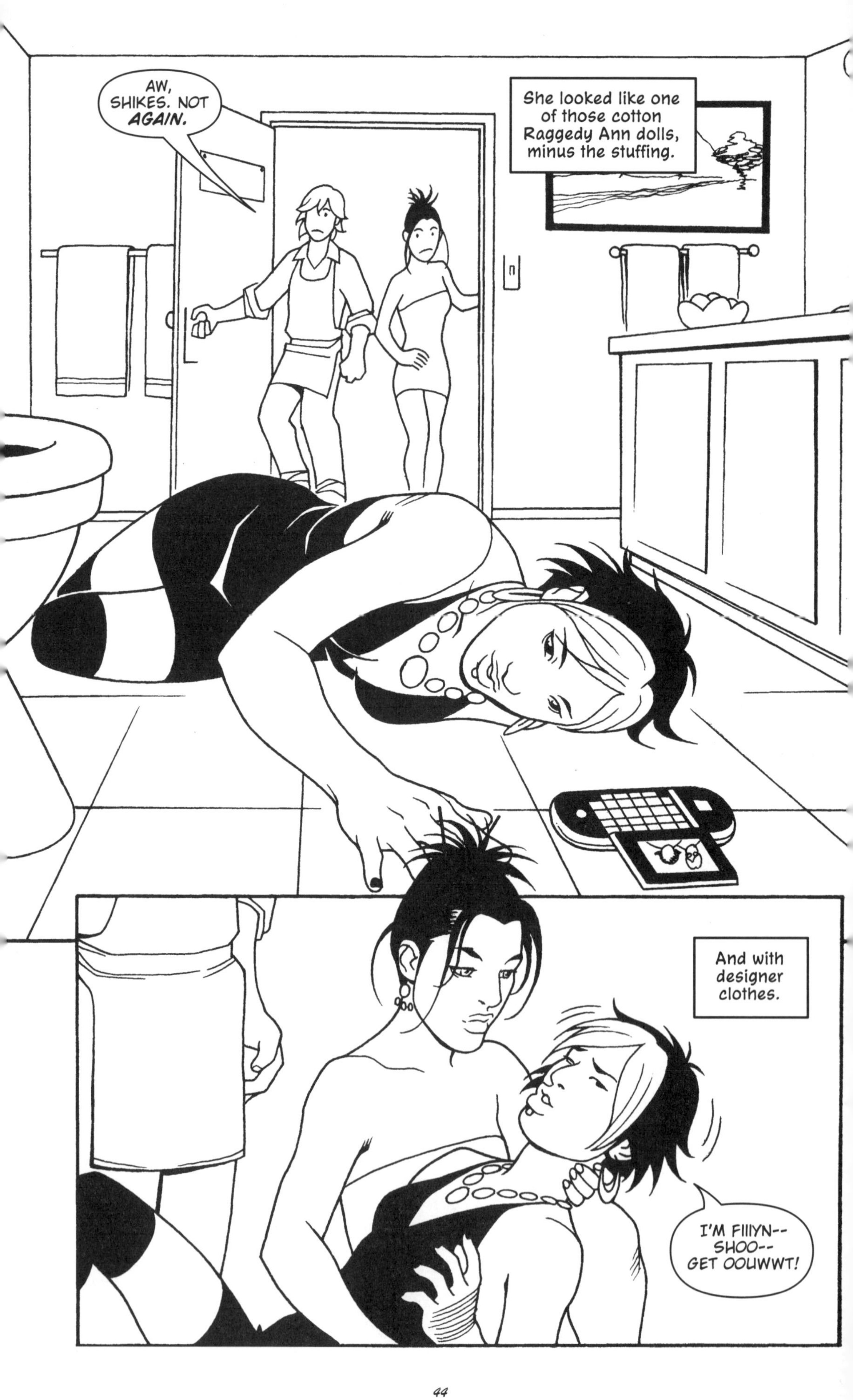
AW, SHIKES. NOT AGAIN.
She looked like one of those cotton Raggedy Ann dolls, minus the stuffing.
And with designer clothes.
I'M FIIIYN-- SHOO-- GET OOUWWT!

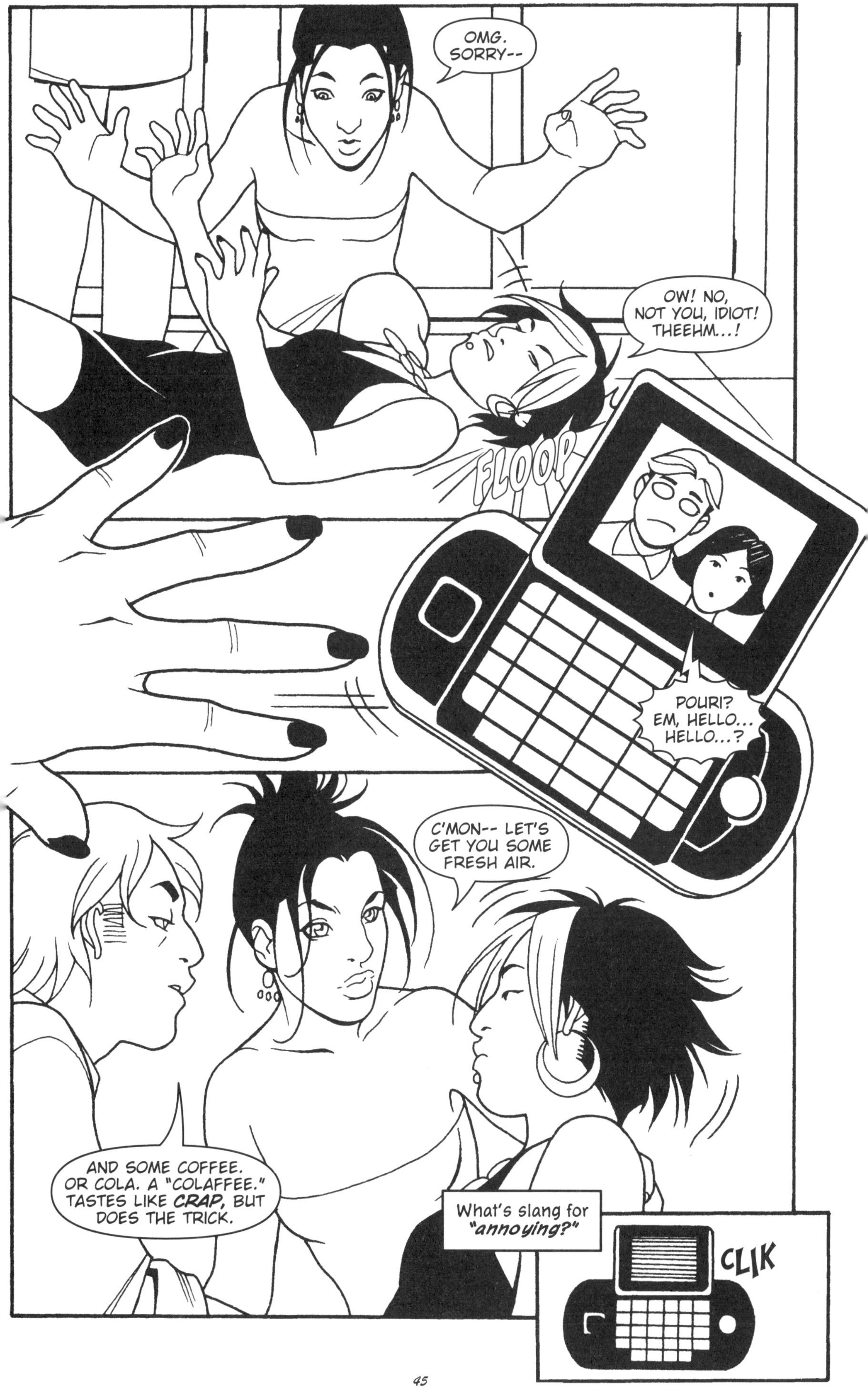
OMG. SORRY--
OW! NO, NOT YOU, IDIOT! THEEHM...!
FLOOP
POURI? EM, HELLO... HELLO...?
C'MON-- LET'S GET YOU SOME FRESH AIR.
AND SOME COFFEE. OR COLA. A "COLAFFEE." TASTES LIKE **CRAP**, BUT DOES THE TRICK.
What's slang for *"annoying?"*
CLIK

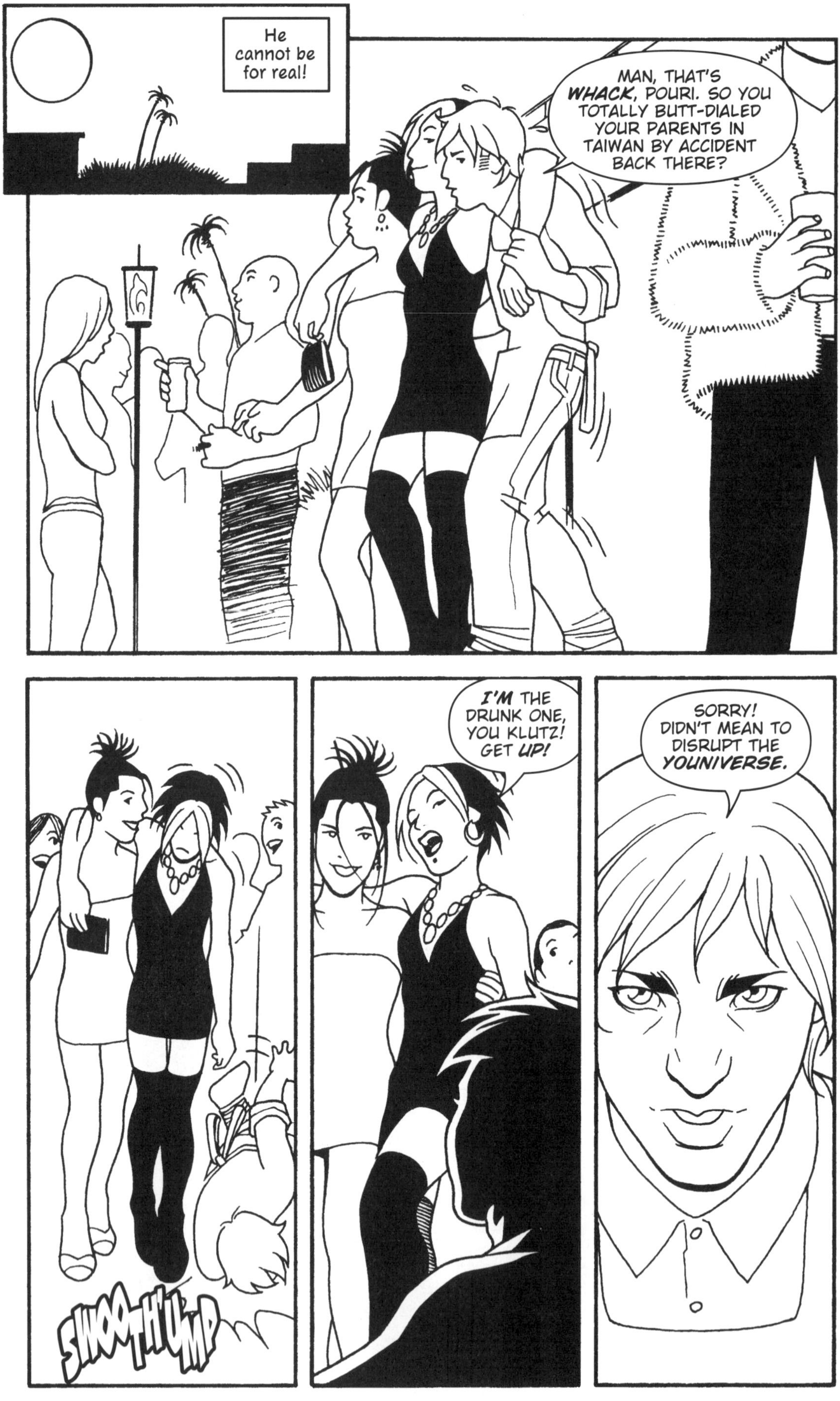

He cannot be for real!
MAN, THAT'S WHACK, POURI. SO YOU TOTALLY BUTT-DIALED YOUR PARENTS IN TAIWAN BY ACCIDENT BACK THERE?
SWOOTHUMP
I'M THE DRUNK ONE, YOU KLUTZ! GET UP!
SORRY! DIDN'T MEAN TO DISRUPT THE YOUNIVERSE.

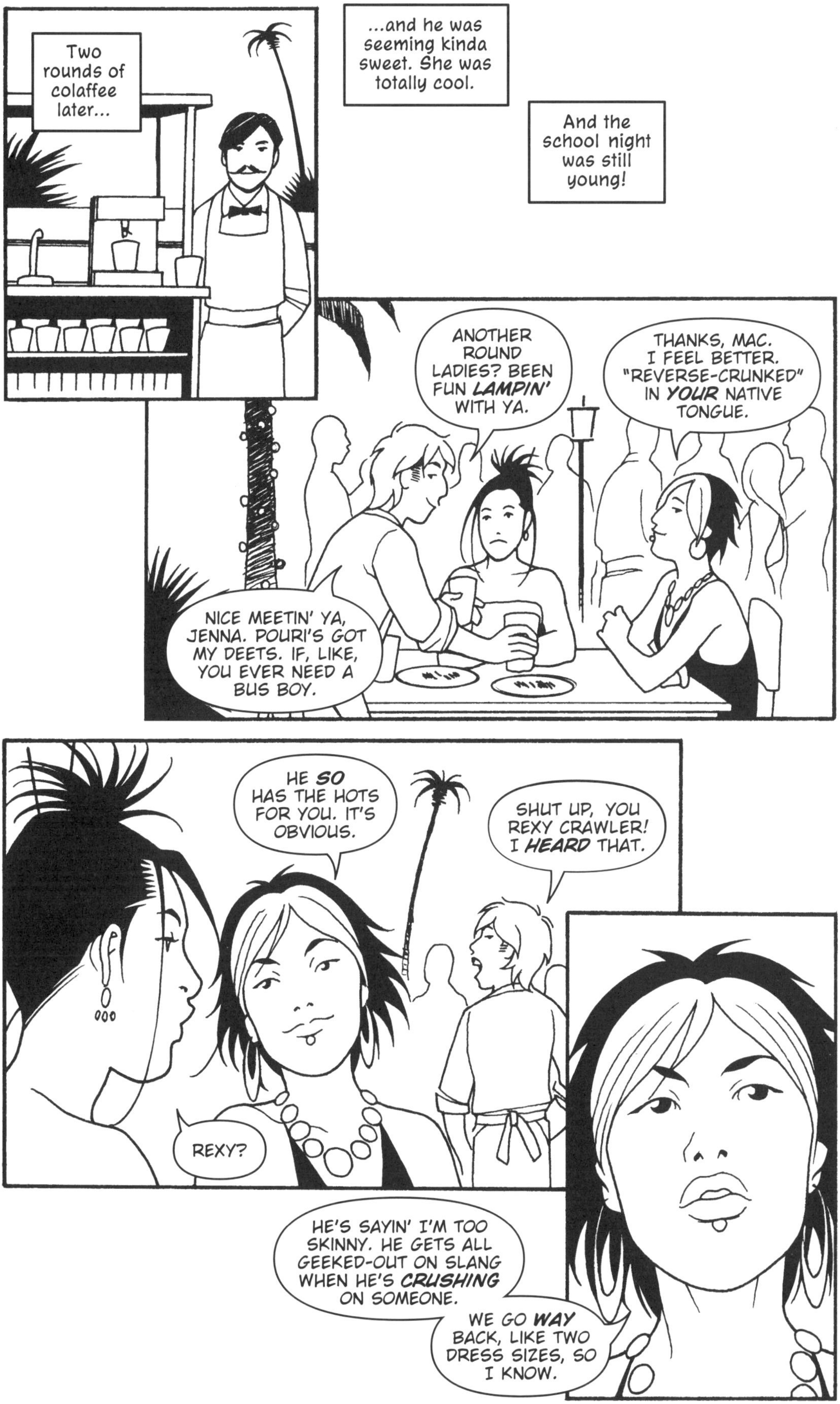

Two rounds of colaffee later...
...and he was seeming kinda sweet. She was totally cool.
And the school night was still young!
ANOTHER ROUND LADIES? BEEN FUN LAMPIN' WITH YA.
THANKS, MAC. I FEEL BETTER. "REVERSE-CRUNKED" IN YOUR NATIVE TONGUE.
NICE MEETIN' YA, JENNA. POURI'S GOT MY DEETS. IF, LIKE, YOU EVER NEED A BUS BOY.
HE SO HAS THE HOTS FOR YOU. IT'S OBVIOUS.
SHUT UP, YOU REXY CRAWLER! I HEARD THAT.
REXY?
HE'S SAYIN' I'M TOO SKINNY. HE GETS ALL GEEKED-OUT ON SLANG WHEN HE'S CRUSHING ON SOMEONE.
WE GO WAY BACK, LIKE TWO DRESS SIZES, SO I KNOW.

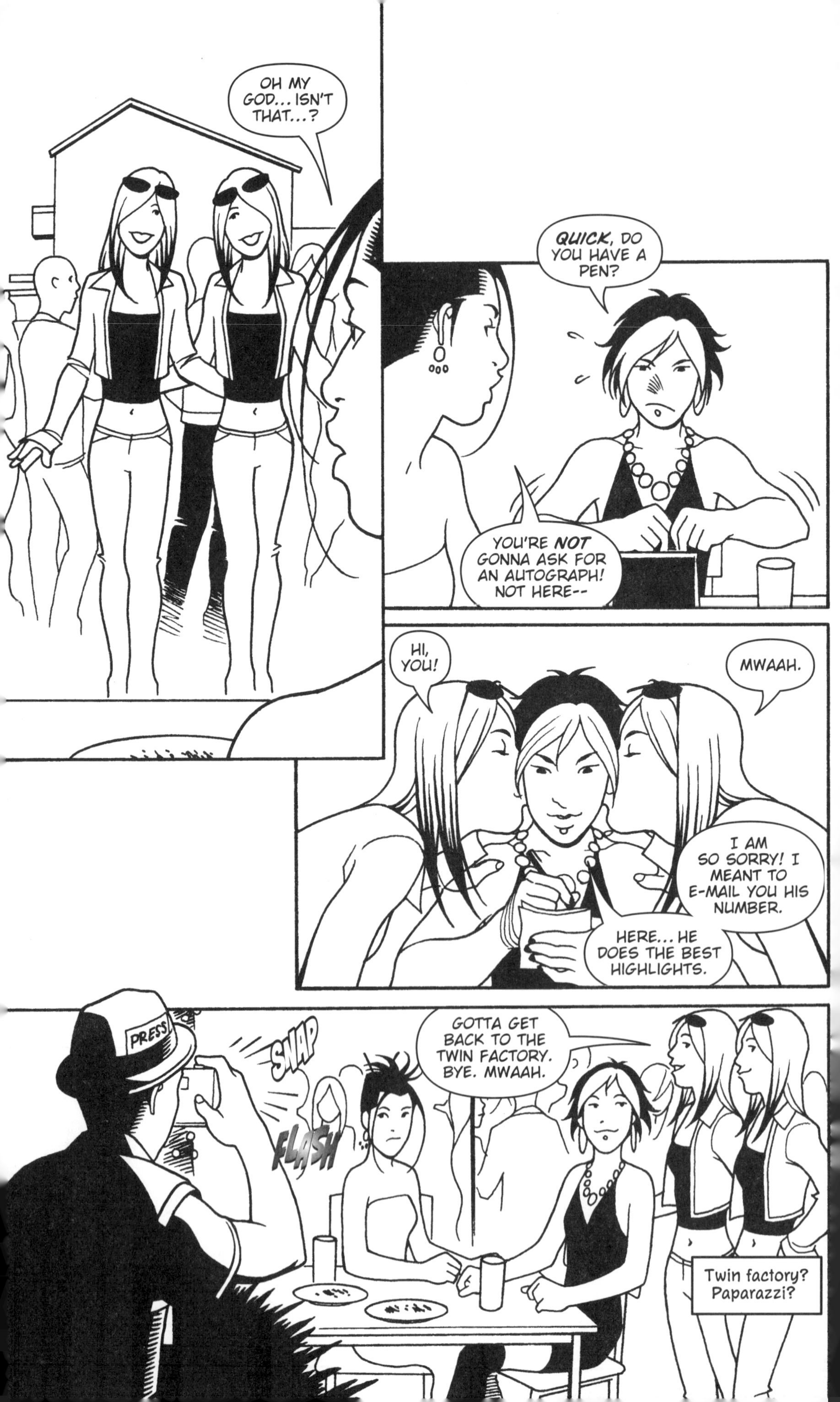
OH MY GOD... ISN'T THAT...?
QUICK, DO YOU HAVE A PEN?
YOU'RE NOT GONNA ASK FOR AN AUTOGRAPH! NOT HERE--
HI, YOU!
MWAAH.
I AM SO SORRY! I MEANT TO E-MAIL YOU HIS NUMBER.
HERE... HE DOES THE BEST HIGHLIGHTS.
PRESS
SNAP
FLASH
GOTTA GET BACK TO THE TWIN FACTORY. BYE. MWAAH.
Twin factory? Paparazzi?

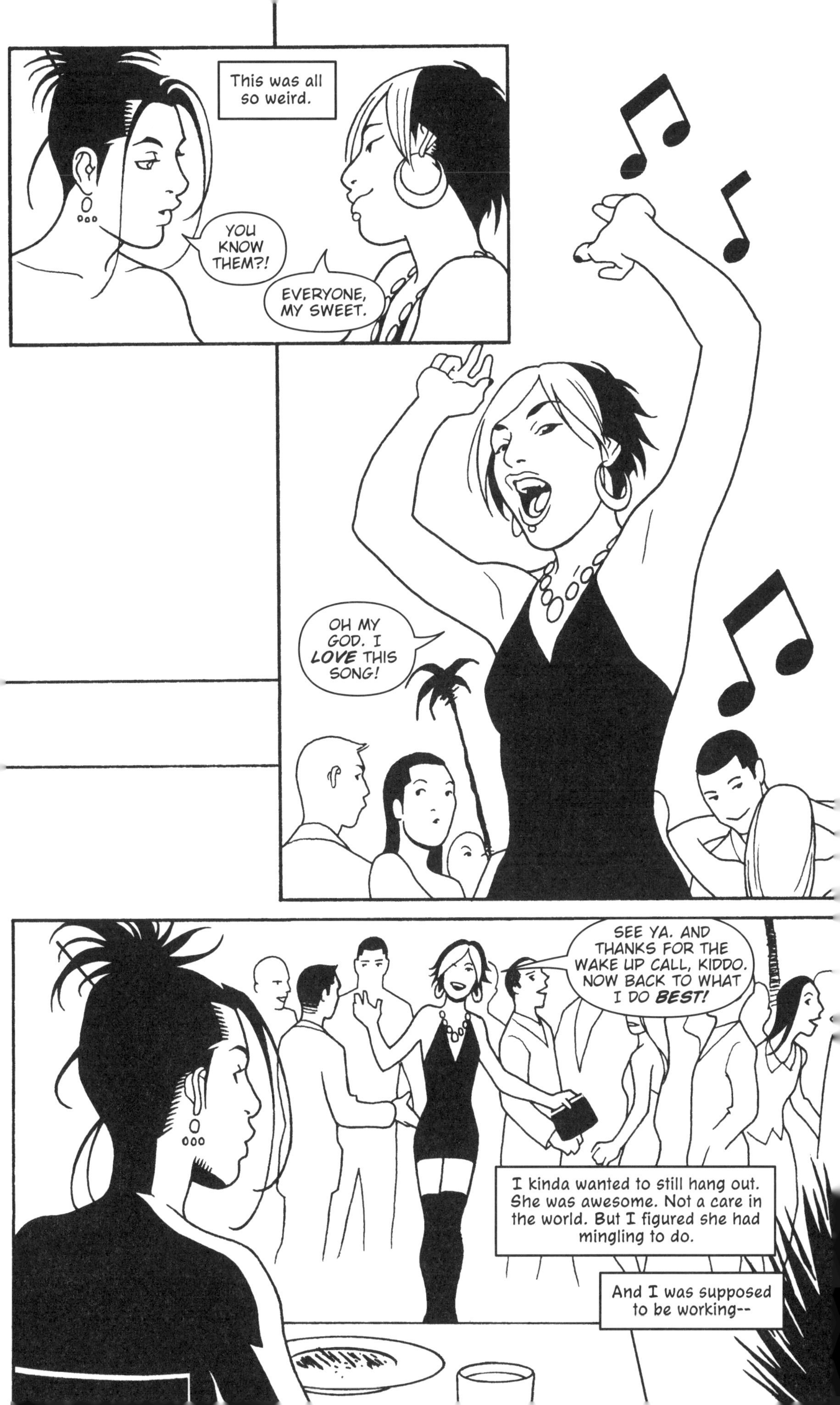

This was all so weird.
YOU KNOW THEM?!
EVERYONE, MY SWEET.
OH MY GOD. I **LOVE** THIS SONG!
SEE YA. AND THANKS FOR THE WAKE UP CALL, KIDDO. NOW BACK TO WHAT I DO **BEST!**
I kinda wanted to still hang out. She was awesome. Not a care in the world. But I figured she had mingling to do.
And I was supposed to be working--

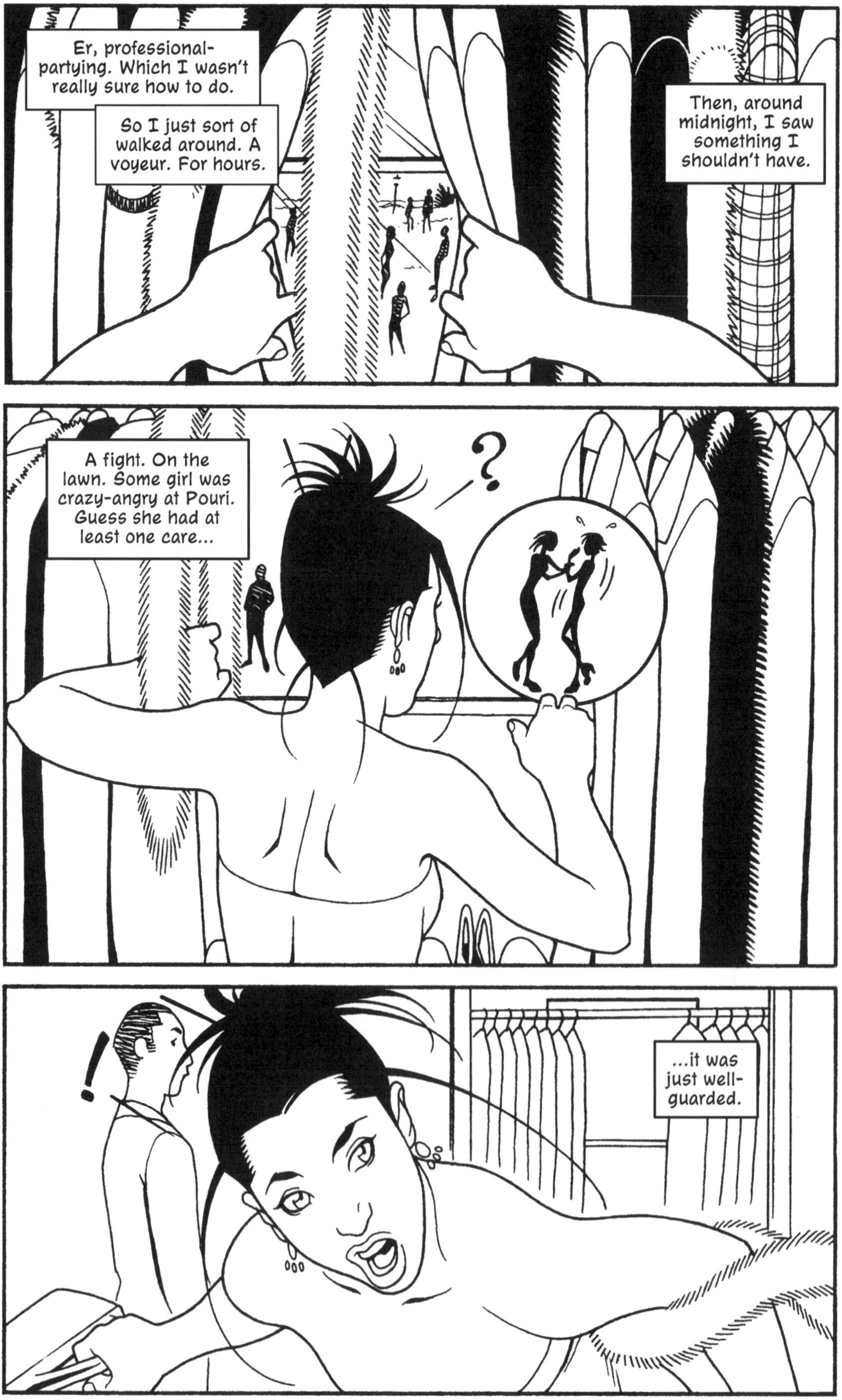
Er, professional-partying. Which I wasn't really sure how to do.
So I just sort of walked around. A voyeur. For hours.
Then, around midnight, I saw something I shouldn't have.
A fight. On the lawn. Some girl was crazy-angry at Pouri. Guess she had at least one care...
?
!
...it was just well-guarded.

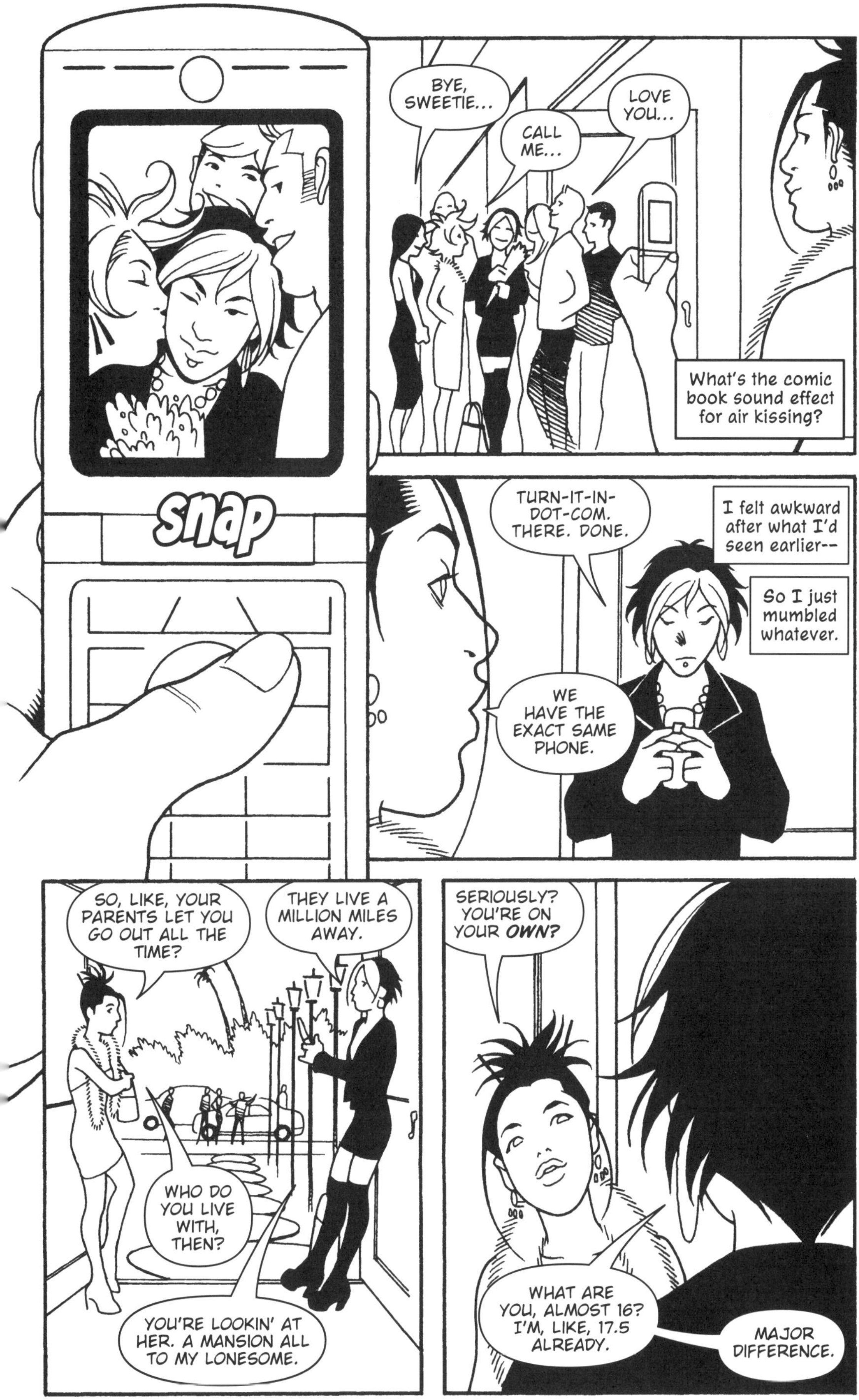

BYE, SWEETIE...
CALL ME...
LOVE YOU...
What's the comic book sound effect for air kissing?
SNAP
TURN-IT-IN-DOT-COM. THERE. DONE.
I felt awkward after what I'd seen earlier--
So I just mumbled whatever.
WE HAVE THE EXACT SAME PHONE.
SO, LIKE, YOUR PARENTS LET YOU GO OUT ALL THE TIME?
THEY LIVE A MILLION MILES AWAY.
WHO DO YOU LIVE WITH, THEN?
YOU'RE LOOKIN' AT HER. A MANSION ALL TO MY LONESOME.
SERIOUSLY? YOU'RE ON YOUR ***OWN?***
WHAT ARE YOU, ALMOST 16? I'M, LIKE, 17.5 ALREADY.
MAJOR DIFFERENCE.

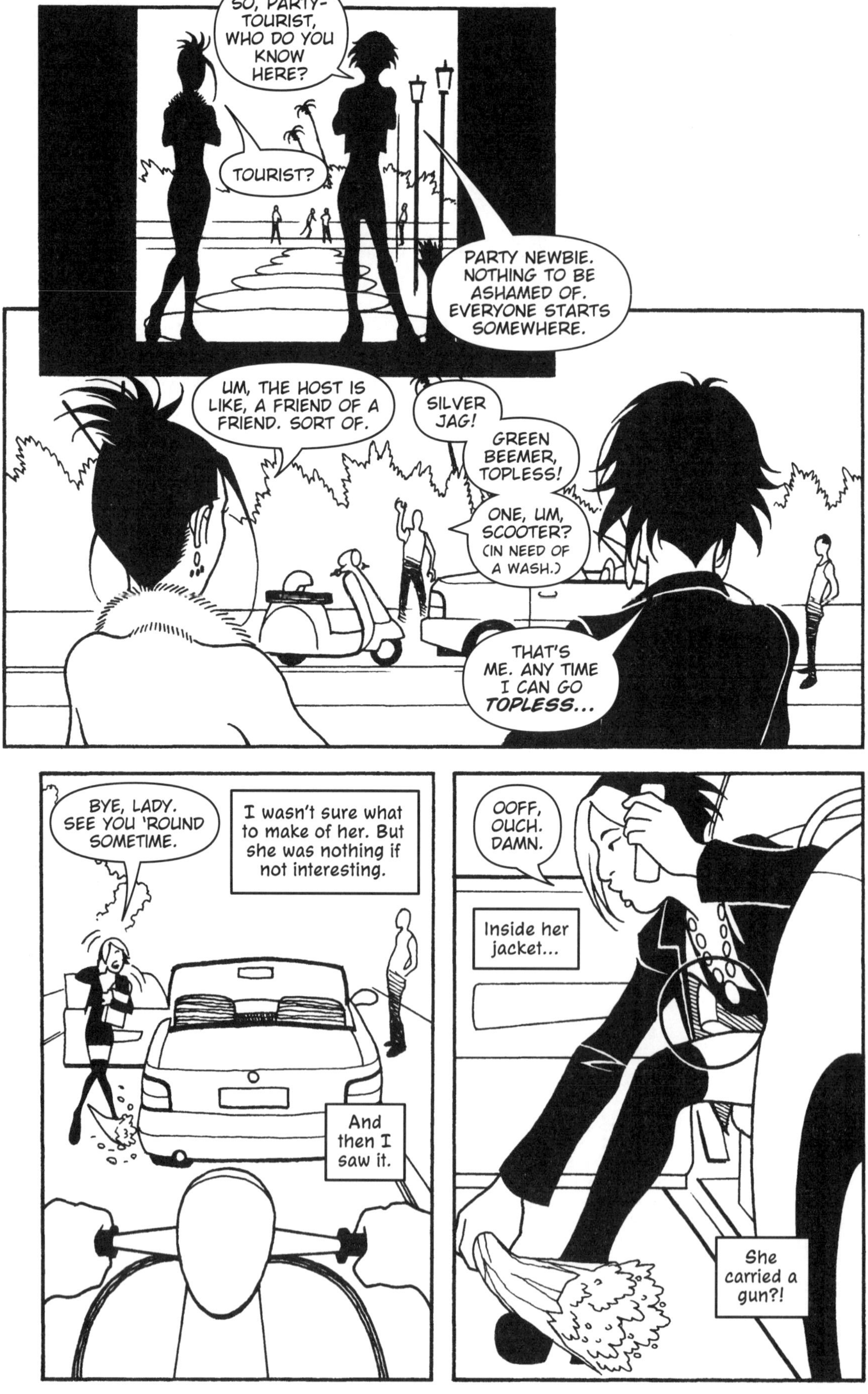
SO, PARTY-TOURIST, WHO DO YOU KNOW HERE?
TOURIST?
PARTY NEWBIE. NOTHING TO BE ASHAMED OF. EVERYONE STARTS SOMEWHERE.
UM, THE HOST IS LIKE, A FRIEND OF A FRIEND. SORT OF.
SILVER JAG!
GREEN BEEMER, TOPLESS!
ONE, UM, SCOOTER? (IN NEED OF A WASH.)
THAT'S ME. ANY TIME I CAN GO *TOPLESS...*
BYE, LADY. SEE YOU 'ROUND SOMETIME.
I wasn't sure what to make of her. But she was nothing if not interesting.
And then I saw it.
OOFF, OUCH. DAMN.
Inside her jacket...
She carried a gun?!

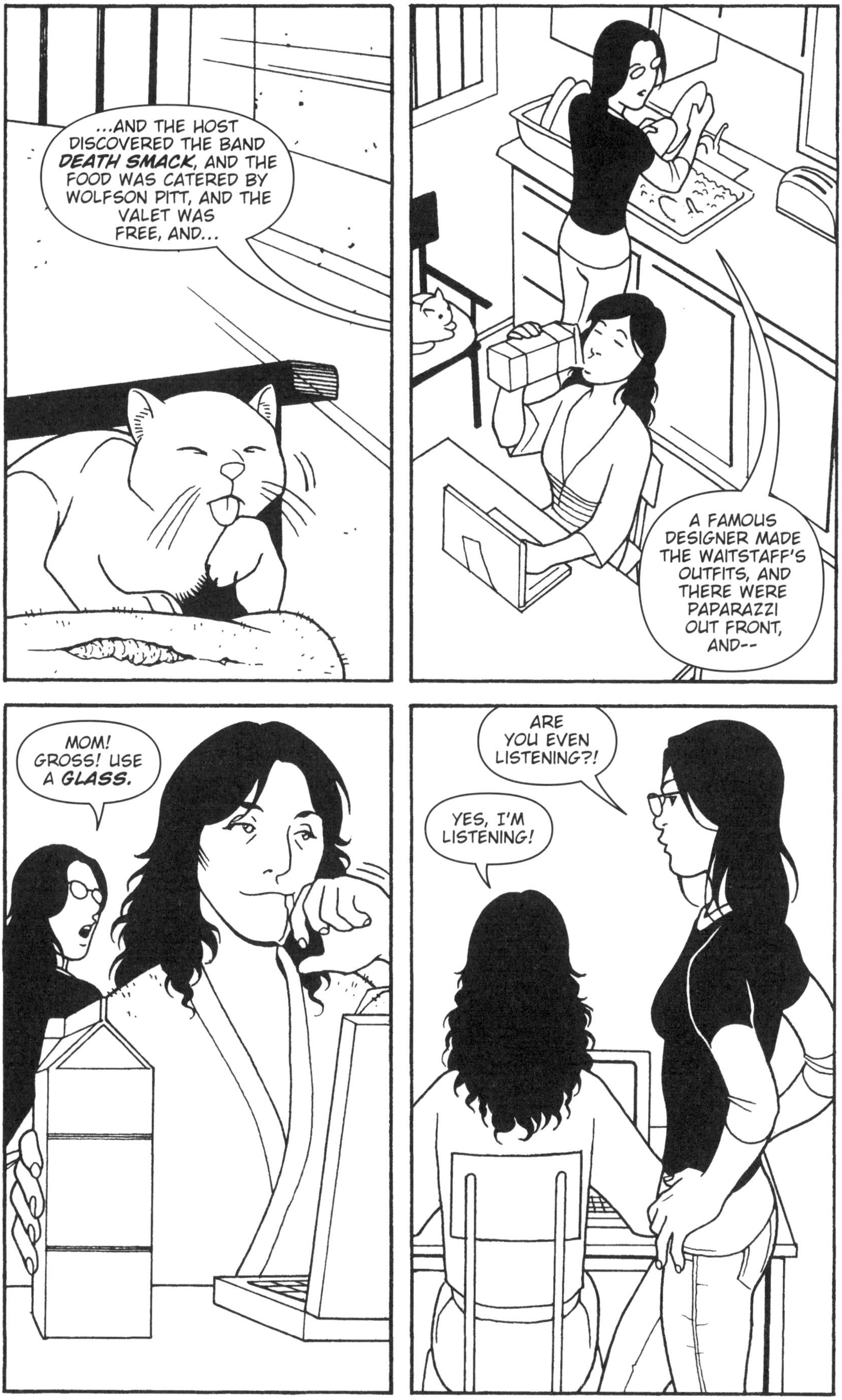
...AND THE HOST DISCOVERED THE BAND DEATH SMACK, AND THE FOOD WAS CATERED BY WOLFSON PITT, AND THE VALET WAS FREE, AND...
A FAMOUS DESIGNER MADE THE WAITSTAFF'S OUTFITS, AND THERE WERE PAPARAZZI OUT FRONT, AND--
MOM! GROSS! USE A GLASS.
ARE YOU EVEN LISTENING?!
YES, I'M LISTENING!

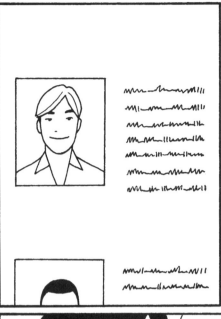

'THERE WERE PAPARAZZI THERE AND...' CUTE HUH? DREEM-DUDE88.

SHOULDN'T *I* BE THE BOY-CRAZY ONE?!

THERE ARE *PLENTY* OF ADORABLE YOUNGER GUYS HERE...

...THEY LIE ABOUT THEIR AGE 'CUZ THEY *LIKE* OLDER--

MOM! STOP, PLEASE!

I'M LATE FOR SCHOOL, REMEMBER?!

YOU SHOULD GET GOING, TOO--YOU HAVE A MEETING AT NINE.

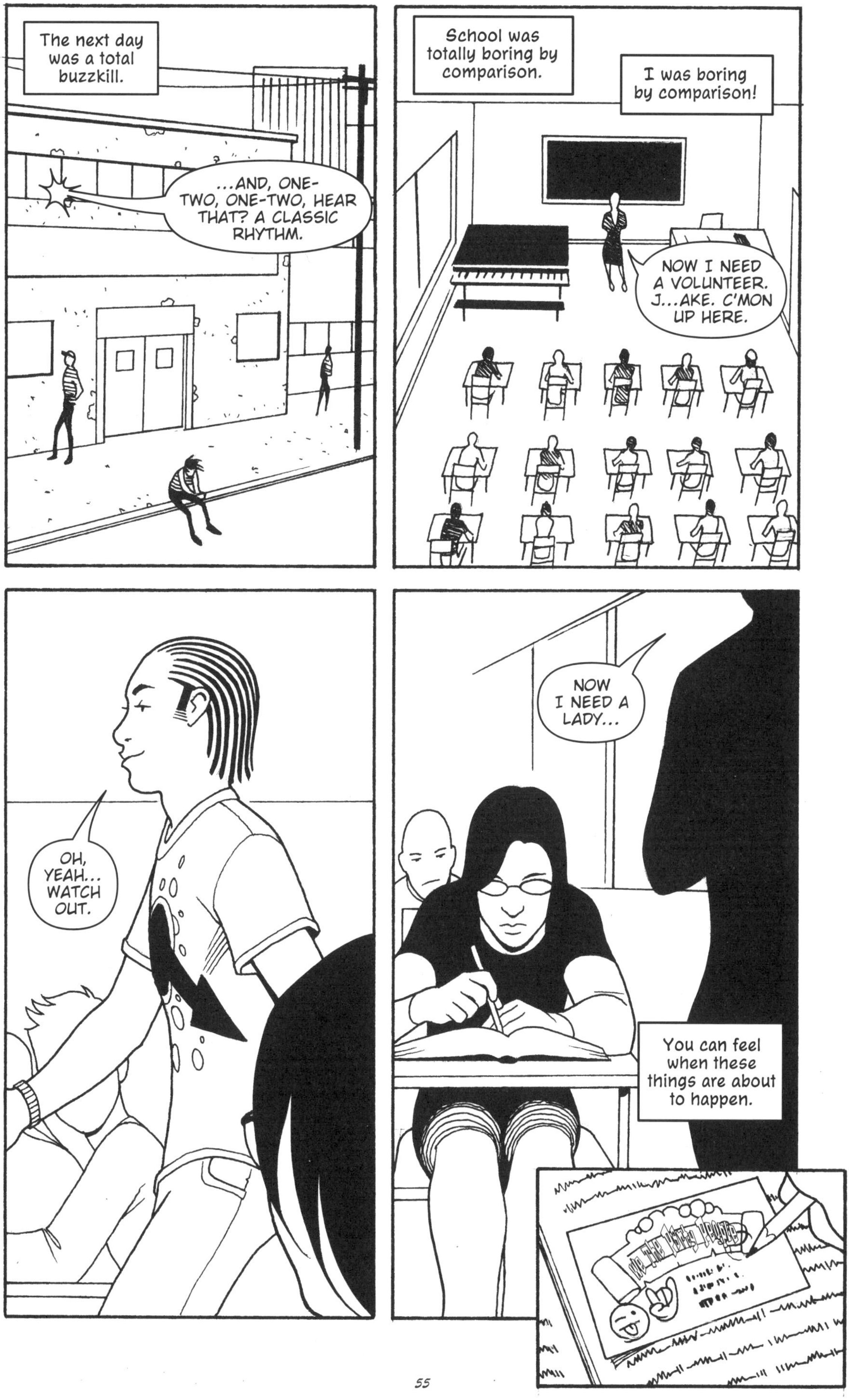

The next day was a total buzzkill.
...AND, ONE-TWO, ONE-TWO, HEAR THAT? A CLASSIC RHYTHM.
School was totally boring by comparison.
I was boring by comparison!
NOW I NEED A VOLUNTEER. J...AKE. C'MON UP HERE.
OH, YEAH... WATCH OUT.
NOW I NEED A LADY...
You can feel when these things are about to happen.

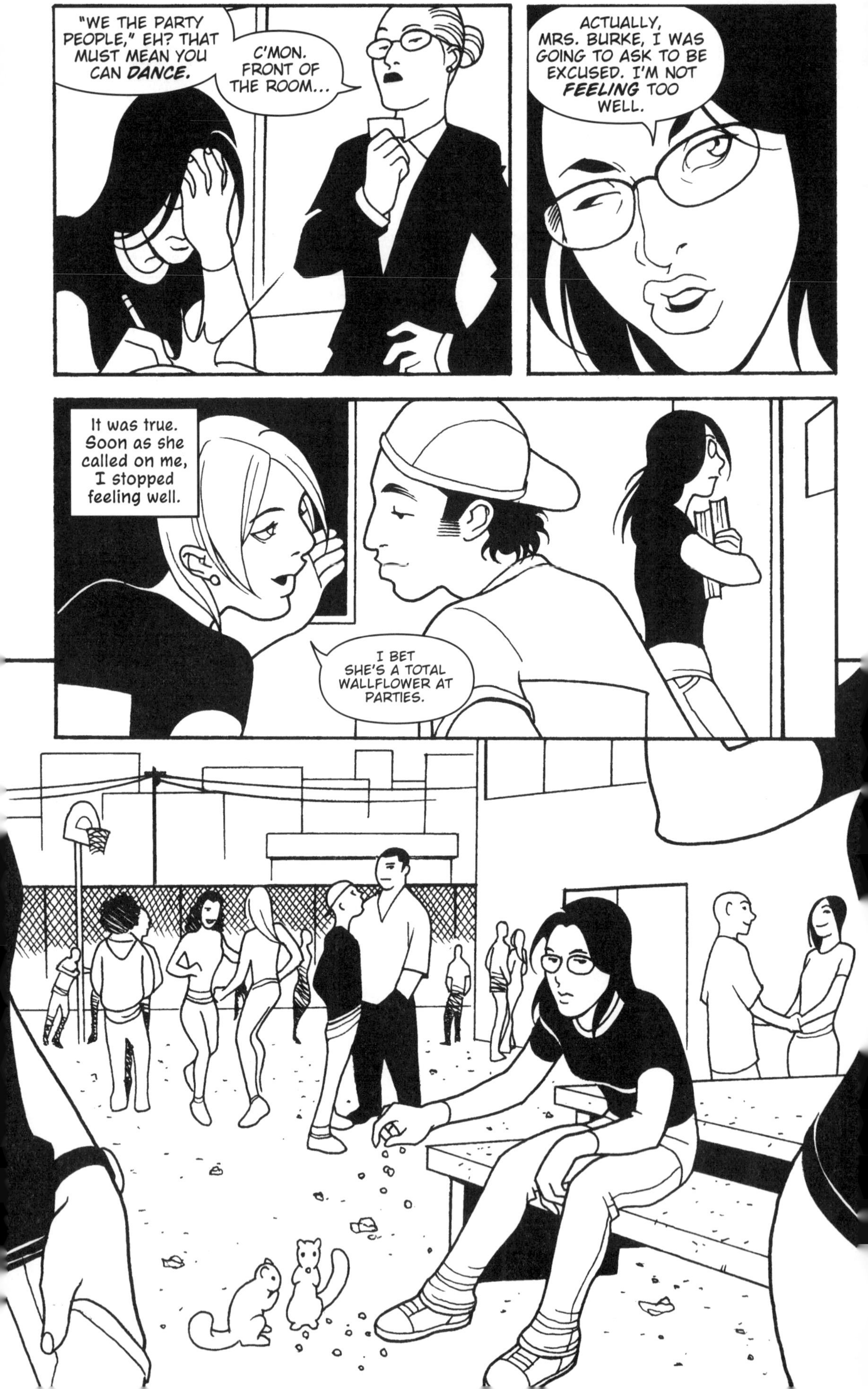
"WE THE PARTY PEOPLE," EH? THAT MUST MEAN YOU CAN DANCE.
C'MON. FRONT OF THE ROOM...
ACTUALLY, MRS. BURKE, I WAS GOING TO ASK TO BE EXCUSED. I'M NOT FEELING TOO WELL.
It was true. Soon as she called on me, I stopped feeling well.
I BET SHE'S A TOTAL WALLFLOWER AT PARTIES.

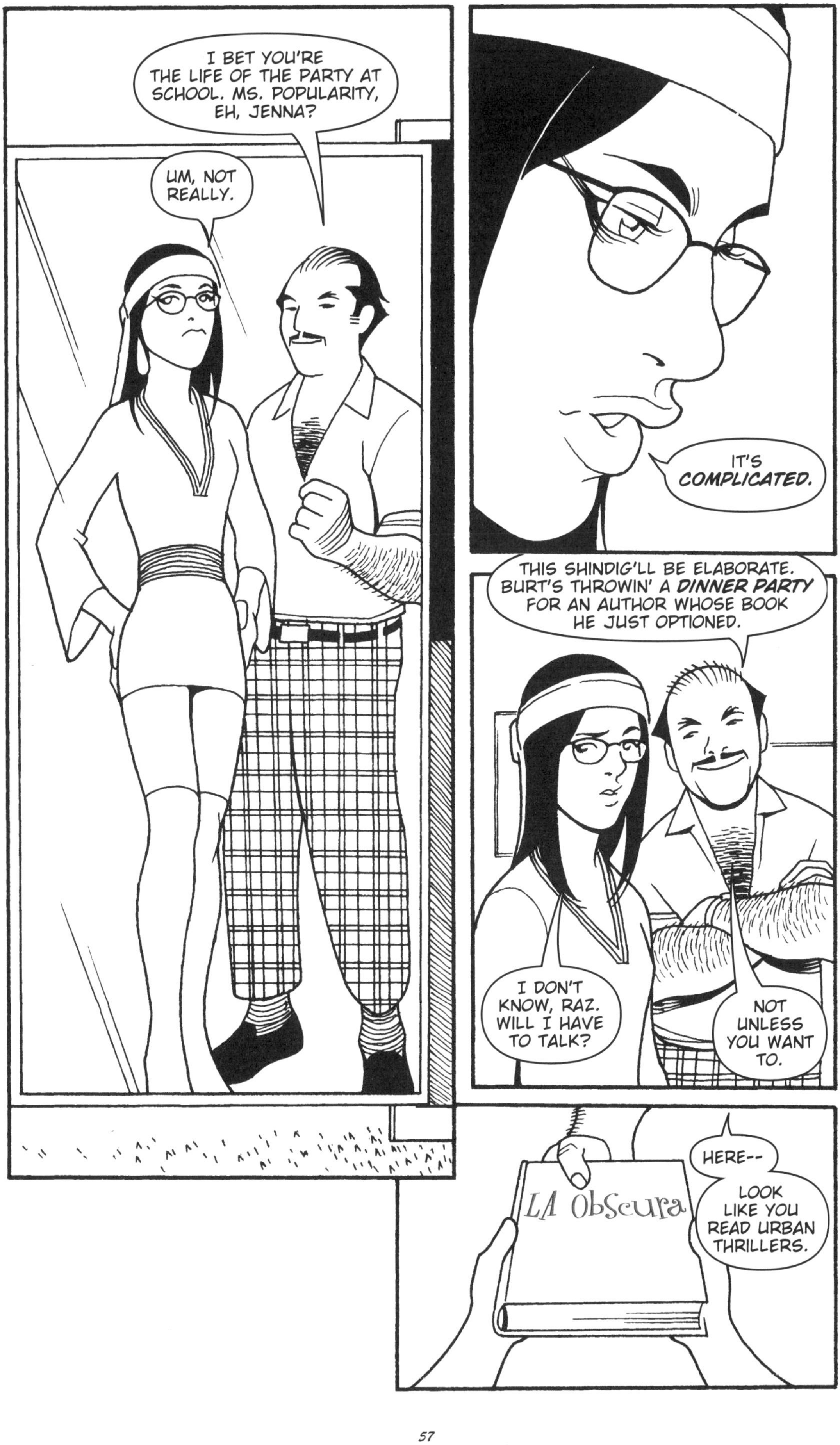
I BET YOU'RE THE LIFE OF THE PARTY AT SCHOOL. MS. POPULARITY, EH, JENNA?
UM, NOT REALLY.
IT'S COMPLICATED.
THIS SHINDIG'LL BE ELABORATE. BURT'S THROWIN' A DINNER PARTY FOR AN AUTHOR WHOSE BOOK HE JUST OPTIONED.
I DON'T KNOW, RAZ. WILL I HAVE TO TALK?
NOT UNLESS YOU WANT TO.
HERE--
LA Obscura
LOOK LIKE YOU READ URBAN THRILLERS.

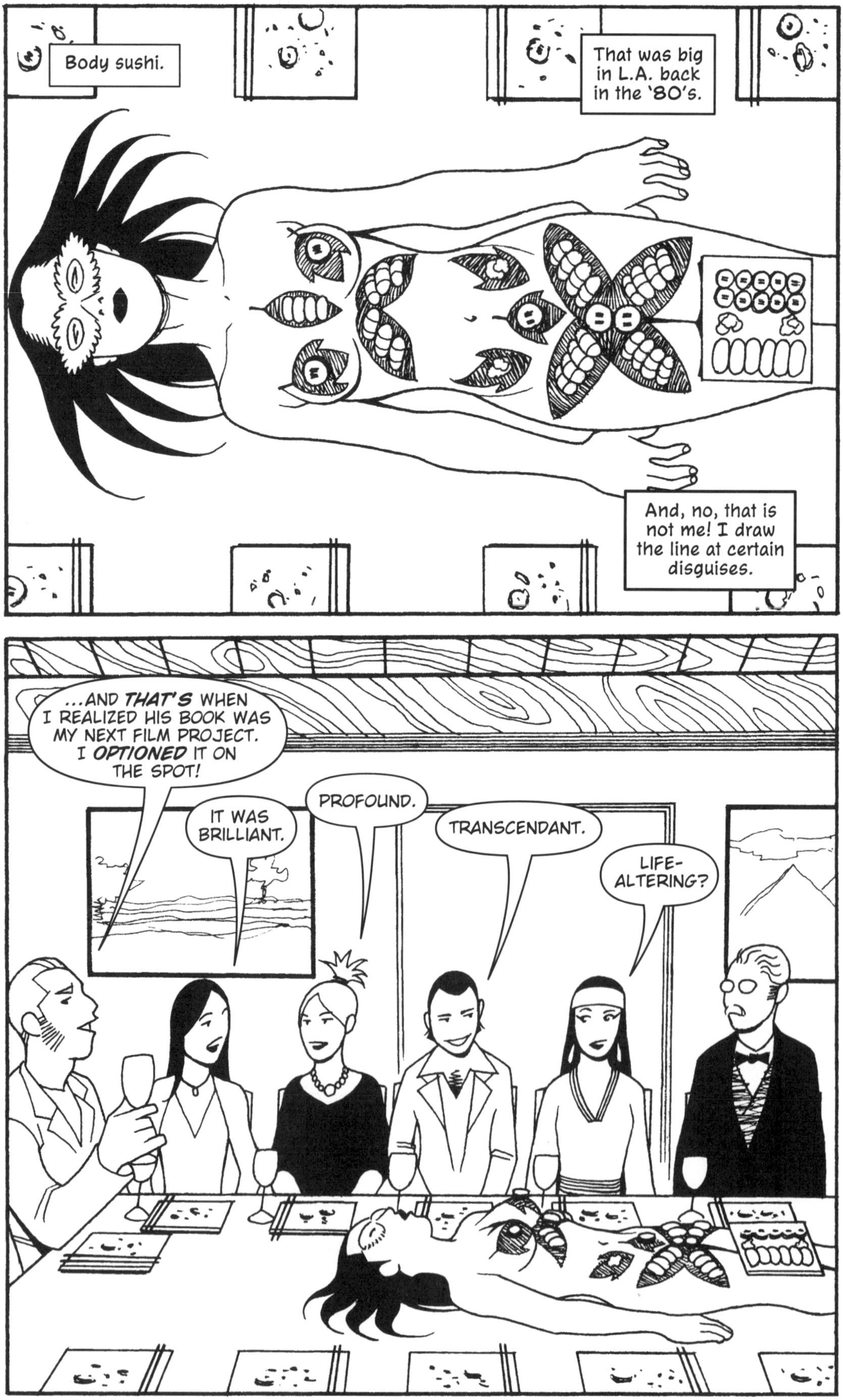
Body sushi.
That was big in L.A. back in the '80's.
And, no, that is not me! I draw the line at certain disguises.
...AND THAT'S WHEN I REALIZED HIS BOOK WAS MY NEXT FILM PROJECT. I OPTIONED IT ON THE SPOT!
IT WAS BRILLIANT.
PROFOUND.
TRANSCENDANT.
LIFE-ALTERING?

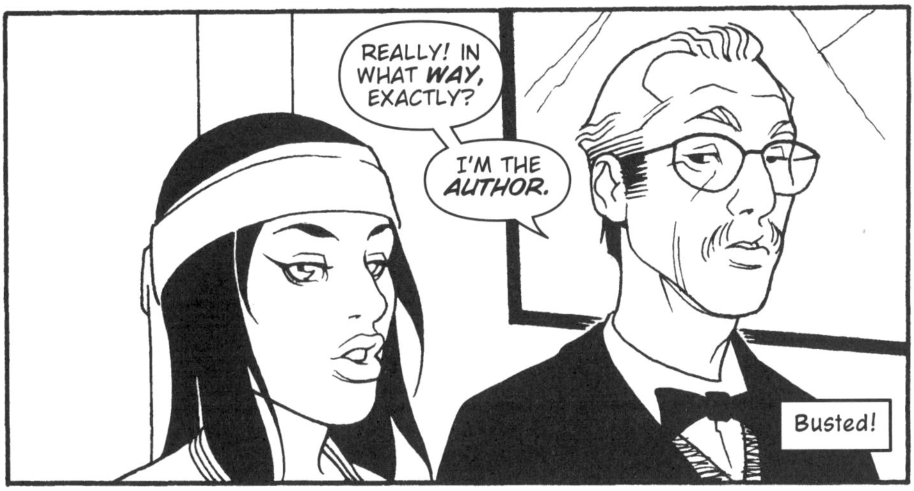
REALLY! IN WHAT WAY, EXACTLY?
I'M THE AUTHOR.
Busted!

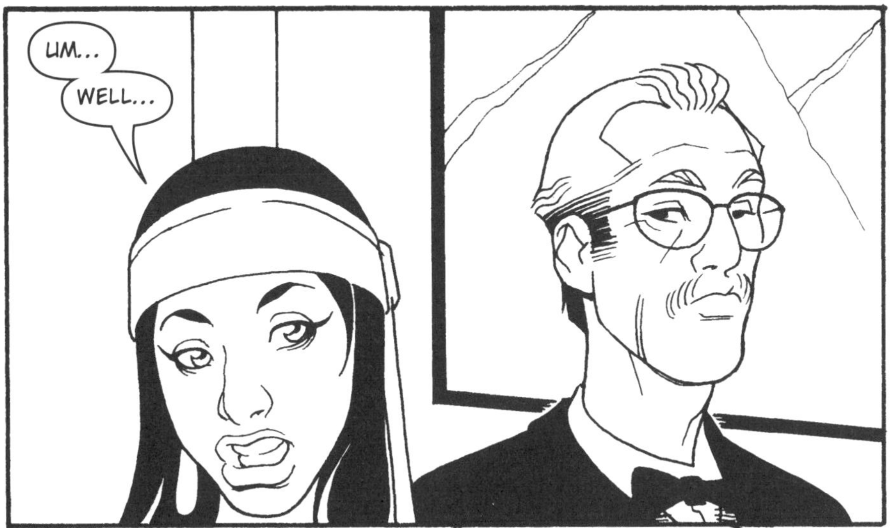
UM...
WELL...

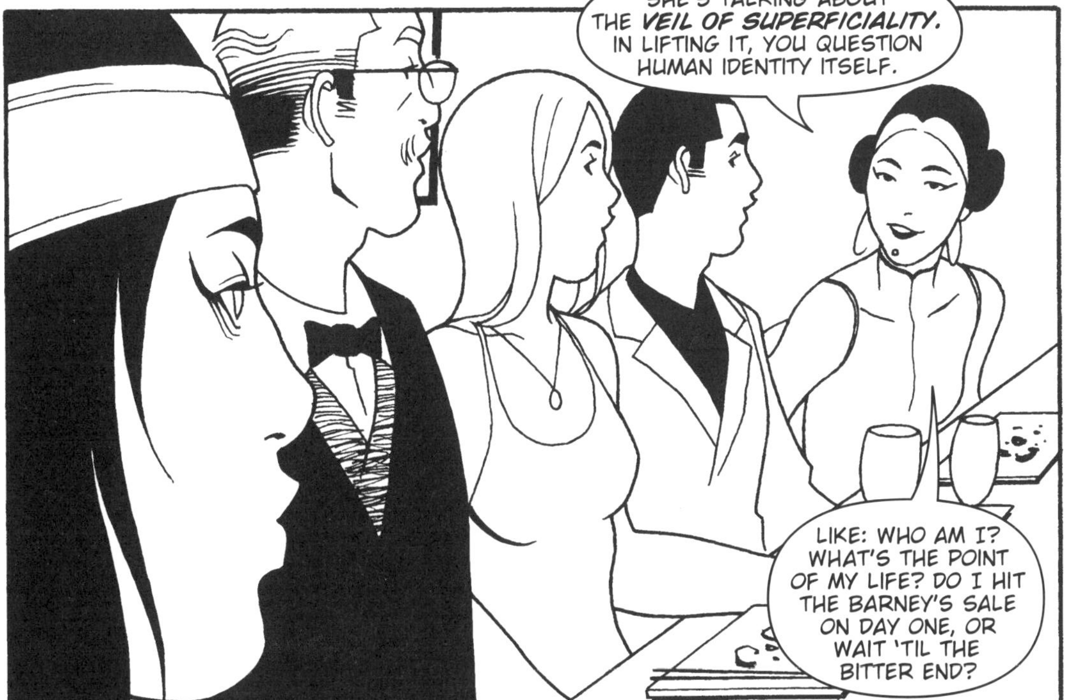
SHE'S TALKING ABOUT THE VEIL OF SUPERFICIALITY. IN LIFTING IT, YOU QUESTION HUMAN IDENTITY ITSELF.
LIKE: WHO AM I? WHAT'S THE POINT OF MY LIFE? DO I HIT THE BARNEY'S SALE ON DAY ONE, OR WAIT 'TIL THE BITTER END?

EXACTLY!

SO, WHAT'S YOUR NAME? I'M *STAN.*

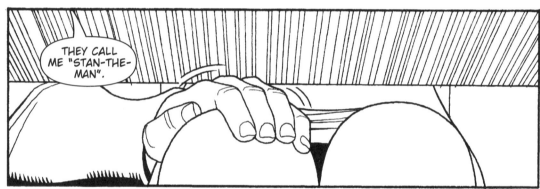

THEY CALL ME "STAN-THE-MAN".

YO, DADDY. *CHILLAX-*OUT.

SURPRISE-- I GET INVITED TO *ALL* THE GOOD PARTIES.

ANYWAY, *WE* GOT YOUR BACK--

--AND HIS LAP!

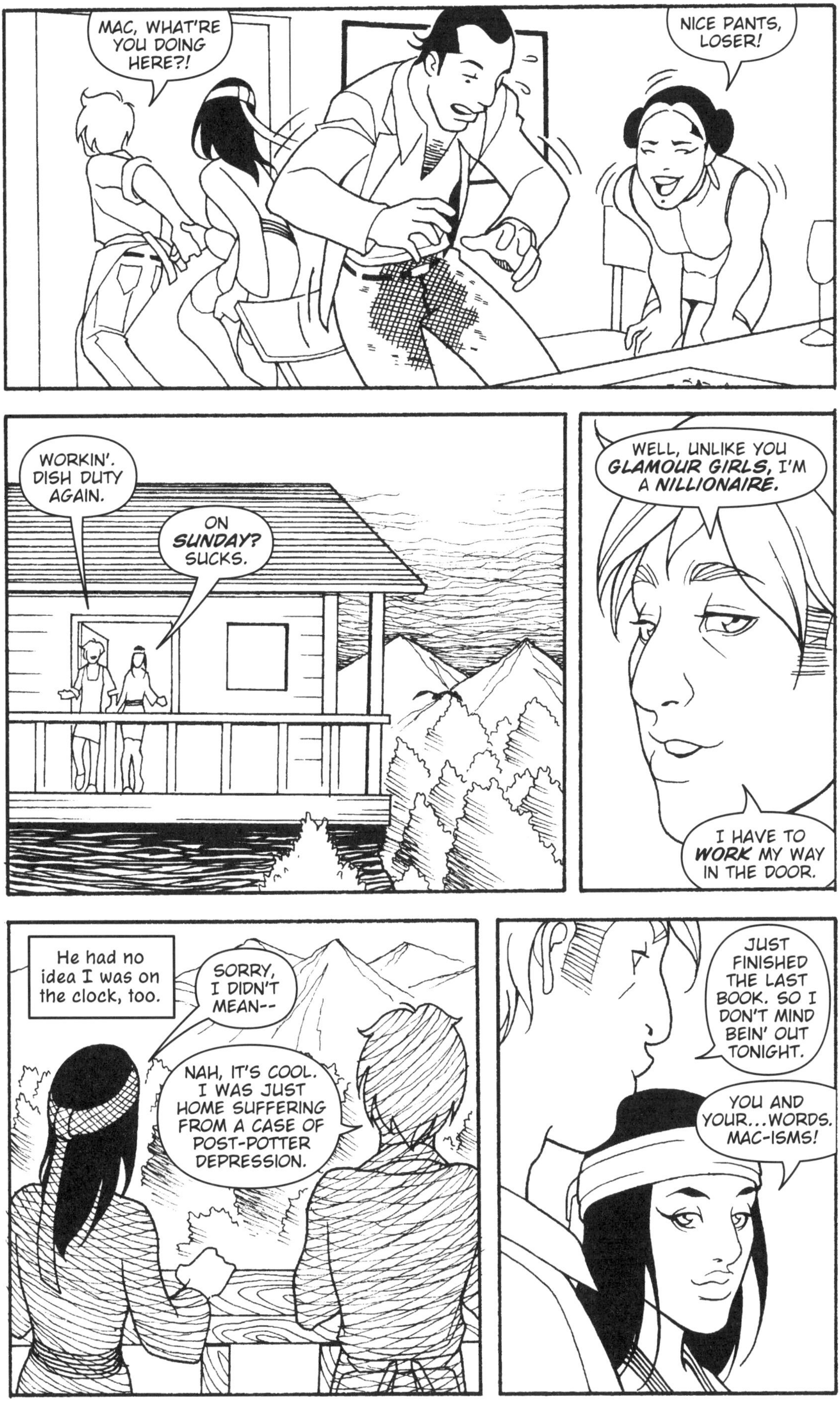
MAC, WHAT'RE YOU DOING HERE?!
NICE PANTS, LOSER!
WORKIN'. DISH DUTY AGAIN.
ON SUNDAY? SUCKS.
WELL, UNLIKE YOU GLAMOUR GIRLS, I'M A NILLIONAIRE.
I HAVE TO WORK MY WAY IN THE DOOR.
He had no idea I was on the clock, too.
SORRY, I DIDN'T MEAN--
NAH, IT'S COOL. I WAS JUST HOME SUFFERING FROM A CASE OF POST-POTTER DEPRESSION.
JUST FINISHED THE LAST BOOK. SO I DON'T MIND BEIN' OUT TONIGHT.
YOU AND YOUR...WORDS. MAC-ISMS!

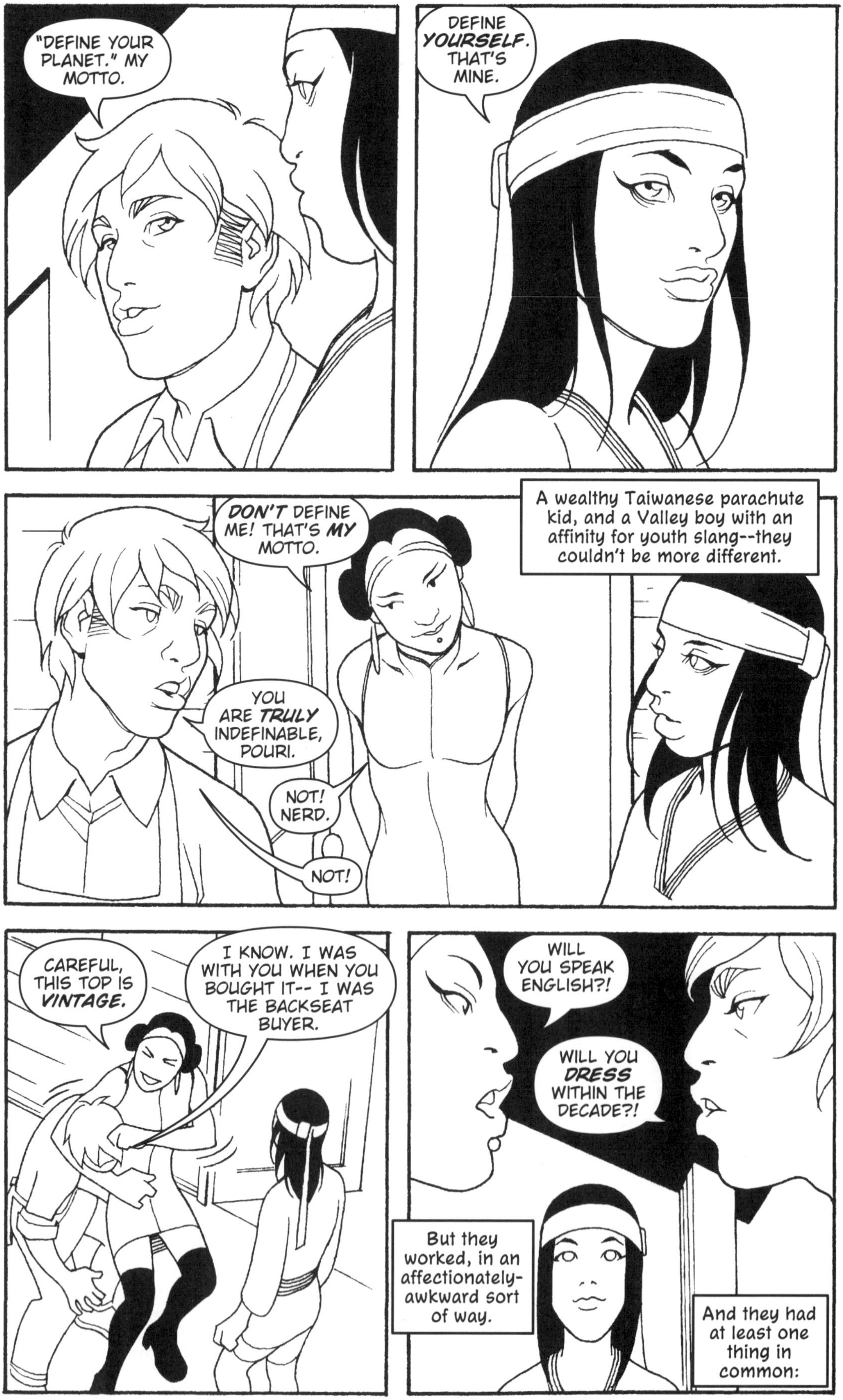
"DEFINE YOUR PLANET." MY MOTTO.
DEFINE YOURSELF. THAT'S MINE.
DON'T DEFINE ME! THAT'S MY MOTTO.
A wealthy Taiwanese parachute kid, and a Valley boy with an affinity for youth slang--they couldn't be more different.
YOU ARE TRULY INDEFINABLE, POURI.
NOT! NERD.
NOT!
CAREFUL, THIS TOP IS VINTAGE.
I KNOW. I WAS WITH YOU WHEN YOU BOUGHT IT-- I WAS THE BACKSEAT BUYER.
WILL YOU SPEAK ENGLISH?!
WILL YOU DRESS WITHIN THE DECADE?!
But they worked, in an affectionately-awkward sort of way.
And they had at least one thing in common:

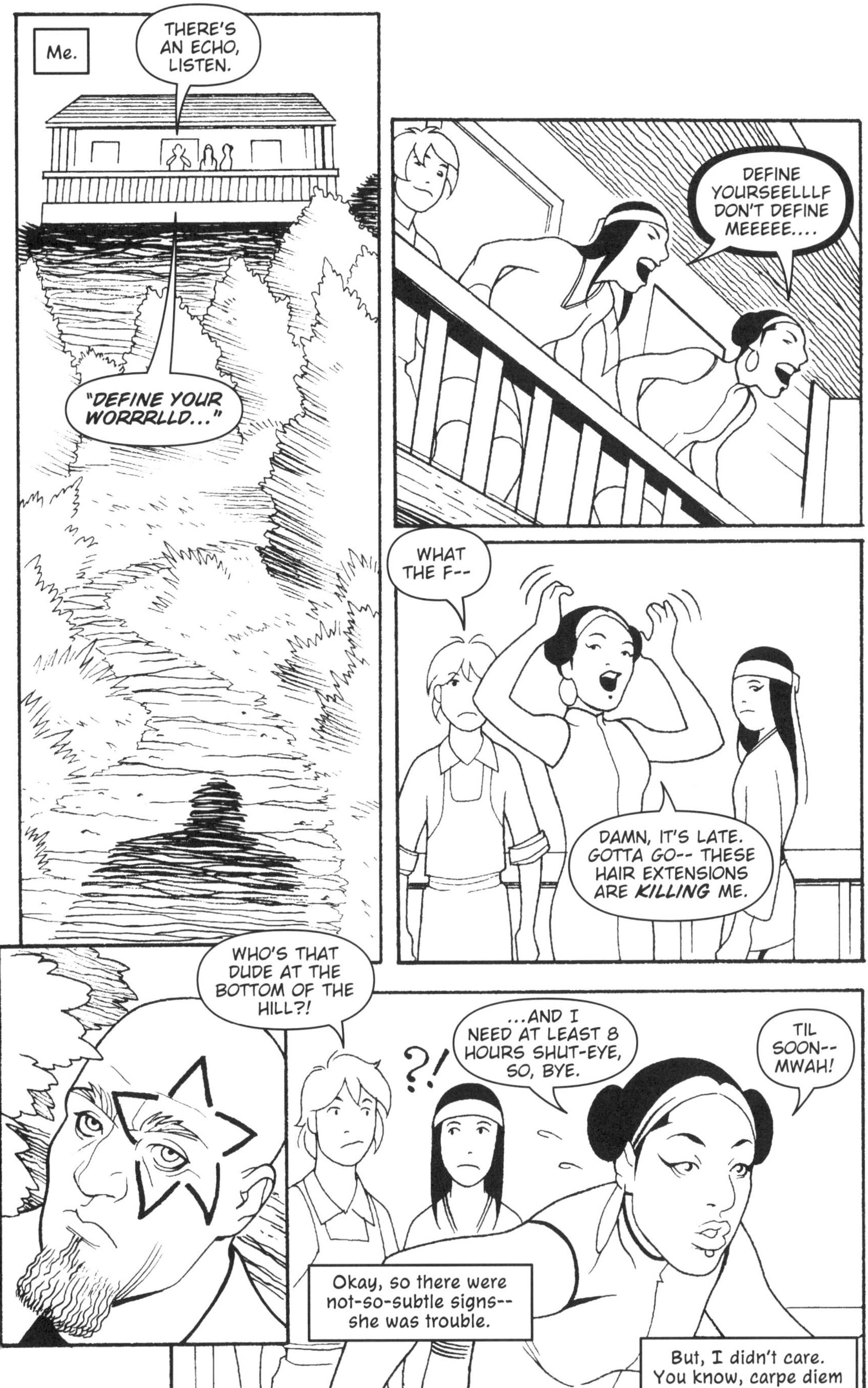
Me.
THERE'S AN ECHO, LISTEN.
"DEFINE YOUR WORRRLLD..."
DEFINE YOURSEELLLF DON'T DEFINE MEEEEE....
WHAT THE F--
DAMN, IT'S LATE. GOTTA GO-- THESE HAIR EXTENSIONS ARE KILLING ME.
WHO'S THAT DUDE AT THE BOTTOM OF THE HILL?!
?!
...AND I NEED AT LEAST 8 HOURS SHUT-EYE, SO, BYE.
TIL SOON-- MWAH!
Okay, so there were not-so-subtle signs-- she was trouble.
But, I didn't care. You know, carpe diem and all that.

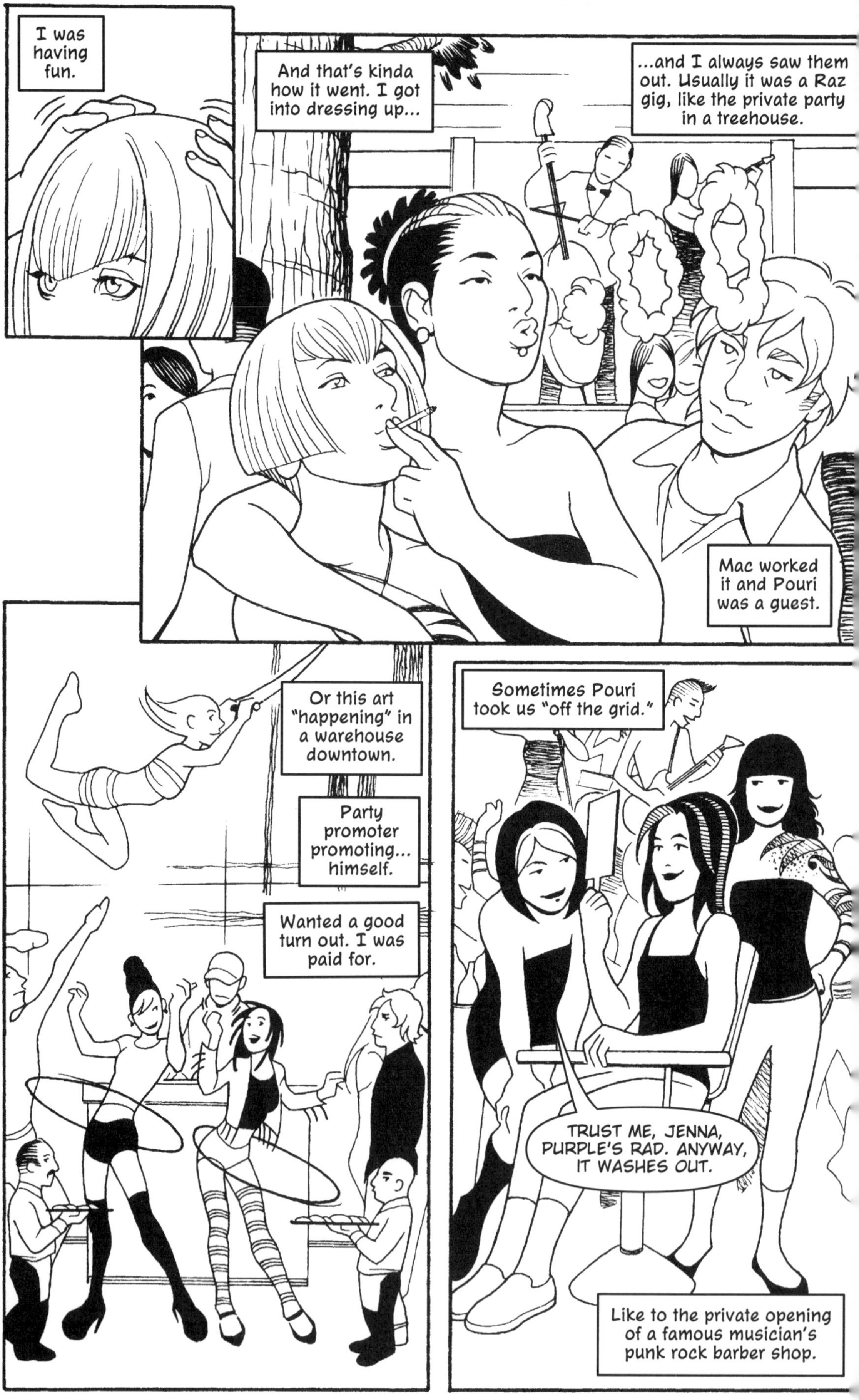

I was having fun.
And that's kinda how it went. I got into dressing up...
...and I always saw them out. Usually it was a Raz gig, like the private party in a treehouse.
Mac worked it and Pouri was a guest.
Or this art "happening" in a warehouse downtown.
Party promoter promoting... himself.
Wanted a good turn out. I was paid for.
Sometimes Pouri took us "off the grid."
TRUST ME, JENNA, PURPLE'S RAD. ANYWAY, IT WASHES OUT.
Like to the private opening of a famous musician's punk rock barber shop.

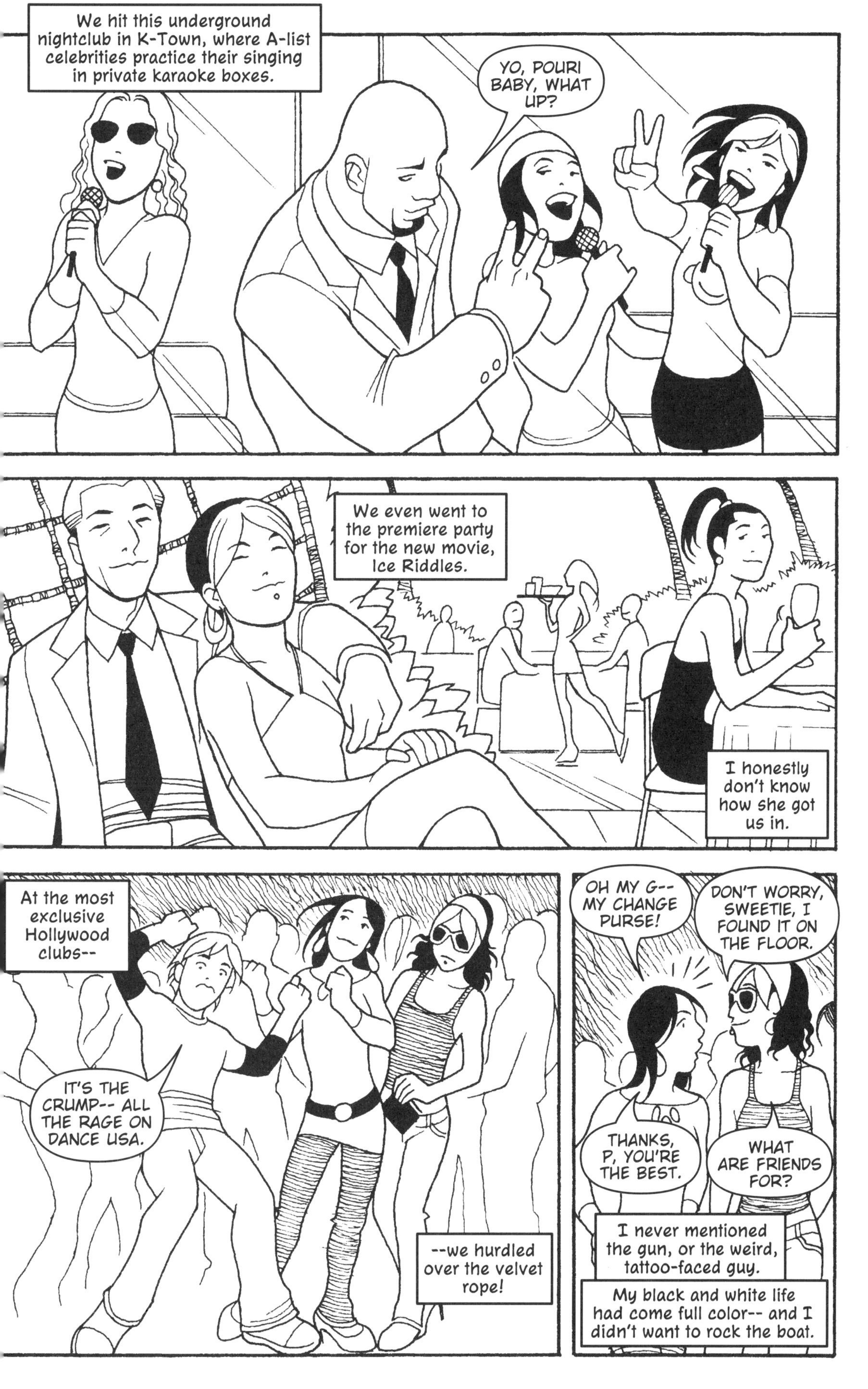
We hit this underground nightclub in K-Town, where A-list celebrities practice their singing in private karaoke boxes.
YO, POURI BABY, WHAT UP?
We even went to the premiere party for the new movie, Ice Riddles.
I honestly don't know how she got us in.
At the most exclusive Hollywood clubs--
IT'S THE CRUMP-- ALL THE RAGE ON DANCE USA.
--we hurdled over the velvet rope!
OH MY G-- MY CHANGE PURSE!
DON'T WORRY, SWEETIE, I FOUND IT ON THE FLOOR.
THANKS, P, YOU'RE THE BEST.
WHAT ARE FRIENDS FOR?
I never mentioned the gun, or the weird, tattoo-faced guy.
My black and white life had come full color-- and I didn't want to rock the boat.

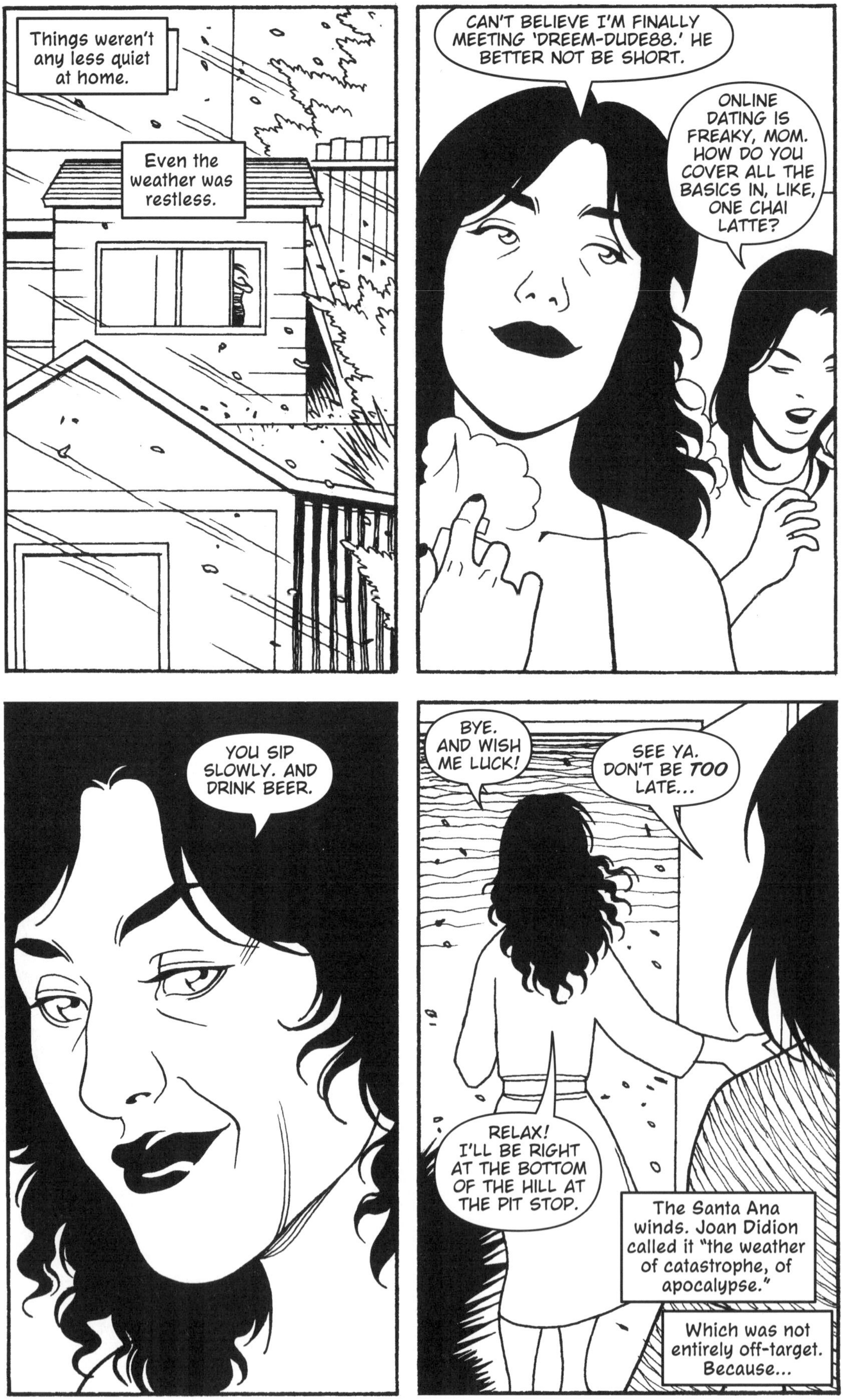
Things weren't any less quiet at home.
Even the weather was restless.
CAN'T BELIEVE I'M FINALLY MEETING 'DREEM-DUDE88.' HE BETTER NOT BE SHORT.
ONLINE DATING IS FREAKY, MOM. HOW DO YOU COVER ALL THE BASICS IN, LIKE, ONE CHAI LATTE?
YOU SIP SLOWLY. AND DRINK BEER.
BYE. AND WISH ME LUCK!
SEE YA. DON'T BE *TOO* LATE...
RELAX! I'LL BE RIGHT AT THE BOTTOM OF THE HILL AT THE PIT STOP.
The Santa Ana winds. Joan Didion called it "the weather of catastrophe, of apocalypse."
Which was not entirely off-target. Because...

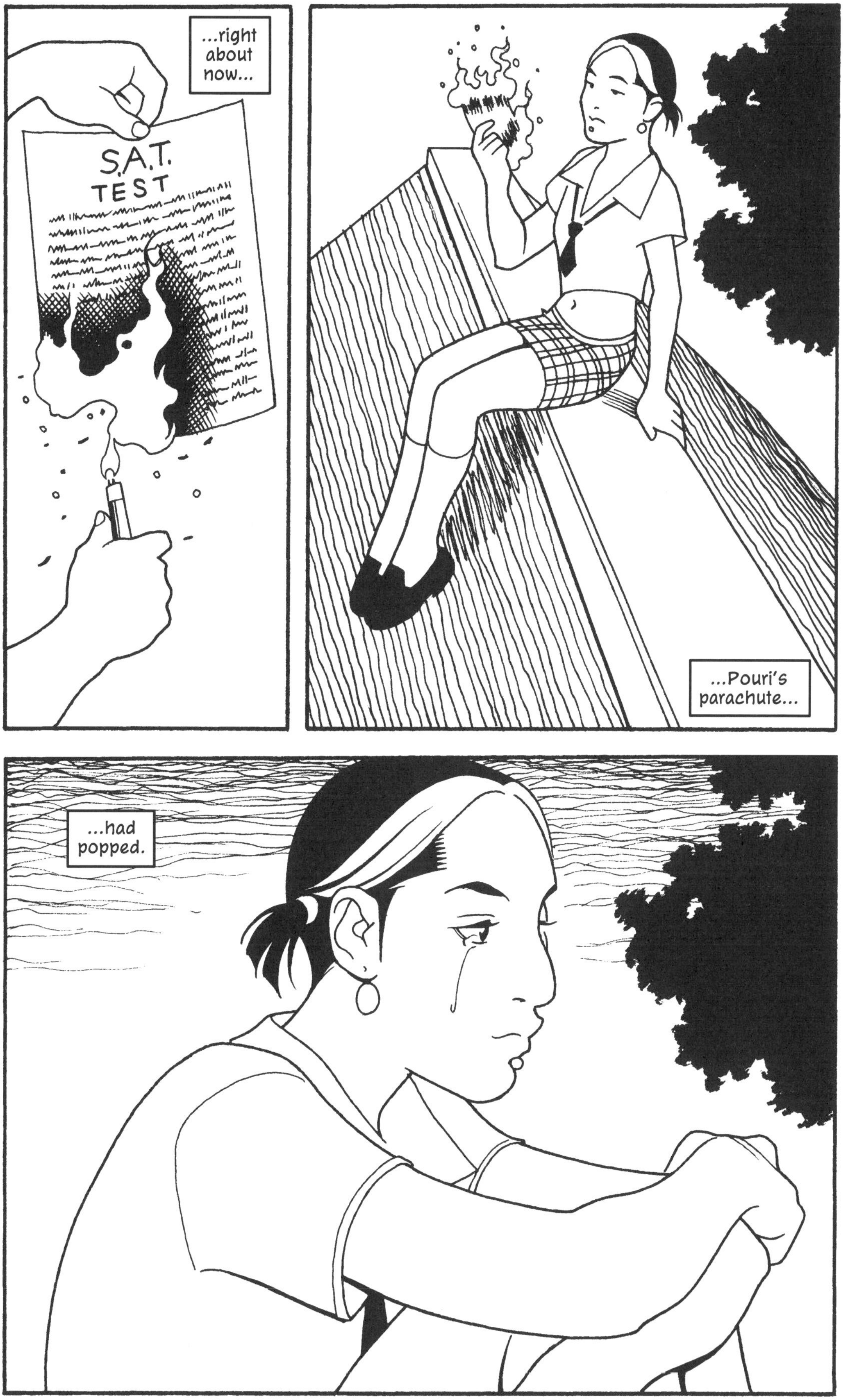
...right about now...
S.A.T. TEST
...Pouri's parachute...
...had popped.

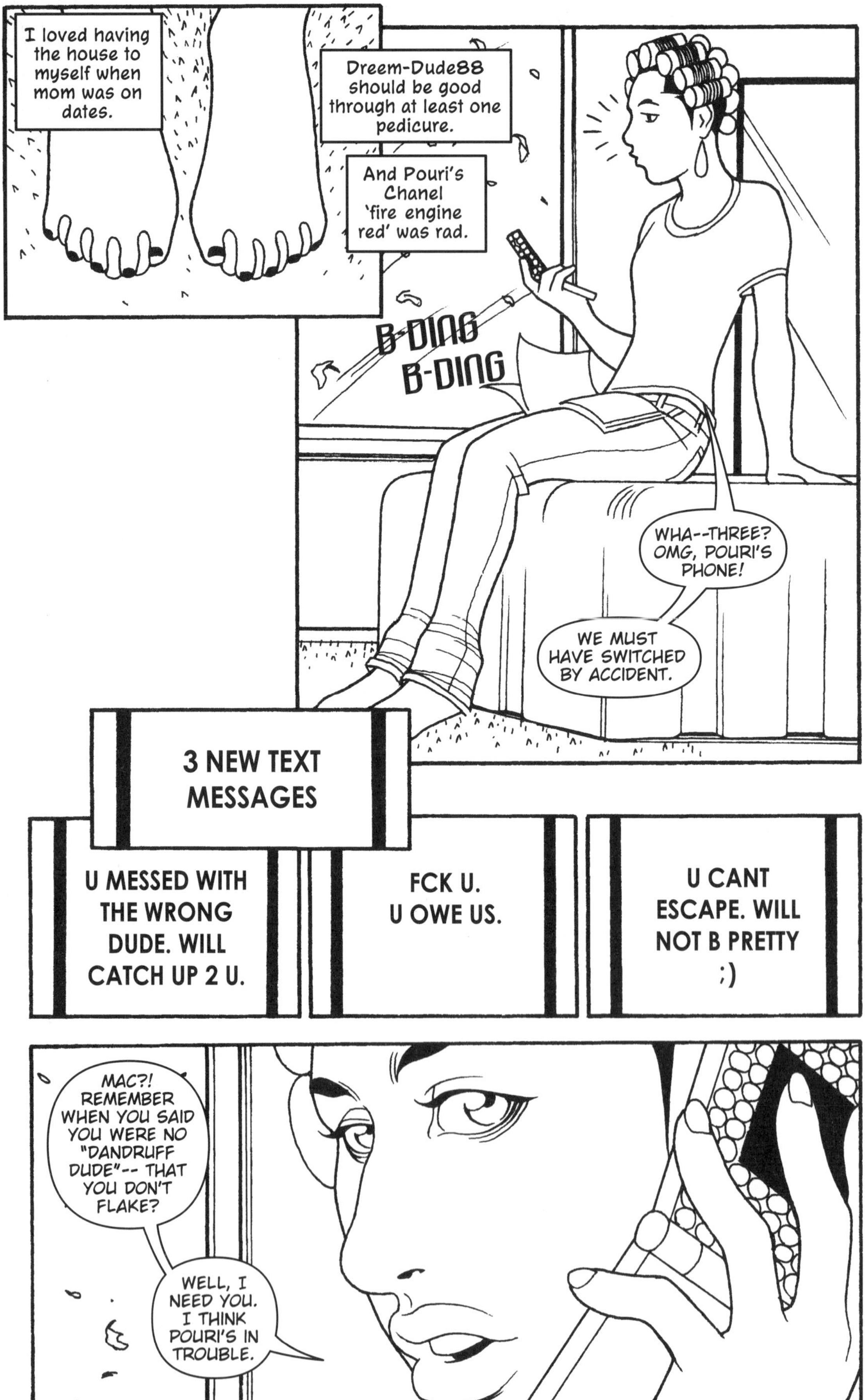

I loved having the house to myself when mom was on dates.
Dreem-Dude88 should be good through at least one pedicure.
And Pouri's Chanel 'fire engine red' was rad.
B-DING B-DING
WHA--THREE? OMG, POURI'S PHONE!
WE MUST HAVE SWITCHED BY ACCIDENT.
3 NEW TEXT MESSAGES
U MESSED WITH THE WRONG DUDE. WILL CATCH UP 2 U.
FCK U. U OWE US.
U CANT ESCAPE. WILL NOT B PRETTY ;)
MAC?! REMEMBER WHEN YOU SAID YOU WERE NO "DANDRUFF DUDE"-- THAT YOU DON'T FLAKE?
WELL, I NEED YOU. I THINK POURI'S IN TROUBLE.

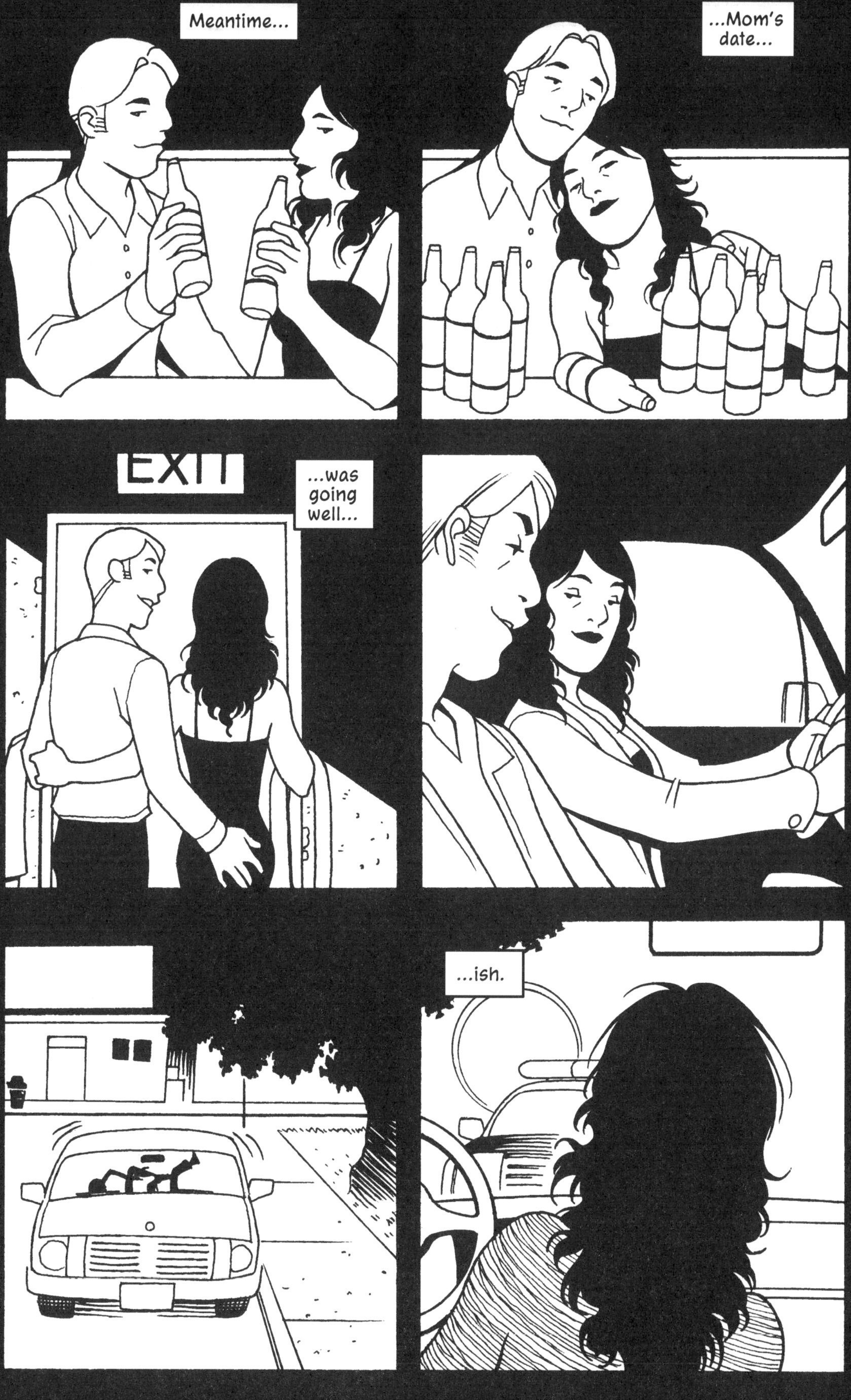
Meantime...
...Mom's date...
EXIT
...was going well...
...ish.

Then trouble collided...

THANKS FOR PICKING ME UP, MAC. YOU SAID YOU KNOW WHERE SHE LIVES, SO--

YEAH, I DROVE HER HOME ONCE.

SHE GAVE ME SOME INTERESTING CARSPECTIVE ON THIS CHICK I LIKED.

OH.

THAT I USED TO LIKE.

ANYWAY.

SO SHE'S GETTING THREATENING *TEXTS?*

YEAH. I'M *FREAKED.* SHE DOESN'T ANSWER THE PHONE, EITHER.

LOOK, I KNOW WE'VE ONLY BEEN HANGING OUT A FEW WEEKS; BUT I KNOW HER. SOMETHING'S WRONG.

NO WAY!

...IS WHY YOU *DON'T* WANT A DUI MA'AM. IS THERE SOMEONE WHO CAN DRIVE YOU BOTH HOME?

OH, THANK *GOD.* YES, MY *DAUGHTER.*

MOM? DRIVE!

Here's where I utter something jaded and disaffected, like, "Typical."

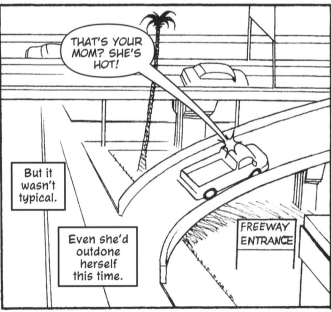

THAT'S YOUR MOM? SHE'S HOT!

But it wasn't typical.

Even she'd outdone herself this time.

FREEWAY ENTRANCE

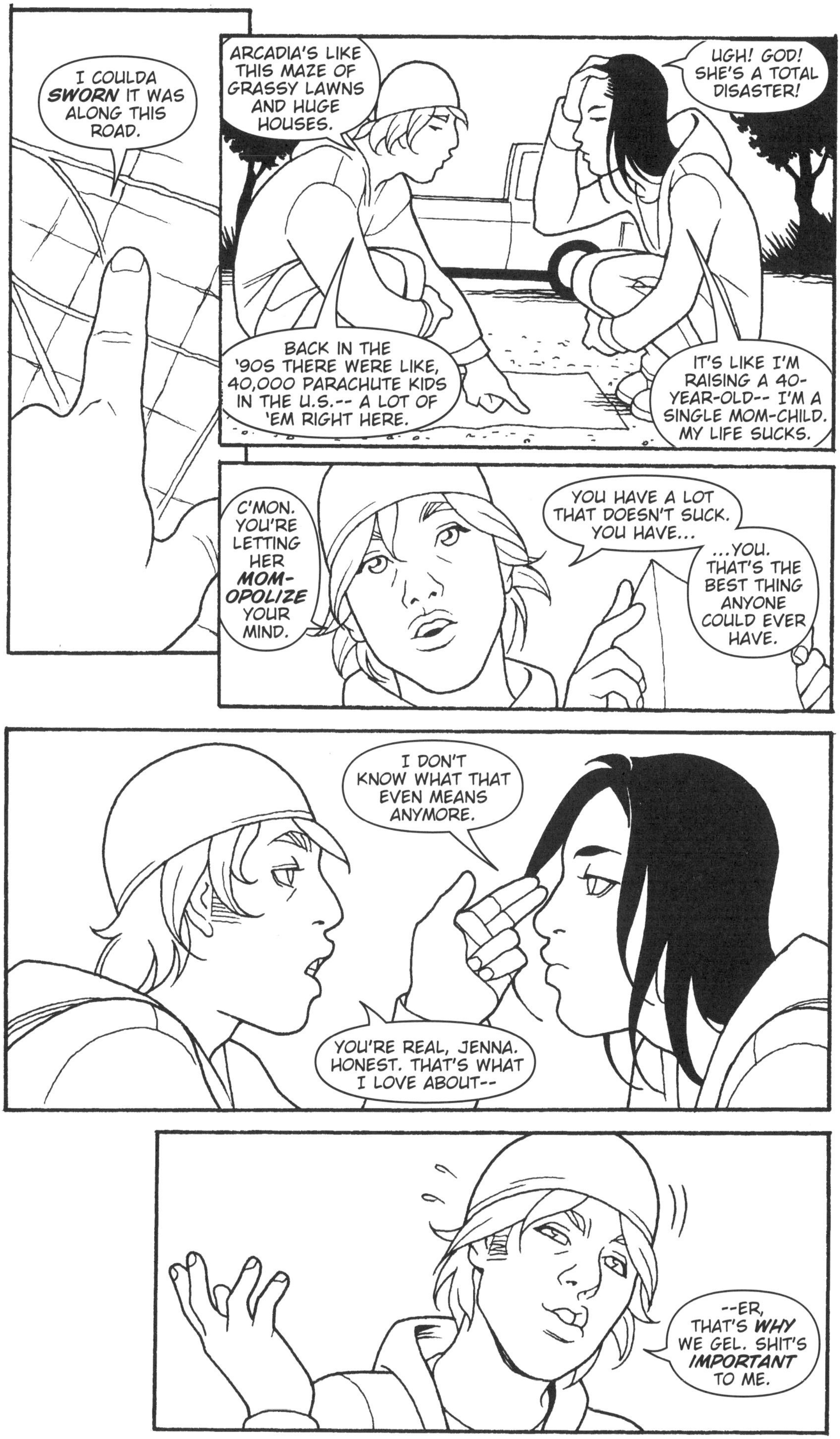
I COULDA SWORN IT WAS ALONG THIS ROAD.
ARCADIA'S LIKE THIS MAZE OF GRASSY LAWNS AND HUGE HOUSES.
BACK IN THE '90S THERE WERE LIKE, 40,000 PARACHUTE KIDS IN THE U.S.-- A LOT OF 'EM RIGHT HERE.
UGH! GOD! SHE'S A TOTAL DISASTER!
IT'S LIKE I'M RAISING A 40-YEAR-OLD-- I'M A SINGLE MOM-CHILD. MY LIFE SUCKS.
C'MON. YOU'RE LETTING HER MOM-OPOLIZE YOUR MIND.
YOU HAVE A LOT THAT DOESN'T SUCK. YOU HAVE...
...YOU. THAT'S THE BEST THING ANYONE COULD EVER HAVE.
I DON'T KNOW WHAT THAT EVEN MEANS ANYMORE.
YOU'RE REAL, JENNA. HONEST. THAT'S WHAT I LOVE ABOUT--
--ER, THAT'S WHY WE GEL. SHIT'S IMPORTANT TO ME.

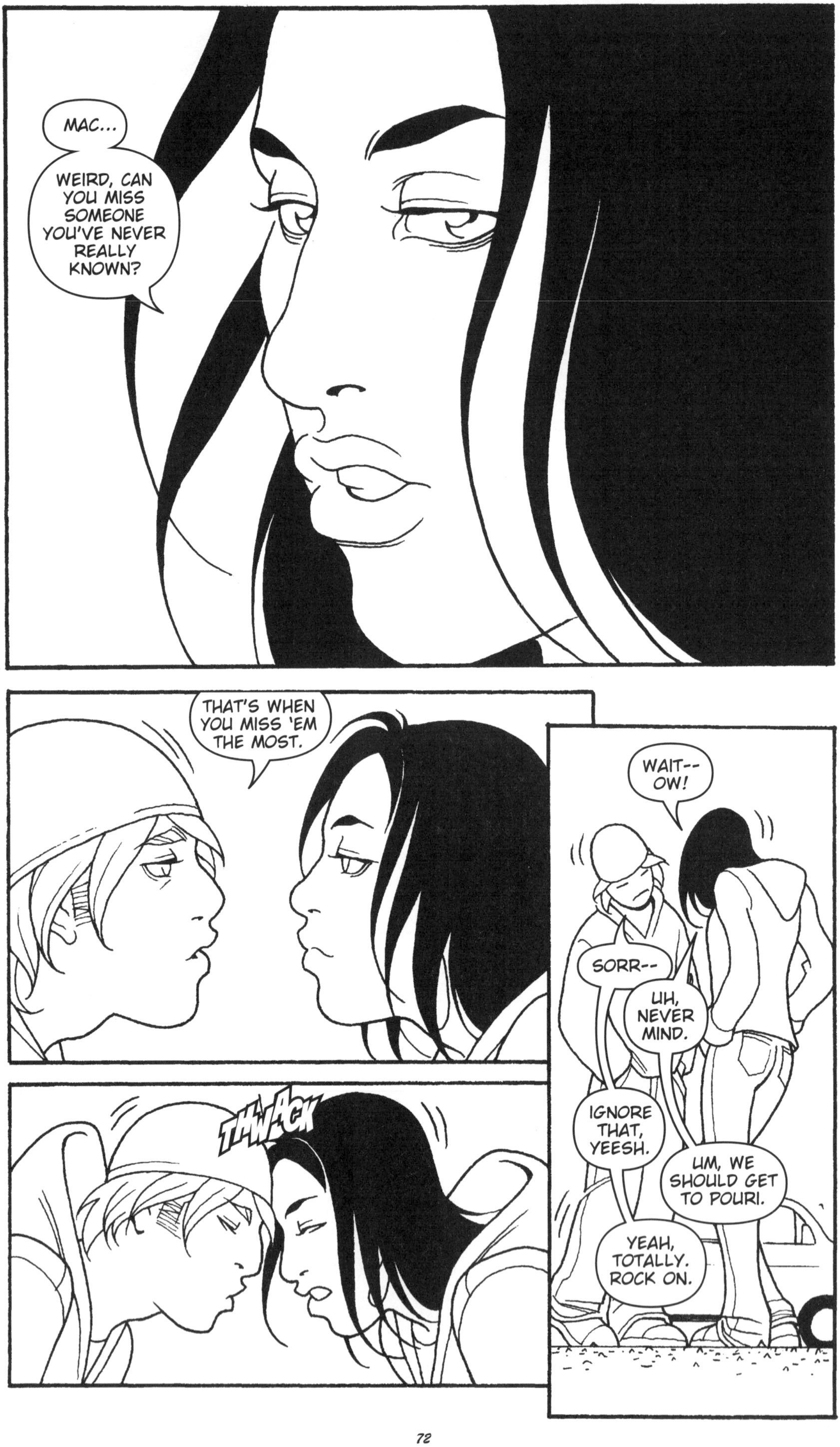
MAC...
WEIRD, CAN YOU MISS SOMEONE YOU'VE NEVER REALLY KNOWN?
THAT'S WHEN YOU MISS 'EM THE MOST.
THWACK
WAIT-- OW!
SORR--
UH, NEVER MIND.
IGNORE THAT, YEESH.
UM, WE SHOULD GET TO POURI.
YEAH, TOTALLY. ROCK ON.

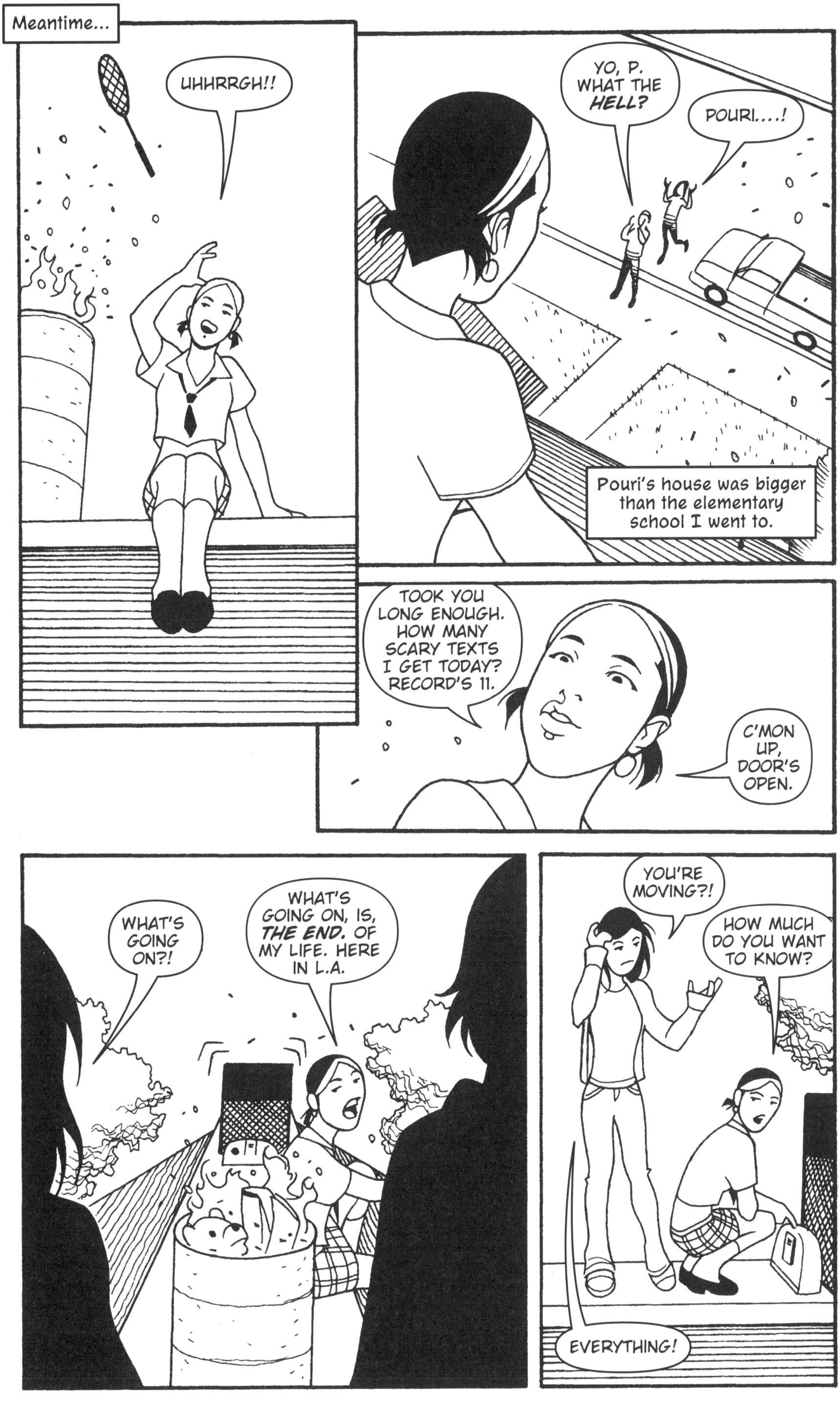

Meantime...
UHHRRGH!!
YO, P. WHAT THE *HELL?*
POURI....!
Pouri's house was bigger than the elementary school I went to.
TOOK YOU LONG ENOUGH. HOW MANY SCARY TEXTS I GET TODAY? RECORD'S 11.
C'MON UP, DOOR'S OPEN.
WHAT'S GOING ON?!
WHAT'S GOING ON, IS, *THE END.* OF MY LIFE. HERE IN L.A.
YOU'RE MOVING?!
HOW MUCH DO YOU WANT TO KNOW?
EVERYTHING!

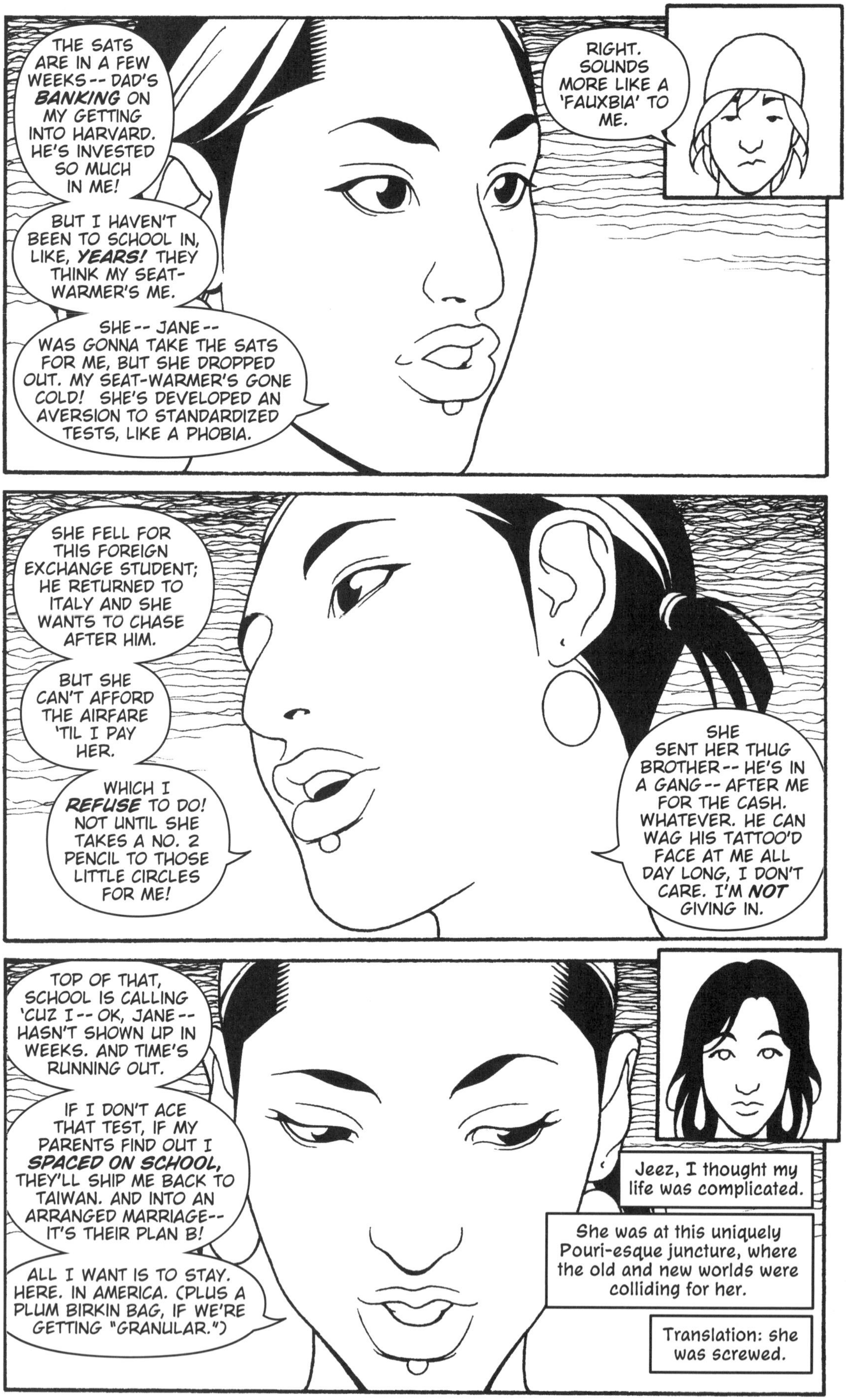
THE SATS ARE IN A FEW WEEKS-- DAD'S BANKING ON MY GETTING INTO HARVARD. HE'S INVESTED SO MUCH IN ME!
BUT I HAVEN'T BEEN TO SCHOOL IN, LIKE, YEARS! THEY THINK MY SEAT-WARMER'S ME.
SHE-- JANE-- WAS GONNA TAKE THE SATS FOR ME, BUT SHE DROPPED OUT. MY SEAT-WARMER'S GONE COLD! SHE'S DEVELOPED AN AVERSION TO STANDARDIZED TESTS, LIKE A PHOBIA.
RIGHT. SOUNDS MORE LIKE A 'FAUXBIA' TO ME.
SHE FELL FOR THIS FOREIGN EXCHANGE STUDENT; HE RETURNED TO ITALY AND SHE WANTS TO CHASE AFTER HIM.
BUT SHE CAN'T AFFORD THE AIRFARE 'TIL I PAY HER.
WHICH I REFUSE TO DO! NOT UNTIL SHE TAKES A NO. 2 PENCIL TO THOSE LITTLE CIRCLES FOR ME!
SHE SENT HER THUG BROTHER-- HE'S IN A GANG-- AFTER ME FOR THE CASH. WHATEVER. HE CAN WAG HIS TATTOO'D FACE AT ME ALL DAY LONG, I DON'T CARE. I'M NOT GIVING IN.
TOP OF THAT, SCHOOL IS CALLING 'CUZ I-- OK, JANE-- HASN'T SHOWN UP IN WEEKS. AND TIME'S RUNNING OUT.
IF I DON'T ACE THAT TEST, IF MY PARENTS FIND OUT I SPACED ON SCHOOL, THEY'LL SHIP ME BACK TO TAIWAN. AND INTO AN ARRANGED MARRIAGE-- IT'S THEIR PLAN B!
ALL I WANT IS TO STAY. HERE. IN AMERICA. (PLUS A PLUM BIRKIN BAG, IF WE'RE GETTING "GRANULAR.")
Jeez, I thought my life was complicated.
She was at this uniquely Pouri-esque juncture, where the old and new worlds were colliding for her.
Translation: she was screwed.

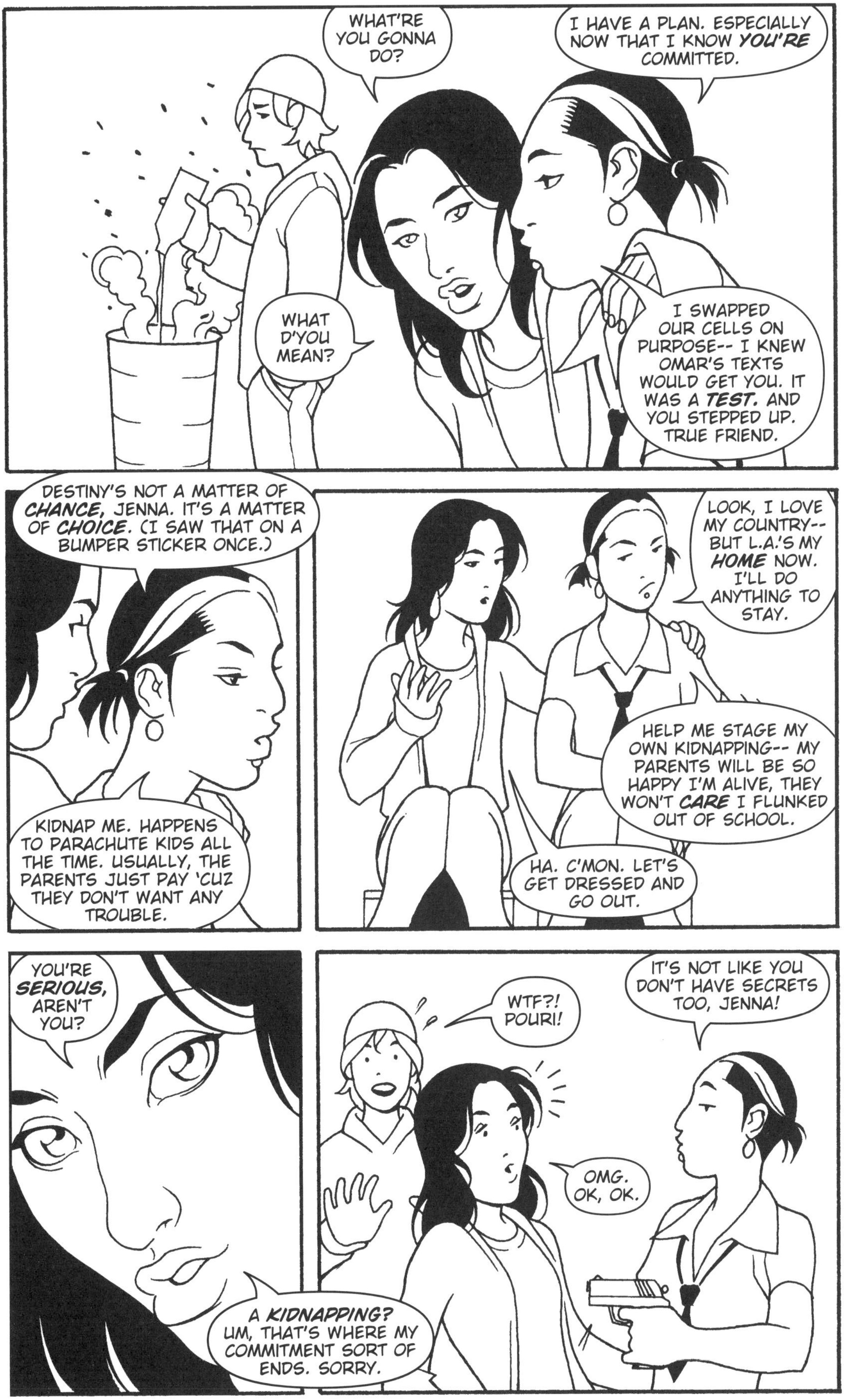
WHAT'RE YOU GONNA DO?
I HAVE A PLAN. ESPECIALLY NOW THAT I KNOW *YOU'RE* COMMITTED.
WHAT D'YOU MEAN?
I SWAPPED OUR CELLS ON PURPOSE-- I KNEW OMAR'S TEXTS WOULD GET YOU. IT WAS A *TEST.* AND YOU STEPPED UP. TRUE FRIEND.
DESTINY'S NOT A MATTER OF *CHANCE,* JENNA. IT'S A MATTER OF *CHOICE.* (I SAW THAT ON A BUMPER STICKER ONCE.)
LOOK, I LOVE MY COUNTRY-- BUT L.A.'S MY *HOME* NOW. I'LL DO ANYTHING TO STAY.
HELP ME STAGE MY OWN KIDNAPPING-- MY PARENTS WILL BE SO HAPPY I'M ALIVE, THEY WON'T *CARE* I FLUNKED OUT OF SCHOOL.
KIDNAP ME. HAPPENS TO PARACHUTE KIDS ALL THE TIME. USUALLY, THE PARENTS JUST PAY 'CUZ THEY DON'T WANT ANY TROUBLE.
HA. C'MON. LET'S GET DRESSED AND GO OUT.
YOU'RE *SERIOUS,* AREN'T YOU?
A *KIDNAPPING?* UM, THAT'S WHERE MY COMMITMENT SORT OF ENDS. SORRY.
WTF?! POURI!
IT'S NOT LIKE YOU DON'T HAVE SECRETS TOO, JENNA!
OMG. OK, OK.

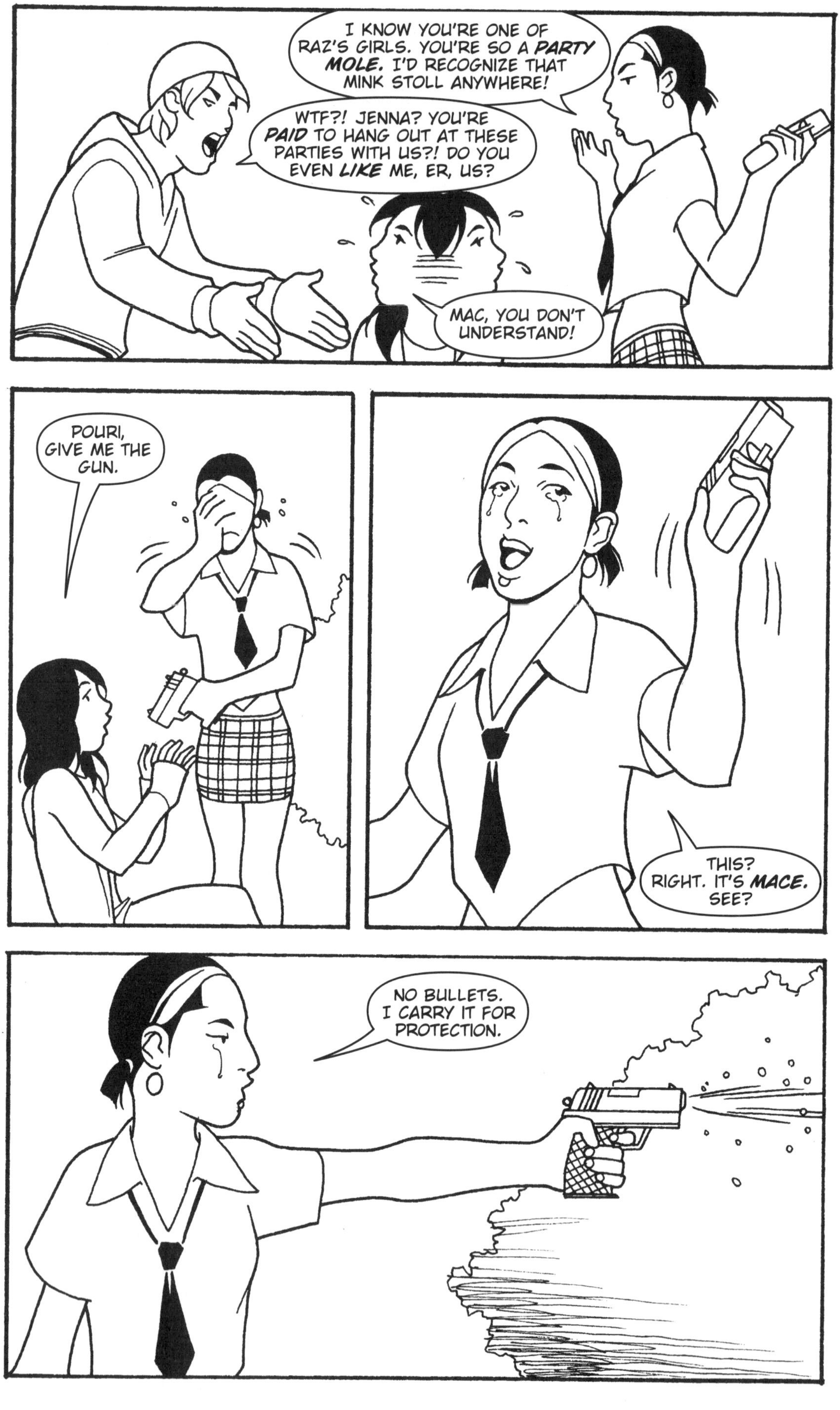
I KNOW YOU'RE ONE OF RAZ'S GIRLS. YOU'RE SO A PARTY MOLE. I'D RECOGNIZE THAT MINK STOLL ANYWHERE!
WTF?! JENNA? YOU'RE PAID TO HANG OUT AT THESE PARTIES WITH US?! DO YOU EVEN LIKE ME, ER, US?
MAC, YOU DON'T UNDERSTAND!
POURI, GIVE ME THE GUN.
THIS? RIGHT. IT'S MACE. SEE?
NO BULLETS. I CARRY IT FOR PROTECTION.

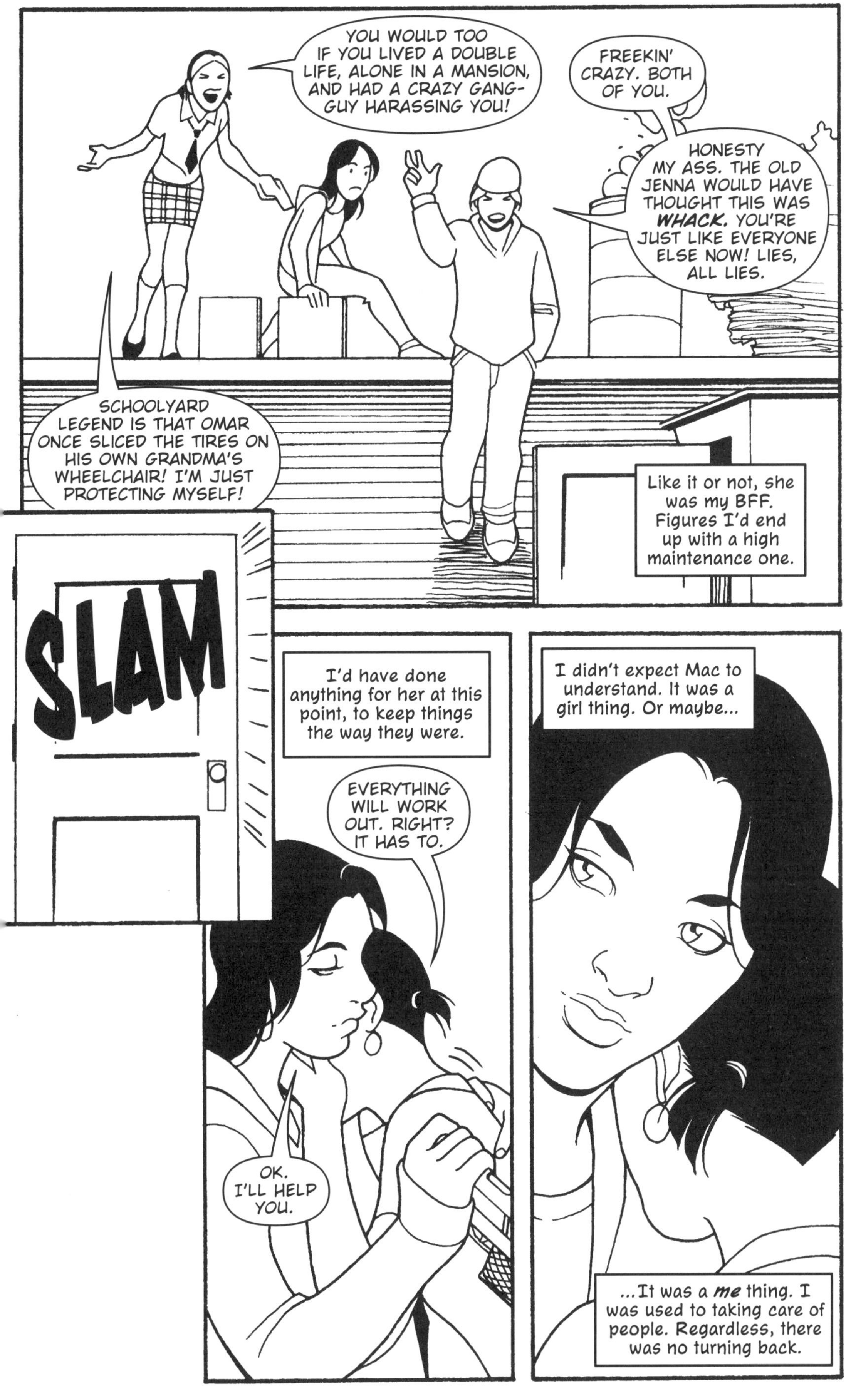
YOU WOULD TOO IF YOU LIVED A DOUBLE LIFE, ALONE IN A MANSION, AND HAD A CRAZY GANG-GUY HARASSING YOU!
FREEKIN' CRAZY. BOTH OF YOU.
HONESTY MY ASS. THE OLD JENNA WOULD HAVE THOUGHT THIS WAS WHACK. YOU'RE JUST LIKE EVERYONE ELSE NOW! LIES, ALL LIES.
SCHOOLYARD LEGEND IS THAT OMAR ONCE SLICED THE TIRES ON HIS OWN GRANDMA'S WHEELCHAIR! I'M JUST PROTECTING MYSELF!
Like it or not, she was my BFF. Figures I'd end up with a high maintenance one.
SLAM
I'd have done anything for her at this point, to keep things the way they were.
EVERYTHING WILL WORK OUT. RIGHT? IT HAS TO.
OK. I'LL HELP YOU.
I didn't expect Mac to understand. It was a girl thing. Or maybe...
...It was a *me* thing. I was used to taking care of people. Regardless, there was no turning back.

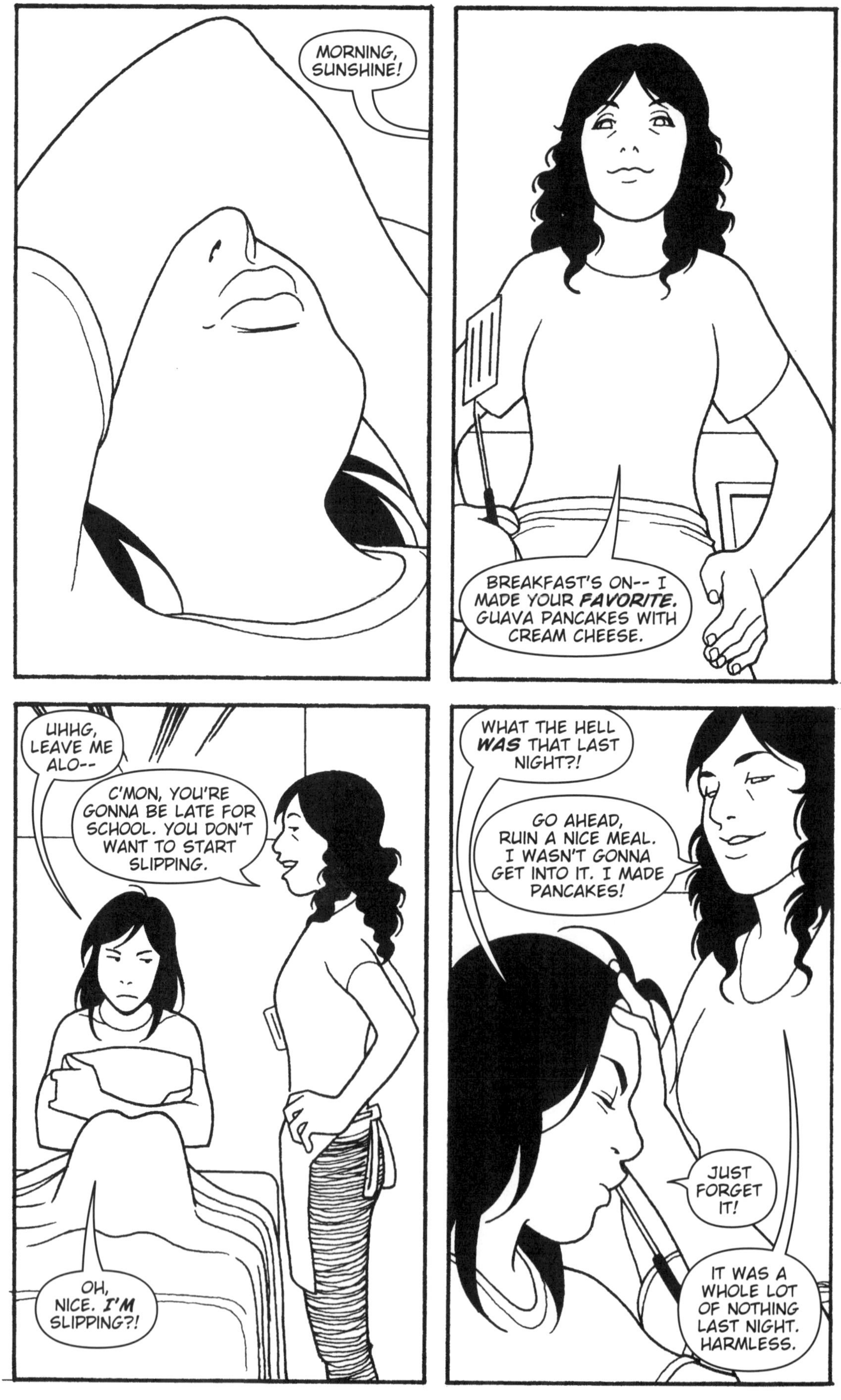
MORNING, SUNSHINE!
BREAKFAST'S ON-- I MADE YOUR ***FAVORITE.*** GUAVA PANCAKES WITH CREAM CHEESE.
UHHG, LEAVE ME ALO--
C'MON, YOU'RE GONNA BE LATE FOR SCHOOL. YOU DON'T WANT TO START SLIPPING.
OH, NICE. ***I'M*** SLIPPING?!
WHAT THE HELL ***WAS*** THAT LAST NIGHT?!
GO AHEAD, RUIN A NICE MEAL. I WASN'T GONNA GET INTO IT. I MADE PANCAKES!
JUST FORGET IT!
IT WAS A WHOLE LOT OF NOTHING LAST NIGHT. HARMLESS.

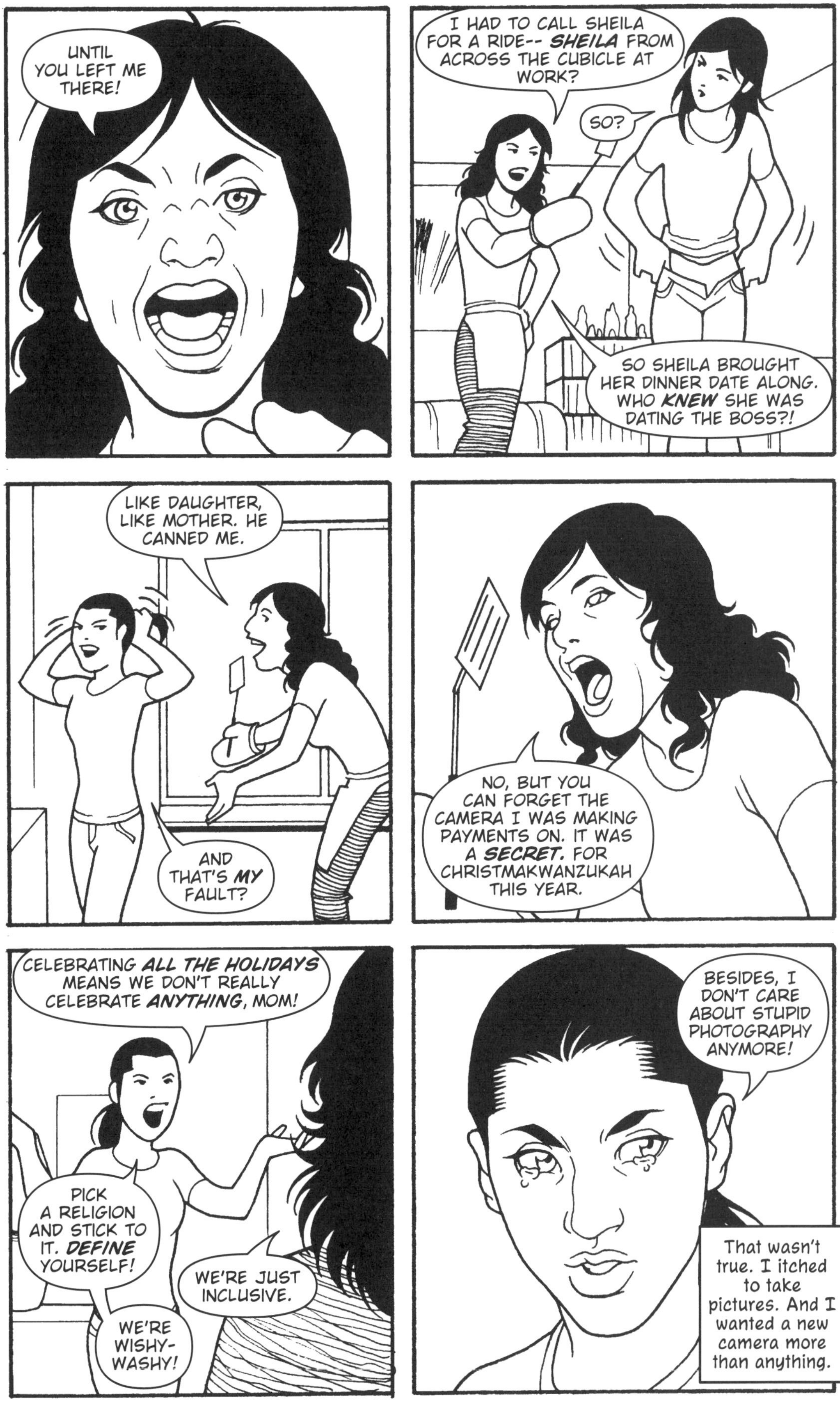
UNTIL YOU LEFT ME THERE!
I HAD TO CALL SHEILA FOR A RIDE-- SHEILA FROM ACROSS THE CUBICLE AT WORK?
SO?
SO SHEILA BROUGHT HER DINNER DATE ALONG. WHO KNEW SHE WAS DATING THE BOSS?!
LIKE DAUGHTER, LIKE MOTHER. HE CANNED ME.
AND THAT'S MY FAULT?
NO, BUT YOU CAN FORGET THE CAMERA I WAS MAKING PAYMENTS ON. IT WAS A SECRET. FOR CHRISTMAKWANZUKAH THIS YEAR.
CELEBRATING ALL THE HOLIDAYS MEANS WE DON'T REALLY CELEBRATE ANYTHING, MOM!
PICK A RELIGION AND STICK TO IT. DEFINE YOURSELF!
WE'RE JUST INCLUSIVE.
WE'RE WISHY-WASHY!
BESIDES, I DON'T CARE ABOUT STUPID PHOTOGRAPHY ANYMORE!
That wasn't true. I itched to take pictures. And I wanted a new camera more than anything.

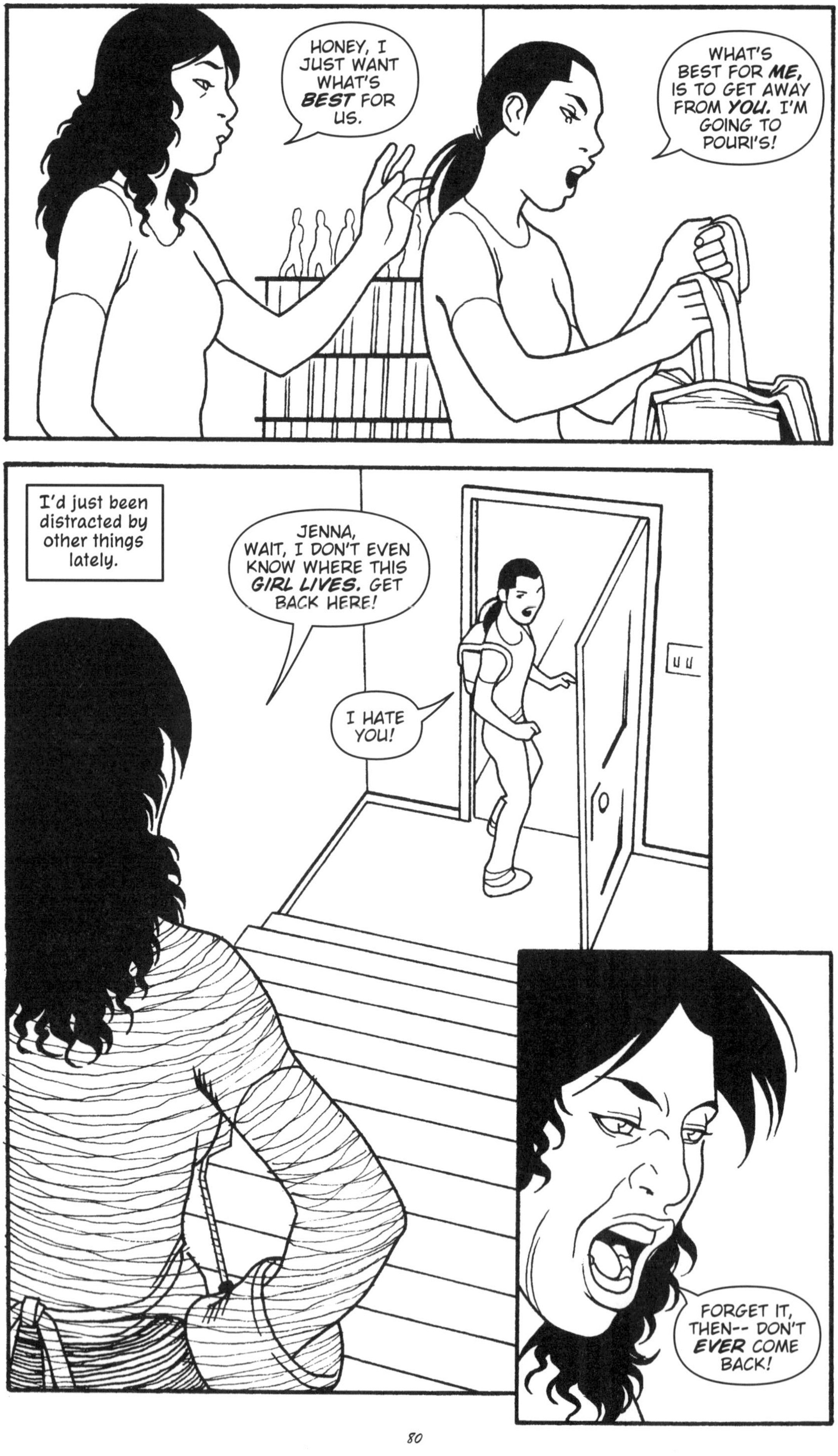

HONEY, I JUST WANT WHAT'S BEST FOR US.
WHAT'S BEST FOR ME, IS TO GET AWAY FROM YOU. I'M GOING TO POURI'S!
I'd just been distracted by other things lately.
JENNA, WAIT, I DON'T EVEN KNOW WHERE THIS GIRL LIVES. GET BACK HERE!
I HATE YOU!
FORGET IT, THEN-- DON'T EVER COME BACK!

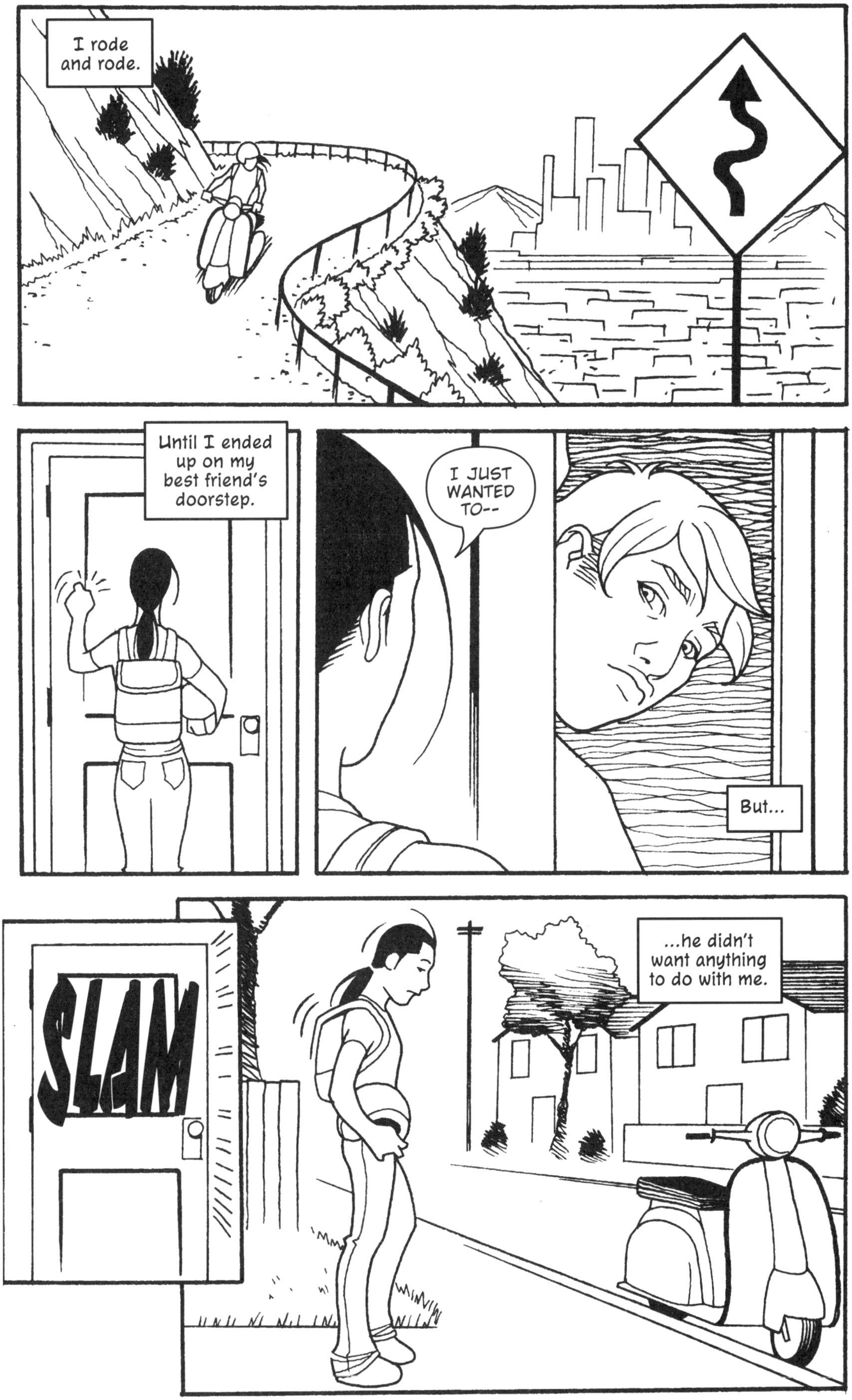
I rode and rode.
Until I ended up on my best friend's doorstep.
I JUST WANTED TO--
But...
SLAM
...he didn't want anything to do with me.

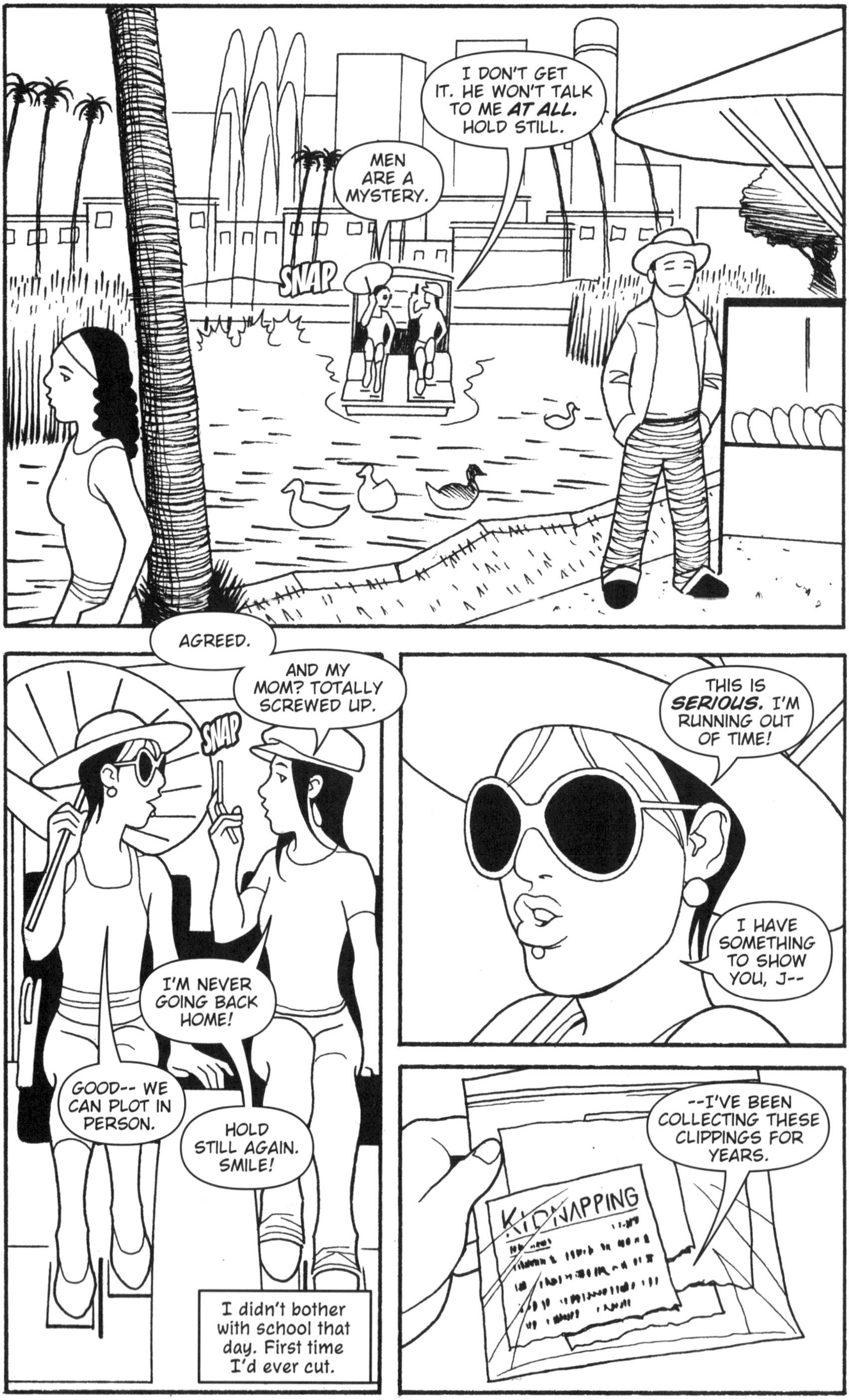
MEN ARE A MYSTERY.
I DON'T GET IT. HE WON'T TALK TO ME AT ALL. HOLD STILL.
SNAP
AGREED.
AND MY MOM? TOTALLY SCREWED UP.
SNAP
I'M NEVER GOING BACK HOME!
GOOD-- WE CAN PLOT IN PERSON.
HOLD STILL AGAIN. SMILE!
I didn't bother with school that day. First time I'd ever cut.
THIS IS SERIOUS. I'M RUNNING OUT OF TIME!
I HAVE SOMETHING TO SHOW YOU, J--
--I'VE BEEN COLLECTING THESE CLIPPINGS FOR YEARS.
KIDNAPPING

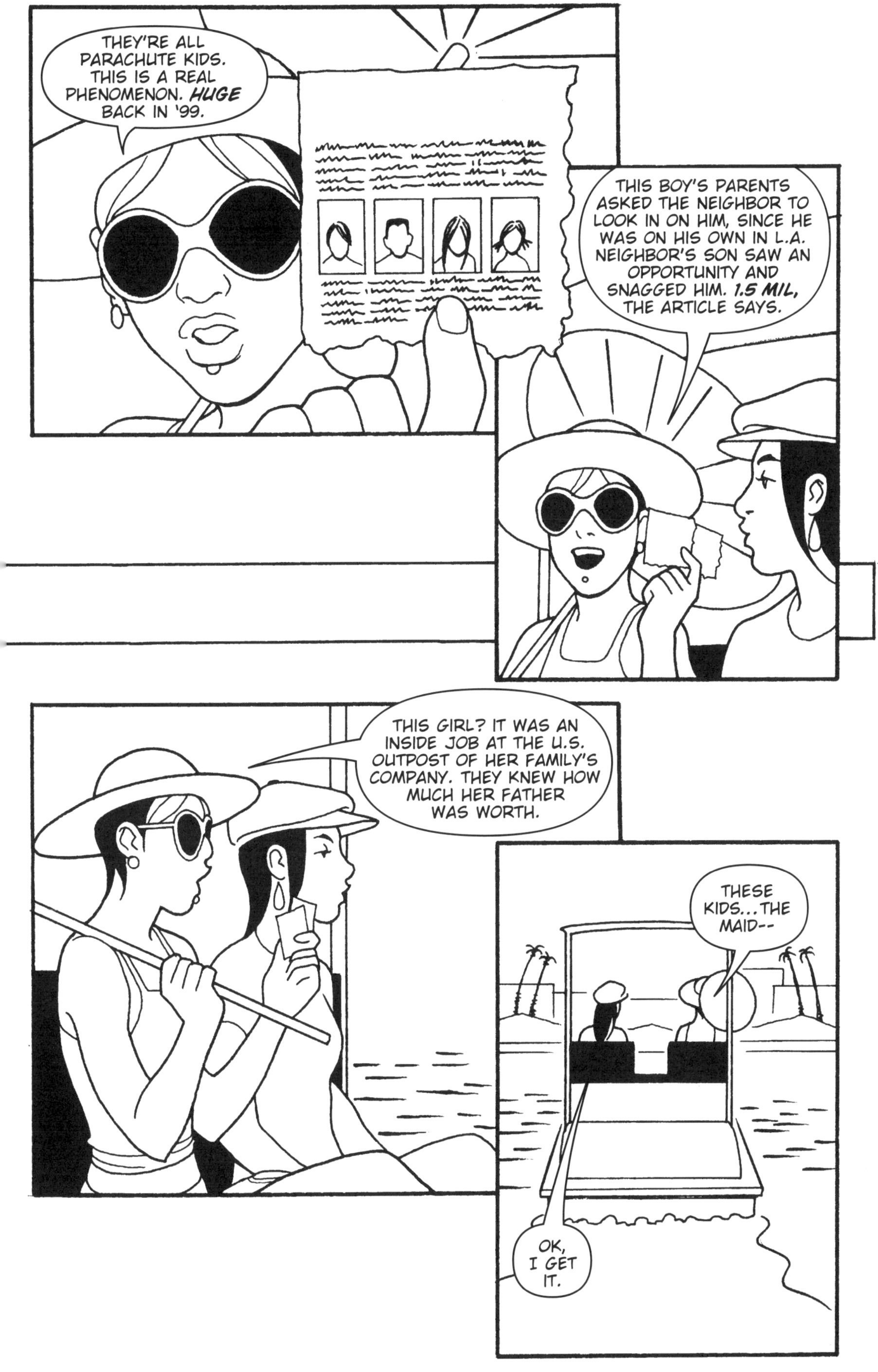
THEY'RE ALL PARACHUTE KIDS. THIS IS A REAL PHENOMENON. HUGE BACK IN '99.
THIS BOY'S PARENTS ASKED THE NEIGHBOR TO LOOK IN ON HIM, SINCE HE WAS ON HIS OWN IN L.A. NEIGHBOR'S SON SAW AN OPPORTUNITY AND SNAGGED HIM. 1.5 MIL, THE ARTICLE SAYS.
THIS GIRL? IT WAS AN INSIDE JOB AT THE U.S. OUTPOST OF HER FAMILY'S COMPANY. THEY KNEW HOW MUCH HER FATHER WAS WORTH.
THESE KIDS...THE MAID--
OK, I GET IT.

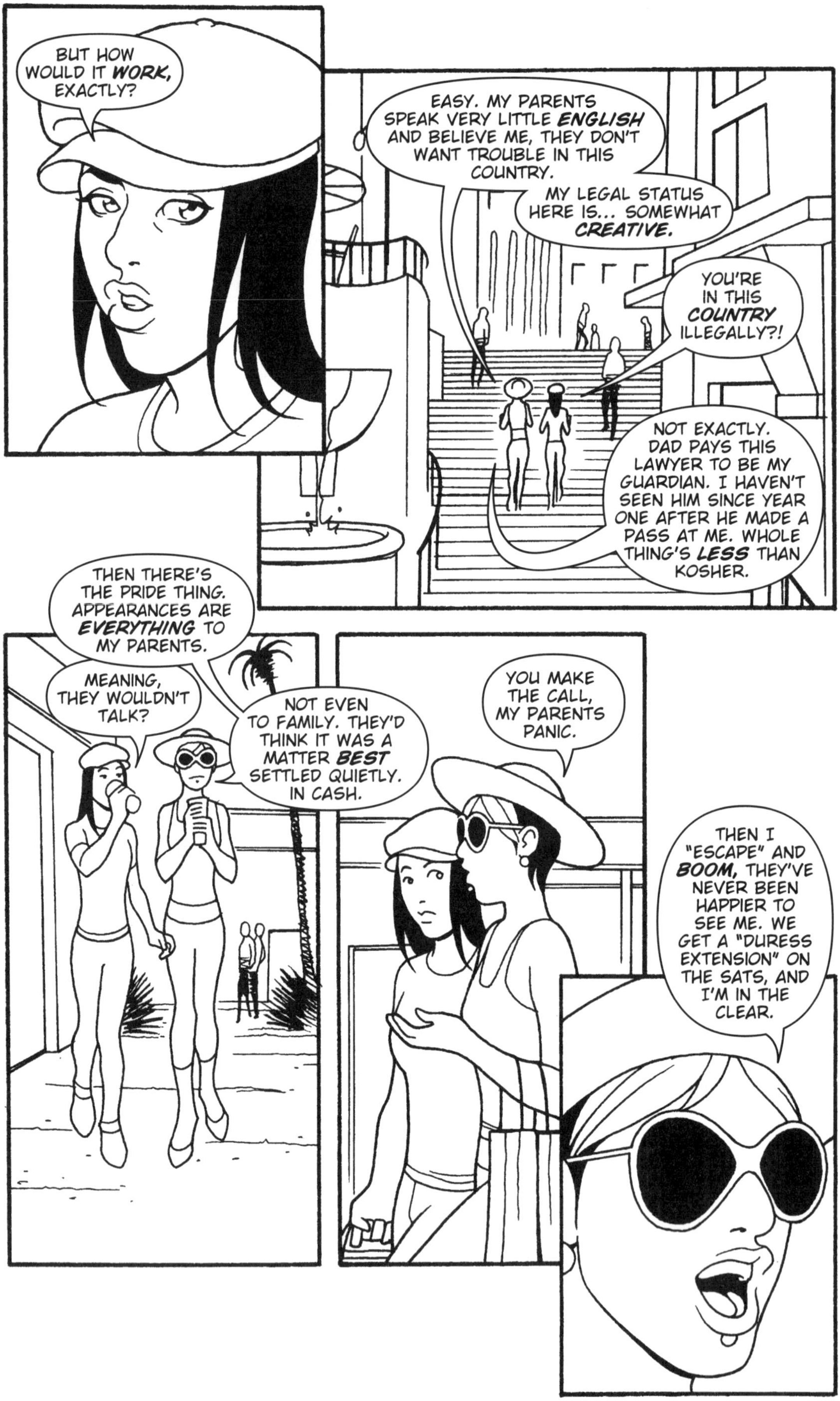
BUT HOW WOULD IT WORK, EXACTLY?
EASY. MY PARENTS SPEAK VERY LITTLE ENGLISH AND BELIEVE ME, THEY DON'T WANT TROUBLE IN THIS COUNTRY.
MY LEGAL STATUS HERE IS... SOMEWHAT CREATIVE.
YOU'RE IN THIS COUNTRY ILLEGALLY?!
NOT EXACTLY. DAD PAYS THIS LAWYER TO BE MY GUARDIAN. I HAVEN'T SEEN HIM SINCE YEAR ONE AFTER HE MADE A PASS AT ME. WHOLE THING'S LESS THAN KOSHER.
THEN THERE'S THE PRIDE THING. APPEARANCES ARE EVERYTHING TO MY PARENTS.
MEANING, THEY WOULDN'T TALK?
NOT EVEN TO FAMILY. THEY'D THINK IT WAS A MATTER BEST SETTLED QUIETLY. IN CASH.
YOU MAKE THE CALL, MY PARENTS PANIC.
THEN I "ESCAPE" AND BOOM, THEY'VE NEVER BEEN HAPPIER TO SEE ME. WE GET A "DURESS EXTENSION" ON THE SATS, AND I'M IN THE CLEAR.

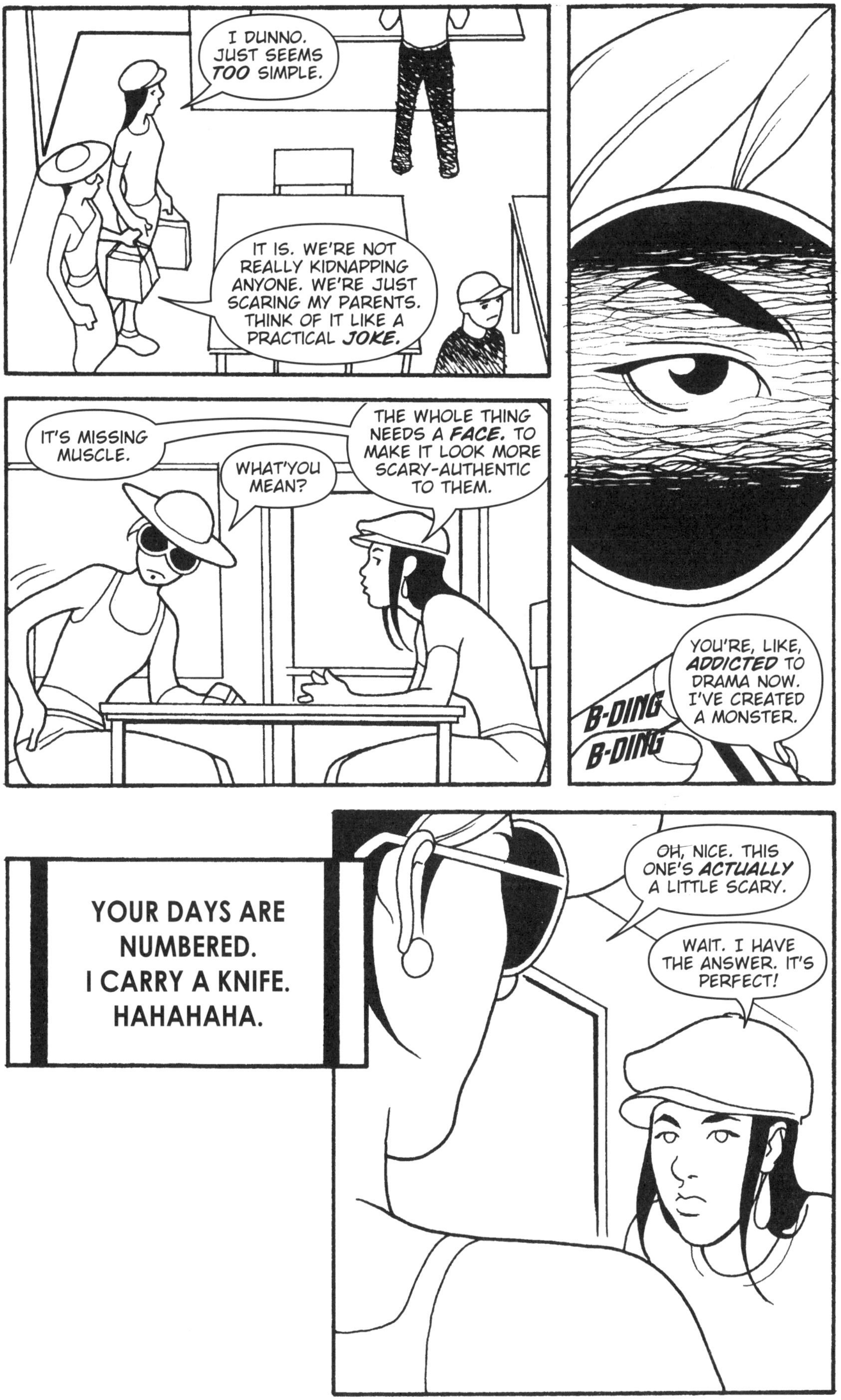
I DUNNO. JUST SEEMS TOO SIMPLE.
IT IS. WE'RE NOT REALLY KIDNAPPING ANYONE. WE'RE JUST SCARING MY PARENTS. THINK OF IT LIKE A PRACTICAL JOKE.
IT'S MISSING MUSCLE.
WHAT'YOU MEAN?
THE WHOLE THING NEEDS A FACE. TO MAKE IT LOOK MORE SCARY-AUTHENTIC TO THEM.
B-DING
B-DING
YOU'RE, LIKE, ADDICTED TO DRAMA NOW. I'VE CREATED A MONSTER.
YOUR DAYS ARE NUMBERED. I CARRY A KNIFE. HAHAHAHA.
OH, NICE. THIS ONE'S ACTUALLY A LITTLE SCARY.
WAIT. I HAVE THE ANSWER. IT'S PERFECT!

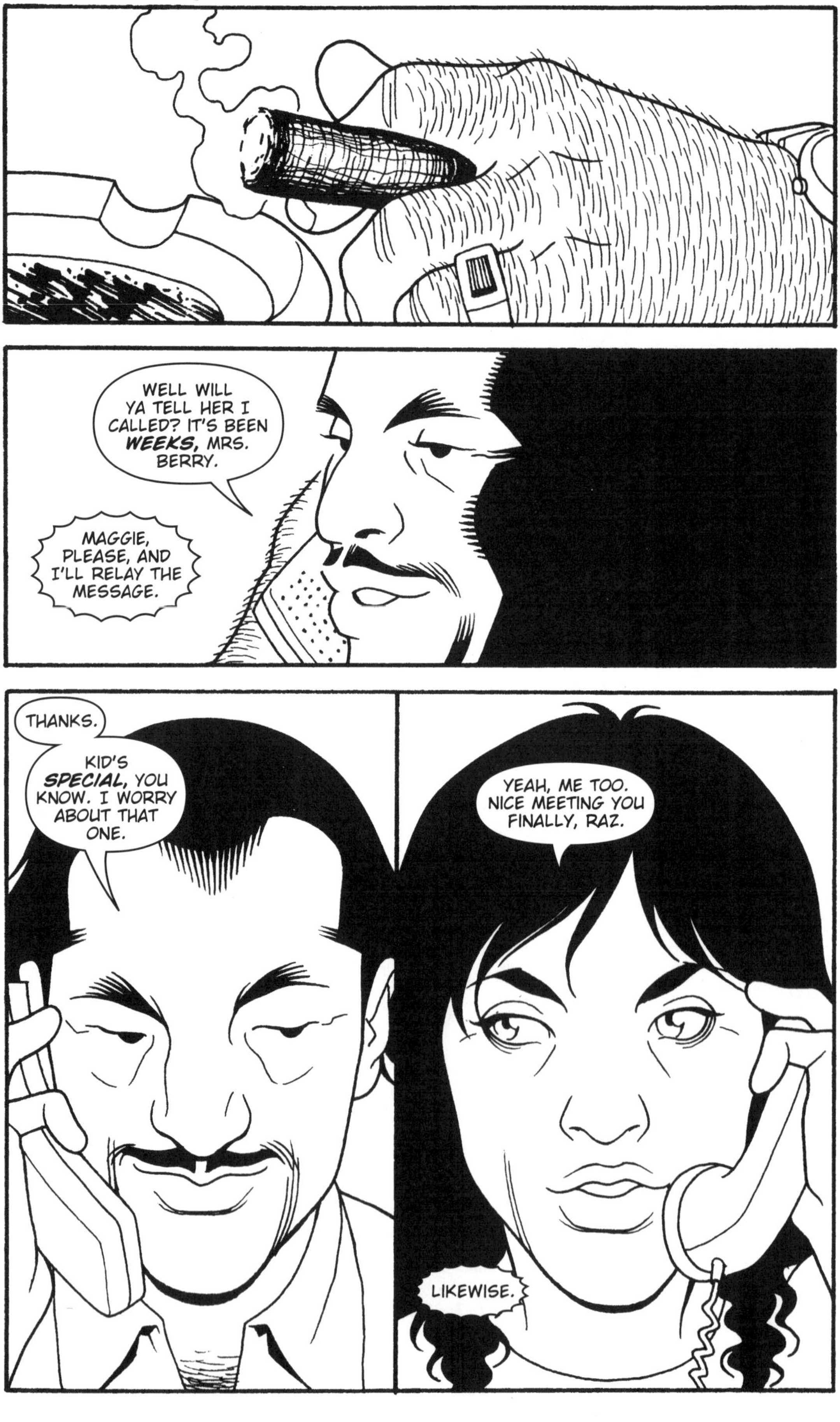
WELL WILL YA TELL HER I CALLED? IT'S BEEN WEEKS, MRS. BERRY.
MAGGIE, PLEASE, AND I'LL RELAY THE MESSAGE.
THANKS.
KID'S SPECIAL, YOU KNOW. I WORRY ABOUT THAT ONE.
YEAH, ME TOO. NICE MEETING YOU FINALLY, RAZ.
LIKEWISE.

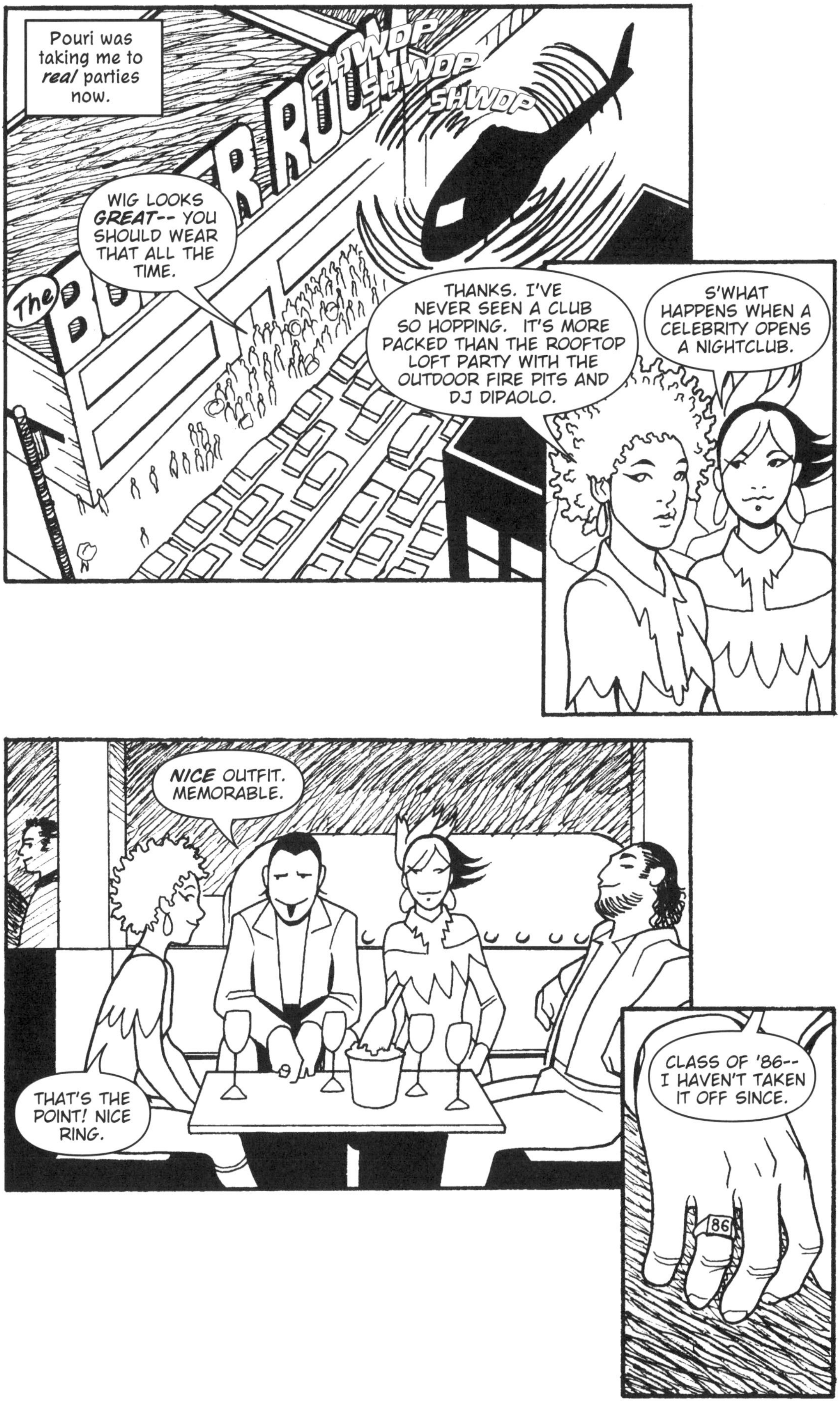
Pouri was taking me to *real* parties now.
SHWDP SHWDP SHWDP
WIG LOOKS **GREAT**-- YOU SHOULD WEAR THAT ALL THE TIME.
THANKS. I'VE NEVER SEEN A CLUB SO HOPPING. IT'S MORE PACKED THAN THE ROOFTOP LOFT PARTY WITH THE OUTDOOR FIRE PITS AND DJ DIPAOLO.
S'WHAT HAPPENS WHEN A CELEBRITY OPENS A NIGHTCLUB.
NICE OUTFIT. MEMORABLE.
THAT'S THE POINT! NICE RING.
CLASS OF '86-- I HAVEN'T TAKEN IT OFF SINCE.
86

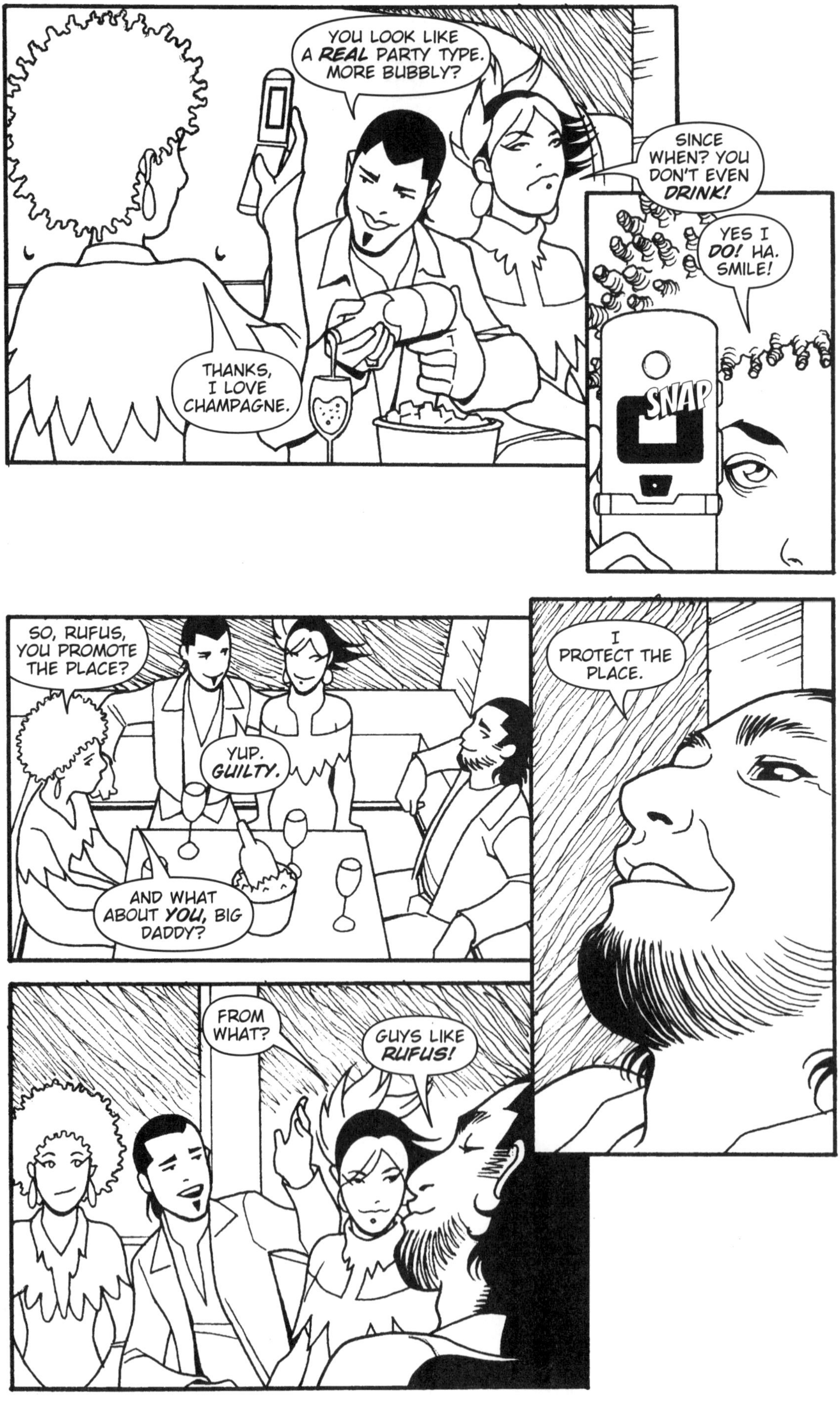
YOU LOOK LIKE A REAL PARTY TYPE. MORE BUBBLY?
THANKS, I LOVE CHAMPAGNE.
SINCE WHEN? YOU DON'T EVEN DRINK!
YES I DO! HA. SMILE!
SNAP
SO, RUFUS, YOU PROMOTE THE PLACE?
YUP. GUILTY.
AND WHAT ABOUT YOU, BIG DADDY?
I PROTECT THE PLACE.
FROM WHAT?
GUYS LIKE RUFUS!

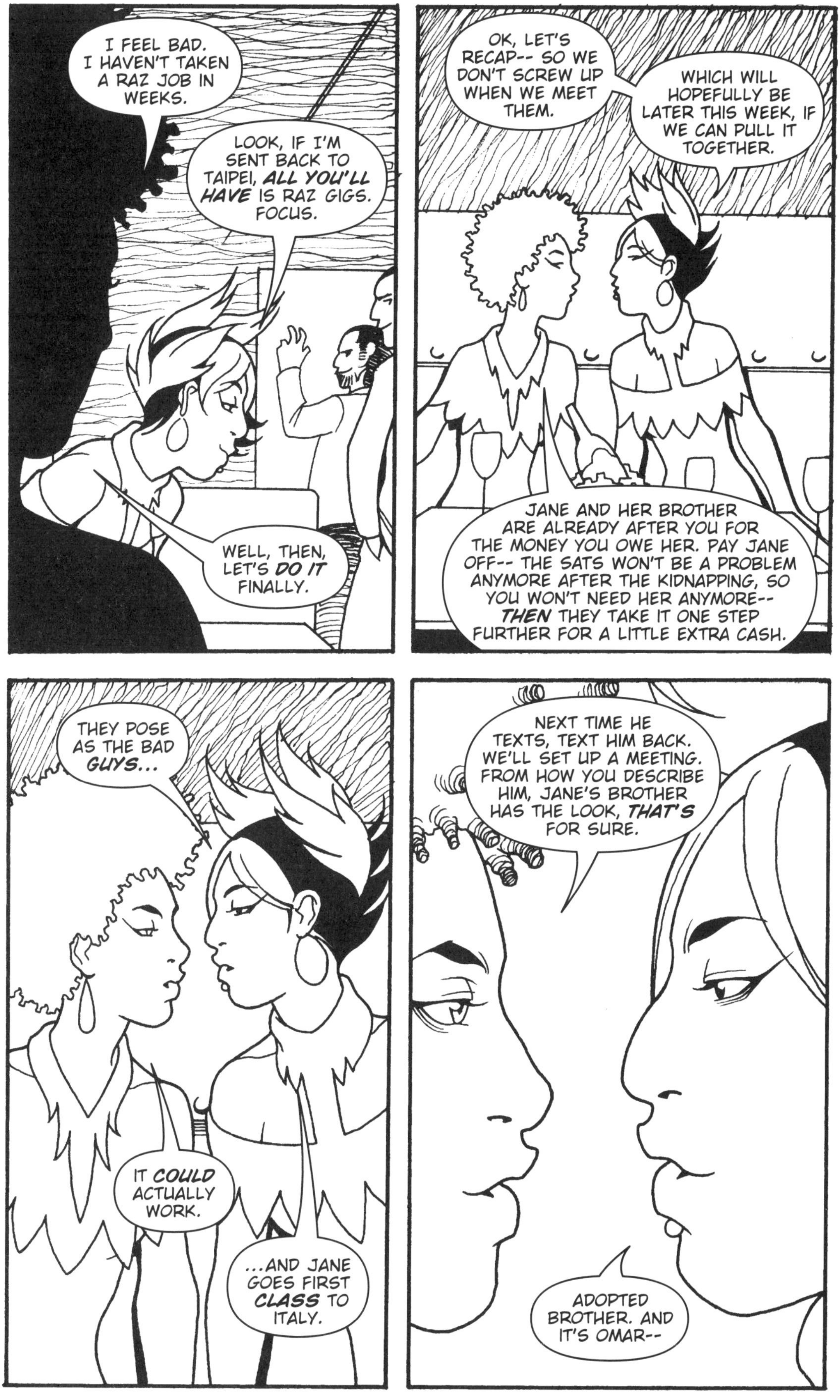
I FEEL BAD. I HAVEN'T TAKEN A RAZ JOB IN WEEKS.
LOOK, IF I'M SENT BACK TO TAIPEI, ALL YOU'LL HAVE IS RAZ GIGS. FOCUS.
WELL, THEN, LET'S DO IT FINALLY.
OK, LET'S RECAP-- SO WE DON'T SCREW UP WHEN WE MEET THEM.
WHICH WILL HOPEFULLY BE LATER THIS WEEK, IF WE CAN PULL IT TOGETHER.
JANE AND HER BROTHER ARE ALREADY AFTER YOU FOR THE MONEY YOU OWE HER. PAY JANE OFF-- THE SATS WON'T BE A PROBLEM ANYMORE AFTER THE KIDNAPPING, SO YOU WON'T NEED HER ANYMORE-- THEN THEY TAKE IT ONE STEP FURTHER FOR A LITTLE EXTRA CASH.
THEY POSE AS THE BAD GUYS...
IT COULD ACTUALLY WORK.
...AND JANE GOES FIRST CLASS TO ITALY.
NEXT TIME HE TEXTS, TEXT HIM BACK. WE'LL SET UP A MEETING. FROM HOW YOU DESCRIBE HIM, JANE'S BROTHER HAS THE LOOK, THAT'S FOR SURE.
ADOPTED BROTHER. AND IT'S OMAR--

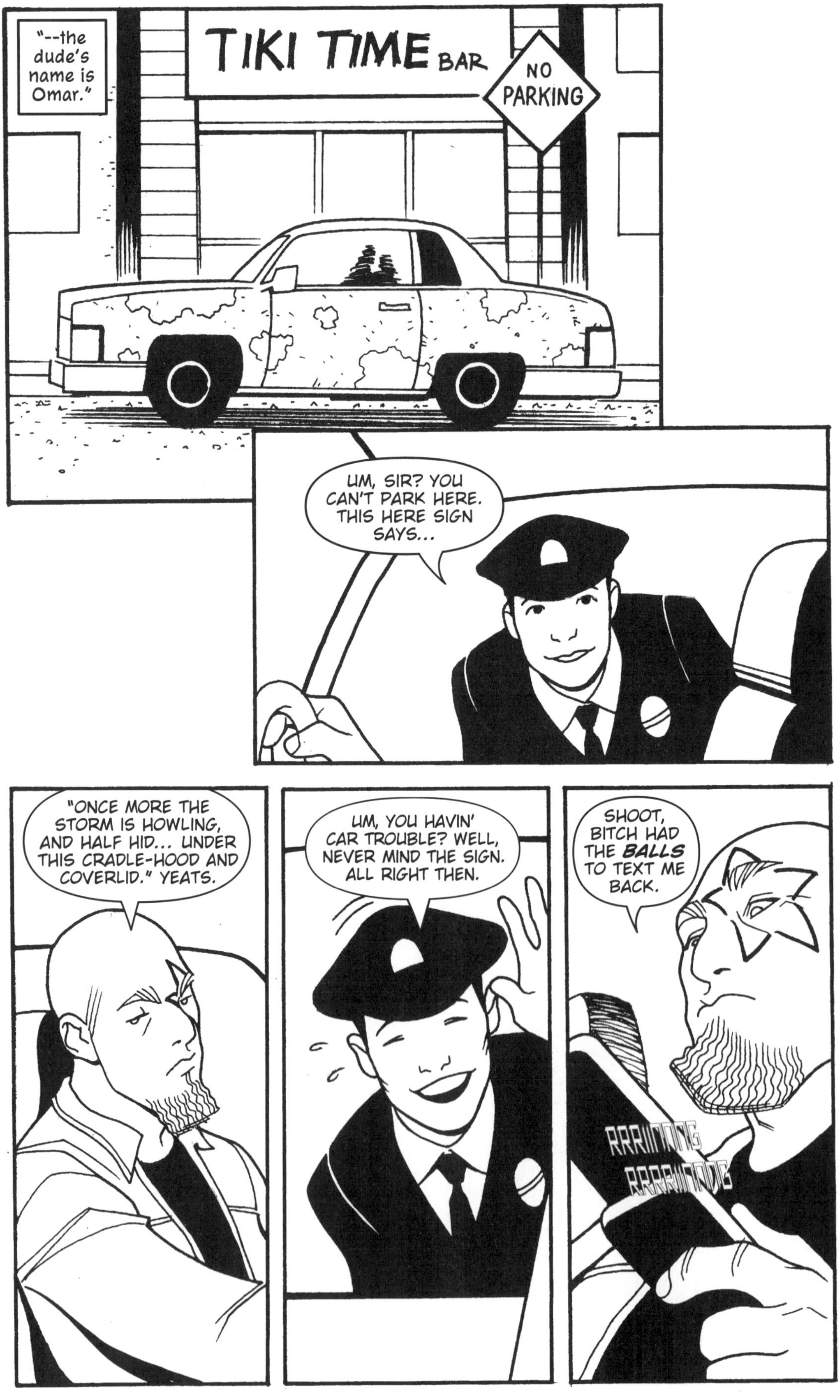
"--the dude's name is Omar."
TIKI TIME BAR
NO PARKING
UM, SIR? YOU CAN'T PARK HERE. THIS HERE SIGN SAYS...
"ONCE MORE THE STORM IS HOWLING, AND HALF HID... UNDER THIS CRADLE-HOOD AND COVERLID." YEATS.
UM, YOU HAVIN' CAR TROUBLE? WELL, NEVER MIND THE SIGN. ALL RIGHT THEN.
SHOOT, BITCH HAD THE **BALLS** TO TEXT ME BACK.
RRRIIINNNG
RRRRIIINNNG

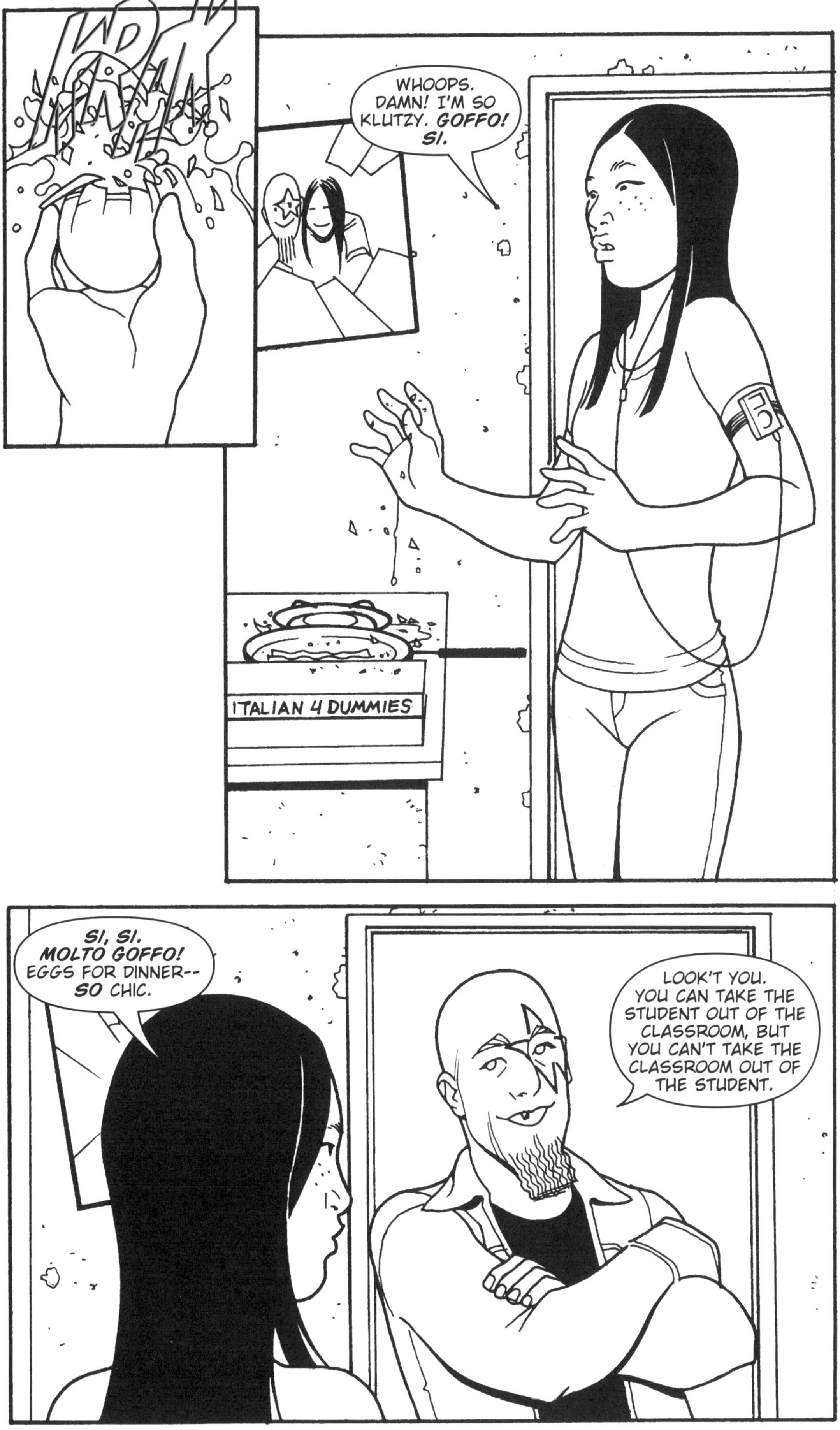
WHOOPS. DAMN! I'M SO KLUTZY. GOFFO! SI.
ITALIAN 4 DUMMIES
SI, SI. MOLTO GOFFO! EGGS FOR DINNER-- SO CHIC.
LOOK'T YOU. YOU CAN TAKE THE STUDENT OUT OF THE CLASSROOM, BUT YOU CAN'T TAKE THE CLASSROOM OUT OF THE STUDENT.

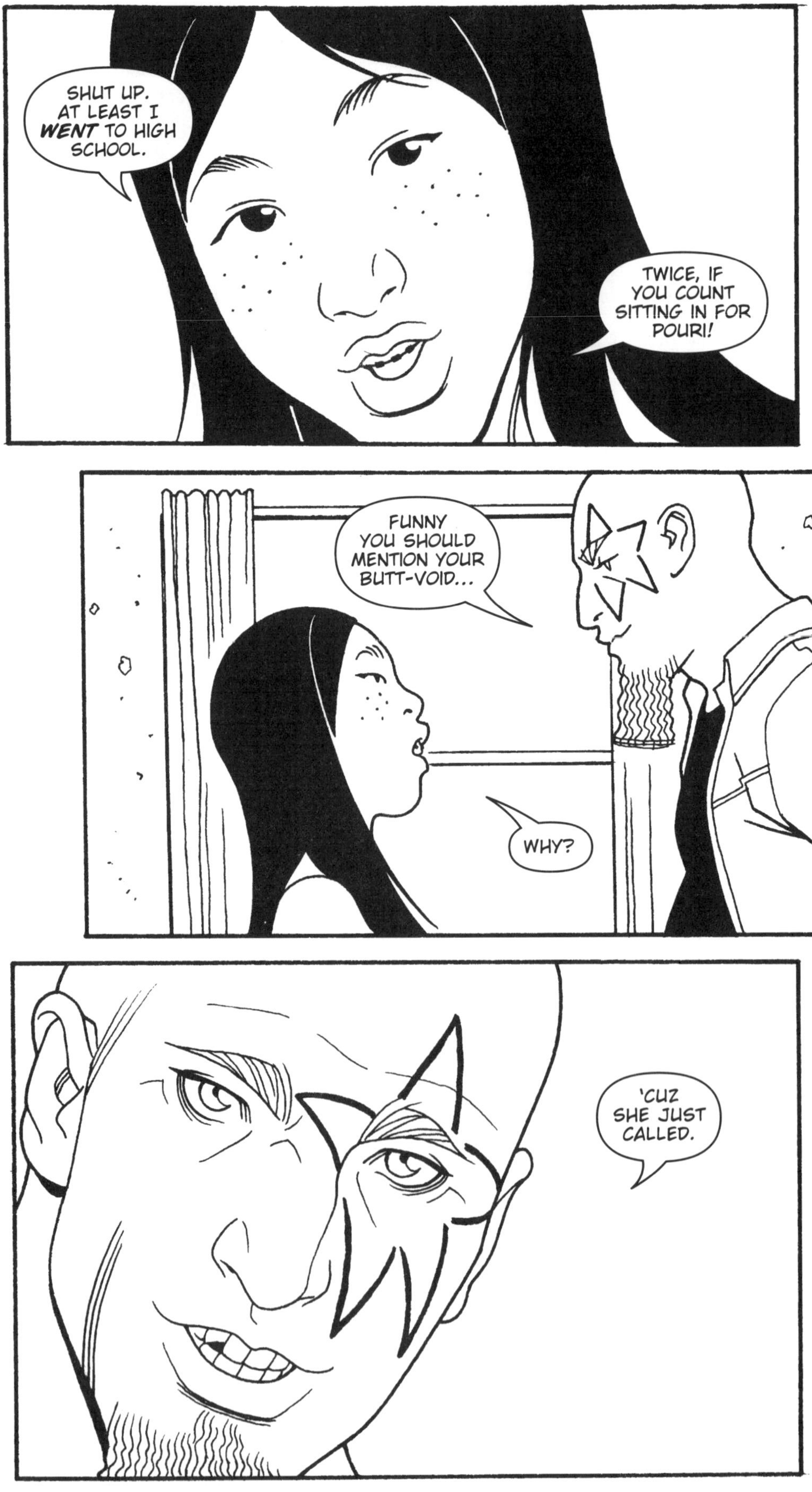
SHUT UP. AT LEAST I *WENT* TO HIGH SCHOOL.
TWICE, IF YOU COUNT SITTING IN FOR POURI!
FUNNY YOU SHOULD MENTION YOUR BUTT-VOID...
WHY?
'CUZ SHE JUST CALLED.

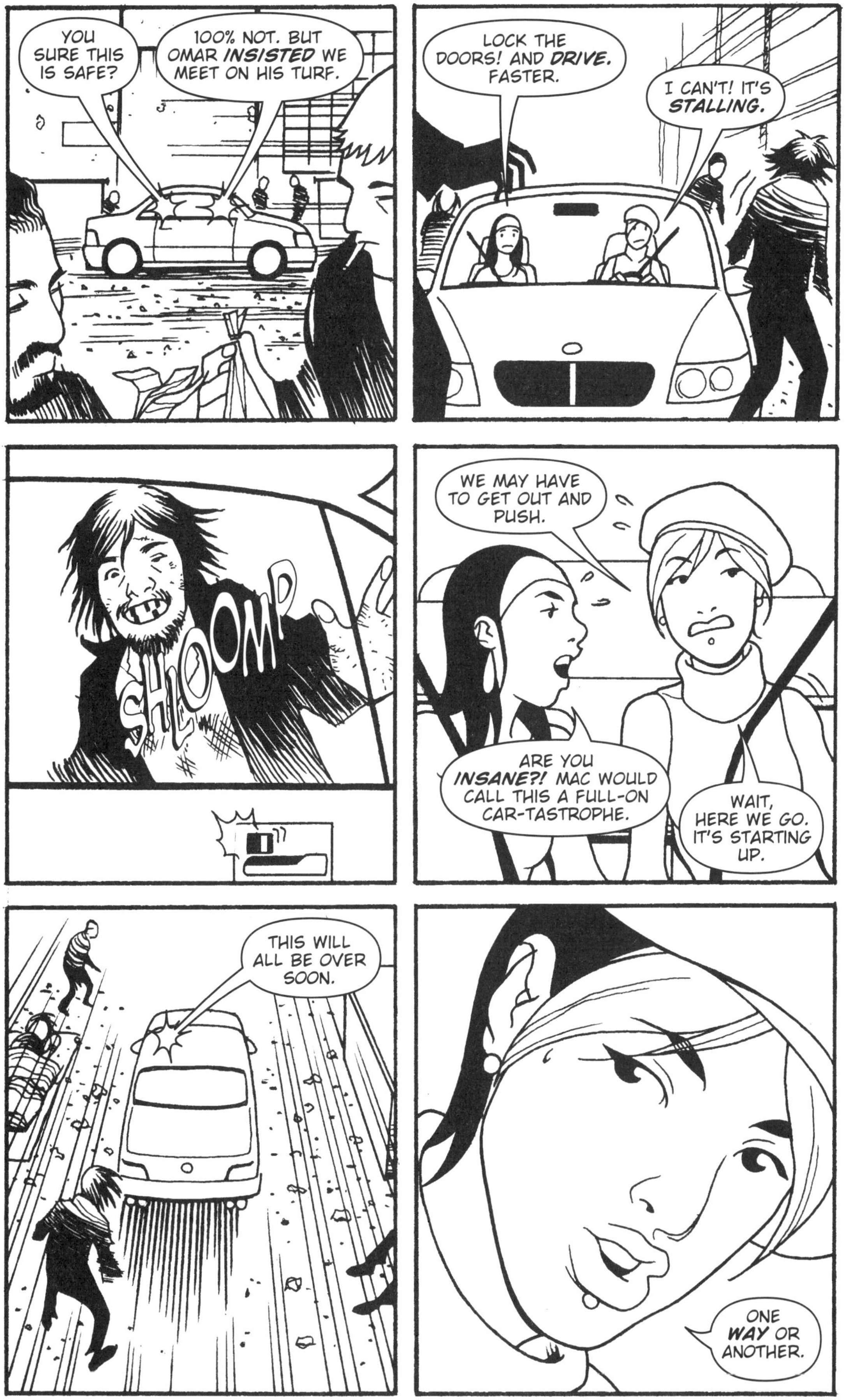
YOU SURE THIS IS SAFE?
100% NOT. BUT OMAR INSISTED WE MEET ON HIS TURF.
LOCK THE DOORS! AND DRIVE. FASTER.
I CAN'T! IT'S STALLING.
SHLOOMP
WE MAY HAVE TO GET OUT AND PUSH.
ARE YOU INSANE?! MAC WOULD CALL THIS A FULL-ON CAR-TASTROPHE.
WAIT, HERE WE GO. IT'S STARTING UP.
THIS WILL ALL BE OVER SOON.
ONE WAY OR ANOTHER.

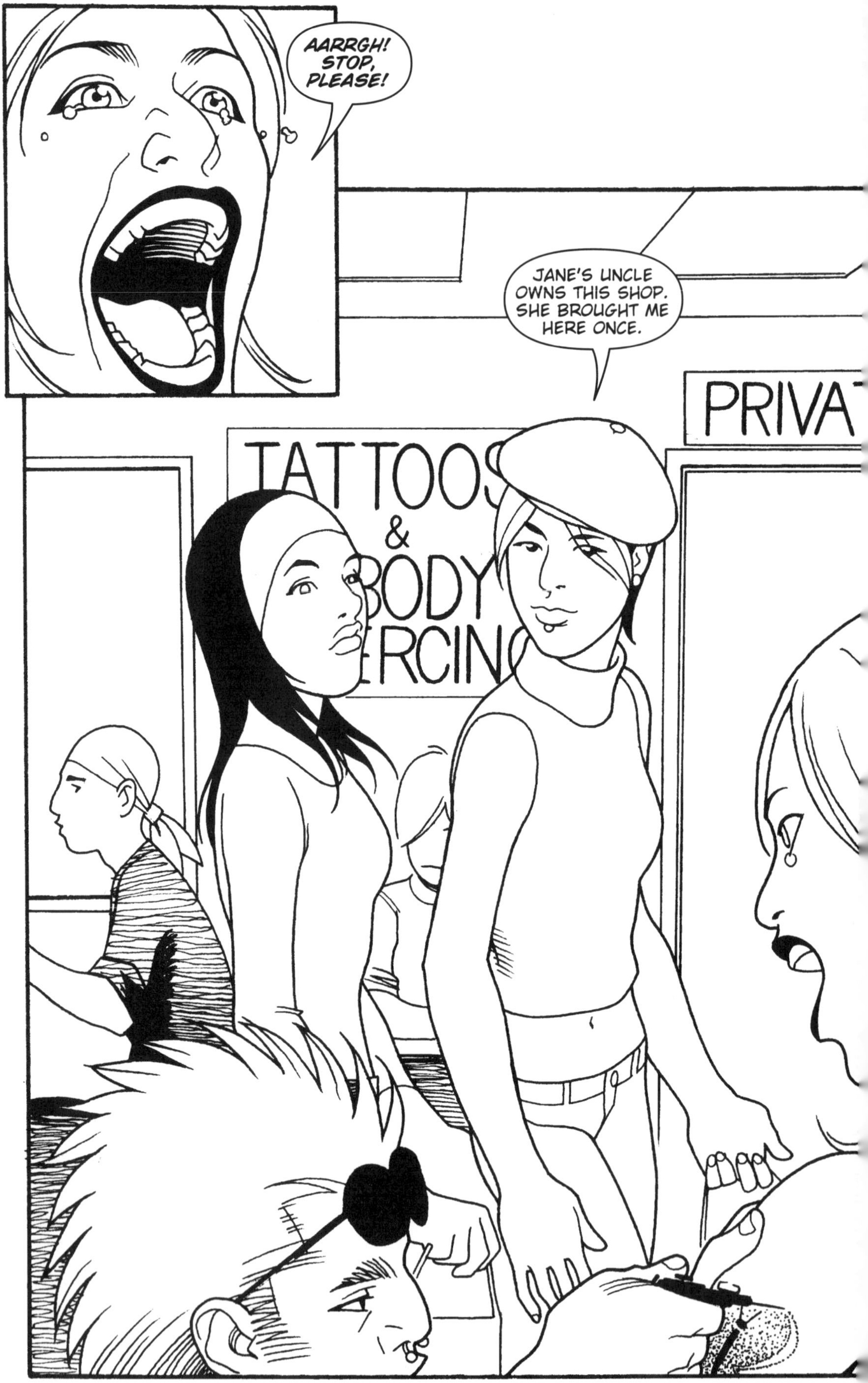
AARRGH! STOP, PLEASE!
JANE'S UNCLE OWNS THIS SHOP. SHE BROUGHT ME HERE ONCE.
PRIVAT
TATTOOS
&
BODY
ERCING

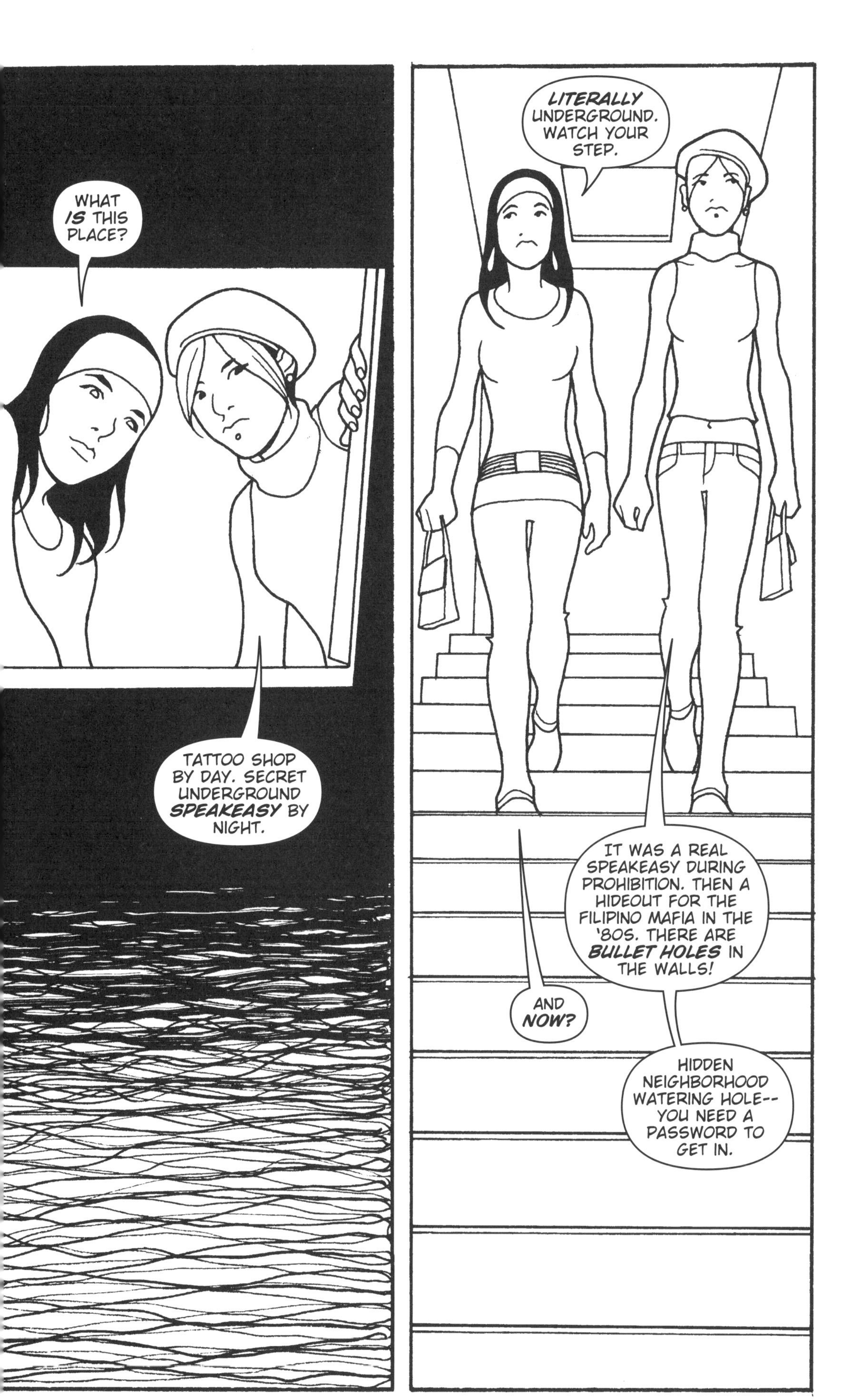
WHAT *IS* THIS PLACE?
TATTOO SHOP BY DAY. SECRET UNDERGROUND ***SPEAKEASY*** BY NIGHT.
LITERALLY UNDERGROUND. WATCH YOUR STEP.
IT WAS A REAL SPEAKEASY DURING PROHIBITION. THEN A HIDEOUT FOR THE FILIPINO MAFIA IN THE '80S. THERE ARE ***BULLET HOLES*** IN THE WALLS!
AND ***NOW?***
HIDDEN NEIGHBORHOOD WATERING HOLE-- YOU NEED A PASSWORD TO GET IN.

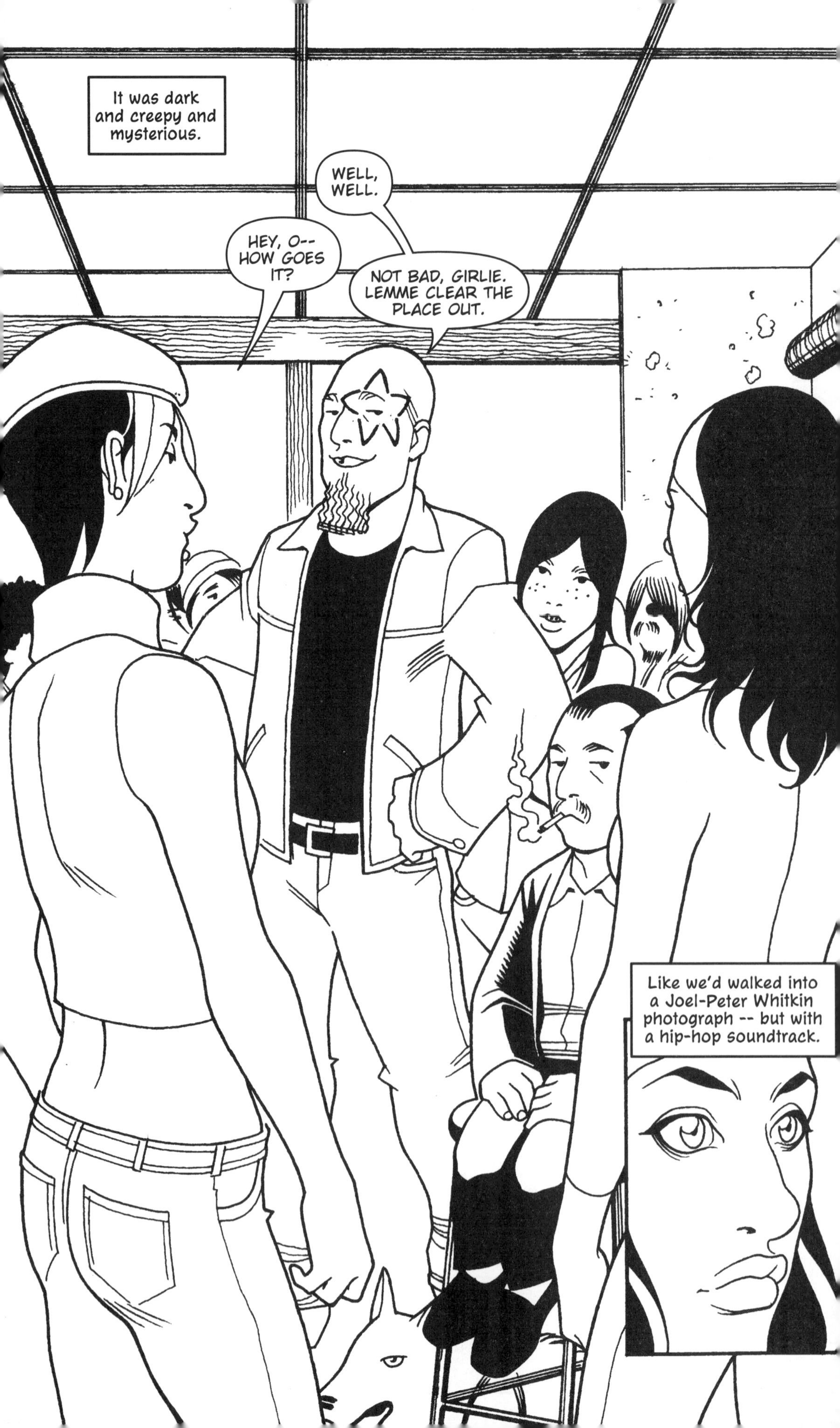
It was dark and creepy and mysterious.
WELL, WELL.
HEY, O-- HOW GOES IT?
NOT BAD, GIRLIE. LEMME CLEAR THE PLACE OUT.
Like we'd walked into a Joel-Peter Whitkin photograph -- but with a hip-hop soundtrack.

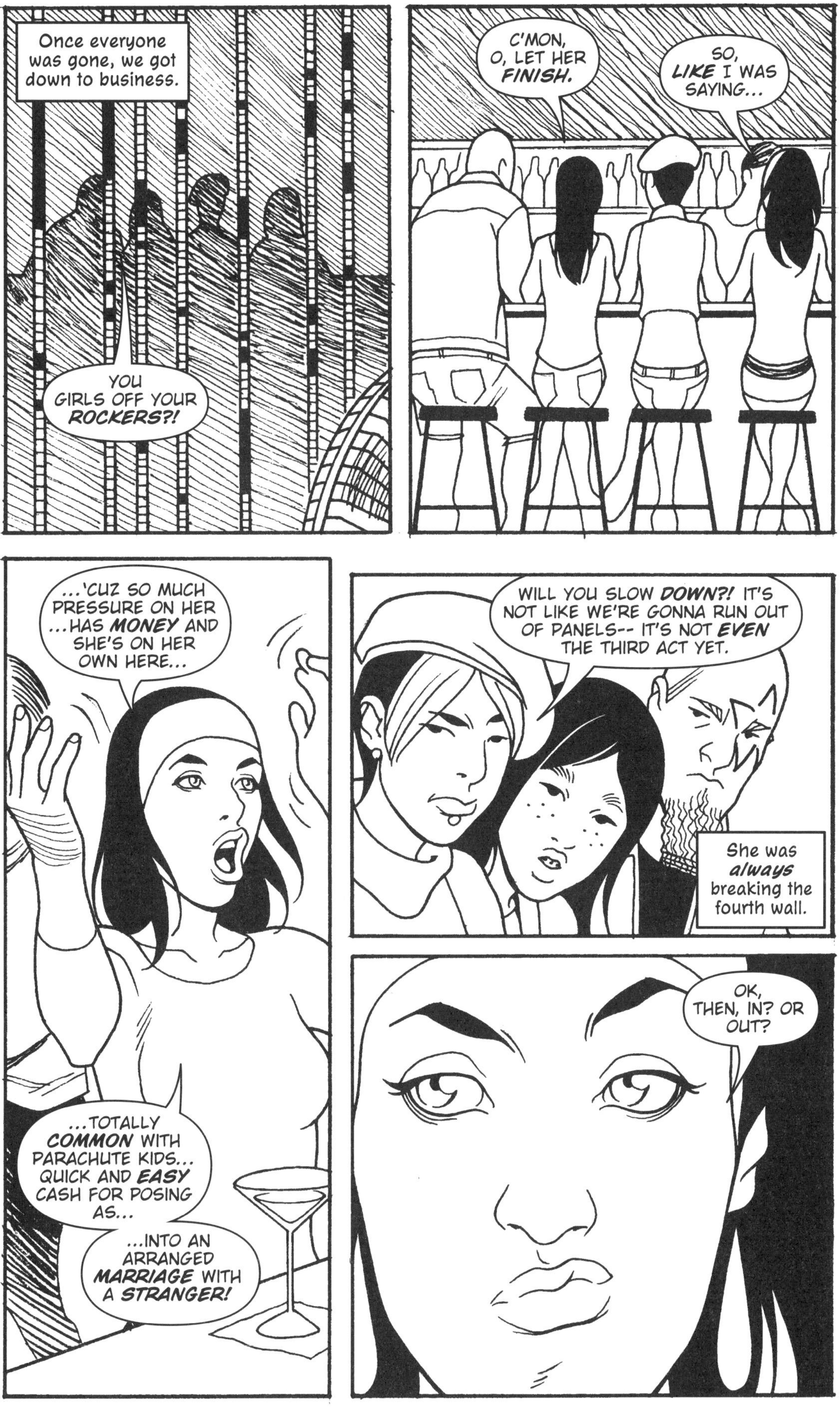

Once everyone was gone, we got down to business.
YOU GIRLS OFF YOUR ROCKERS?!
C'MON, O, LET HER FINISH.
SO, LIKE I WAS SAYING...
...'CUZ SO MUCH PRESSURE ON HER ...HAS MONEY AND SHE'S ON HER OWN HERE...
...TOTALLY COMMON WITH PARACHUTE KIDS... QUICK AND EASY CASH FOR POSING AS...
...INTO AN ARRANGED MARRIAGE WITH A STRANGER!
WILL YOU SLOW DOWN?! IT'S NOT LIKE WE'RE GONNA RUN OUT OF PANELS-- IT'S NOT EVEN THE THIRD ACT YET.
She was always breaking the fourth wall.
OK, THEN, IN? OR OUT?

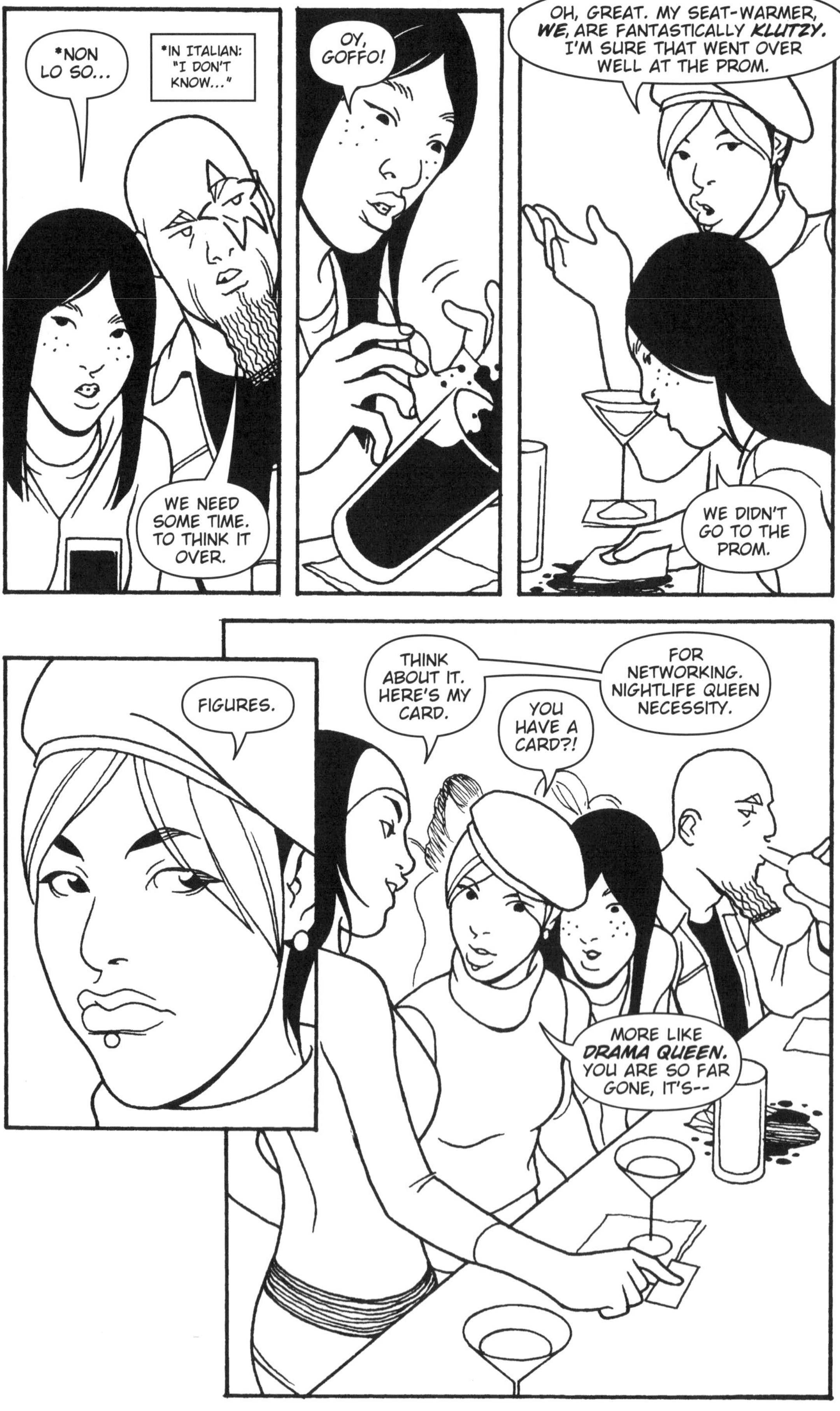
*NON LO SO...
*IN ITALIAN: "I DON'T KNOW..."
WE NEED SOME TIME. TO THINK IT OVER.
OY, GOFFO!
OH, GREAT. MY SEAT-WARMER, **WE**, ARE FANTASTICALLY **KLUTZY.** I'M SURE THAT WENT OVER WELL AT THE PROM.
WE DIDN'T GO TO THE PROM.
FIGURES.
THINK ABOUT IT. HERE'S MY CARD.
YOU HAVE A CARD?!
FOR NETWORKING. NIGHTLIFE QUEEN NECESSITY.
MORE LIKE **DRAMA QUEEN.** YOU ARE SO FAR GONE, IT'S--

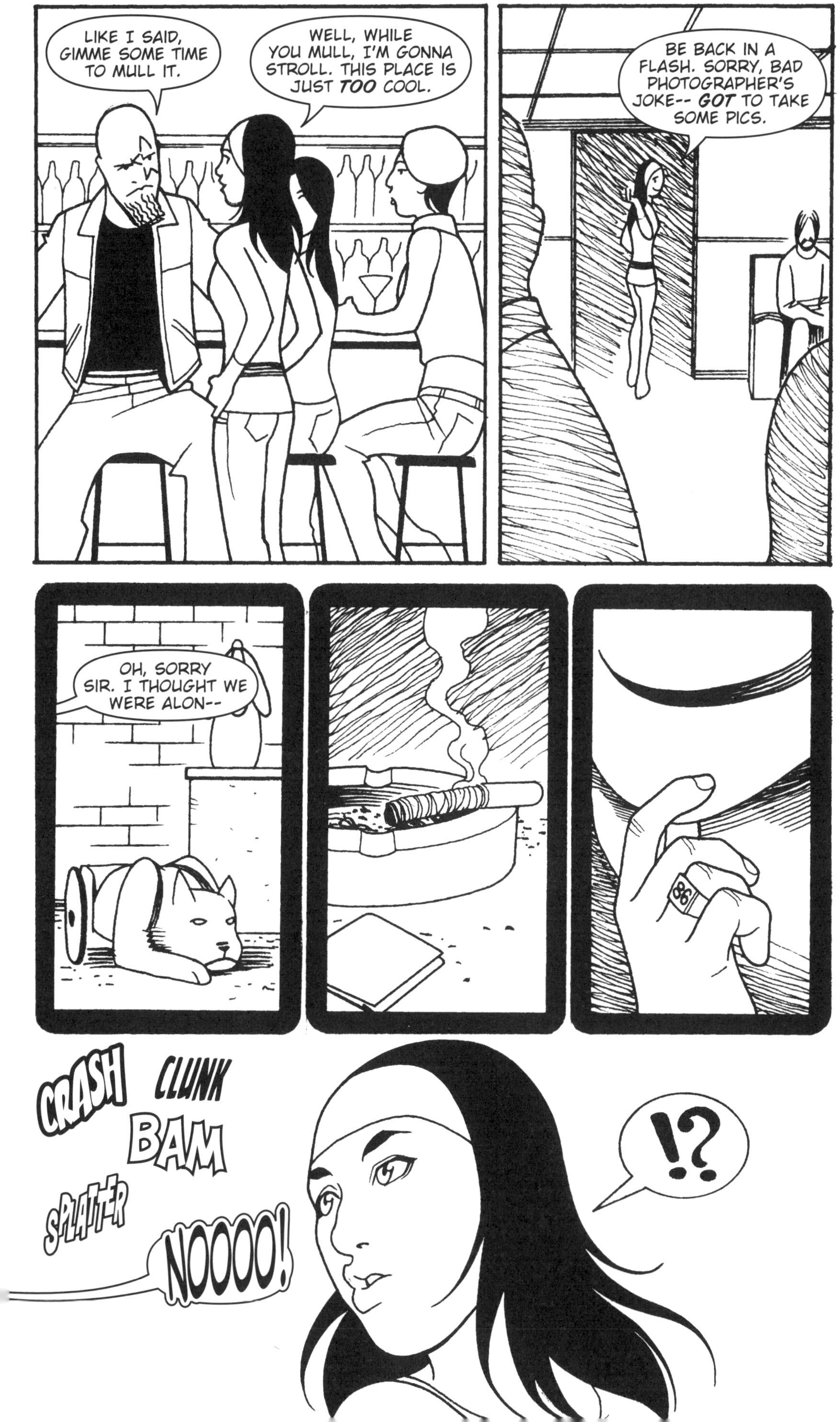
LIKE I SAID, GIMME SOME TIME TO MULL IT.
WELL, WHILE YOU MULL, I'M GONNA STROLL. THIS PLACE IS JUST TOO COOL.
BE BACK IN A FLASH. SORRY, BAD PHOTOGRAPHER'S JOKE-- GOT TO TAKE SOME PICS.
OH, SORRY SIR. I THOUGHT WE WERE ALON--
98
CRASH
CLUNK
BAM
SPLATTER
NOOOO!
!?

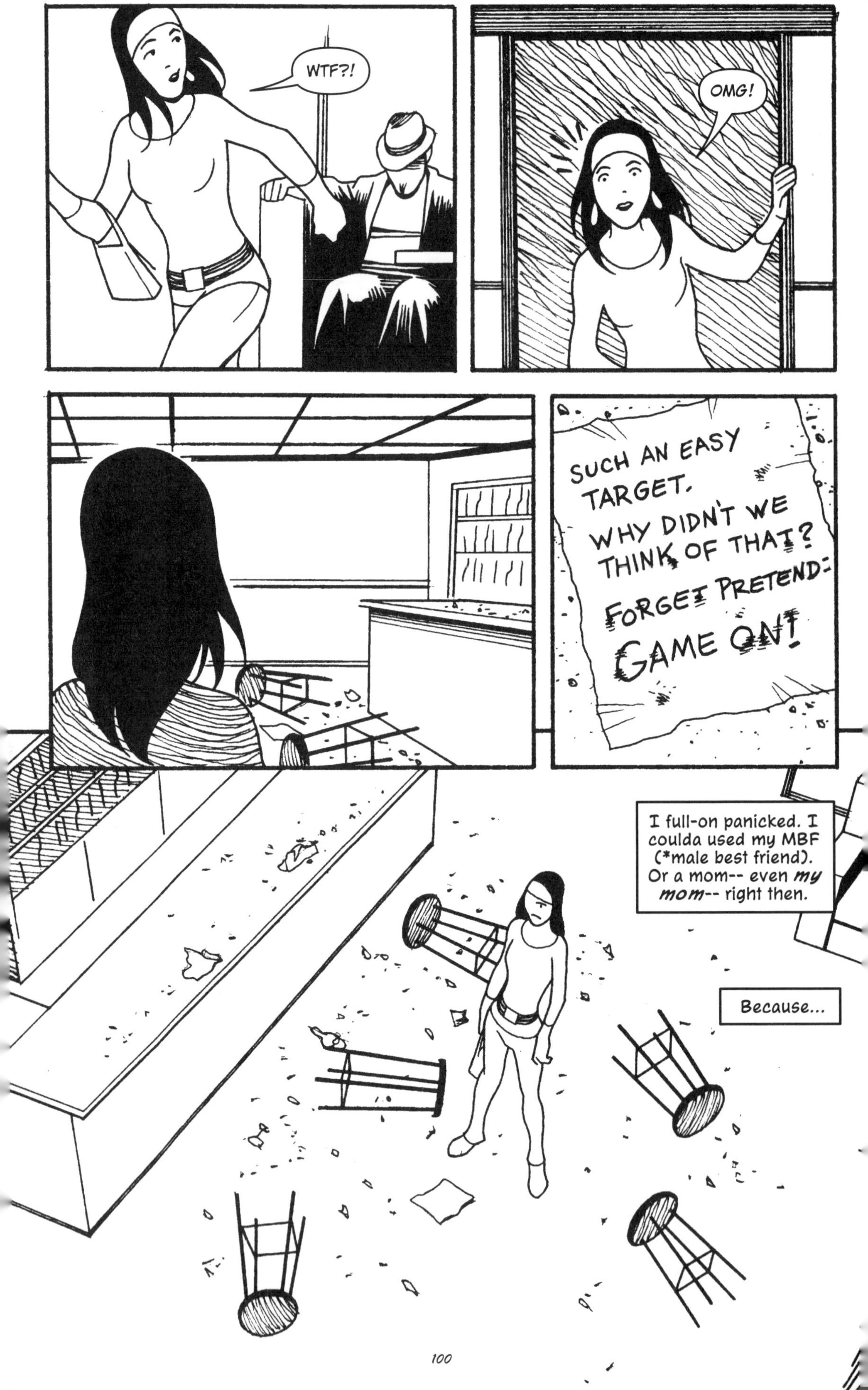
WTF?!
OMG!
SUCH AN EASY TARGET.
WHY DIDN'T WE THINK OF THAT?
FORGET PRETEND:
GAME ON!
I full-on panicked. I coulda used my MBF (*male best friend). Or a mom-- even *my mom*-- right then.
Because...

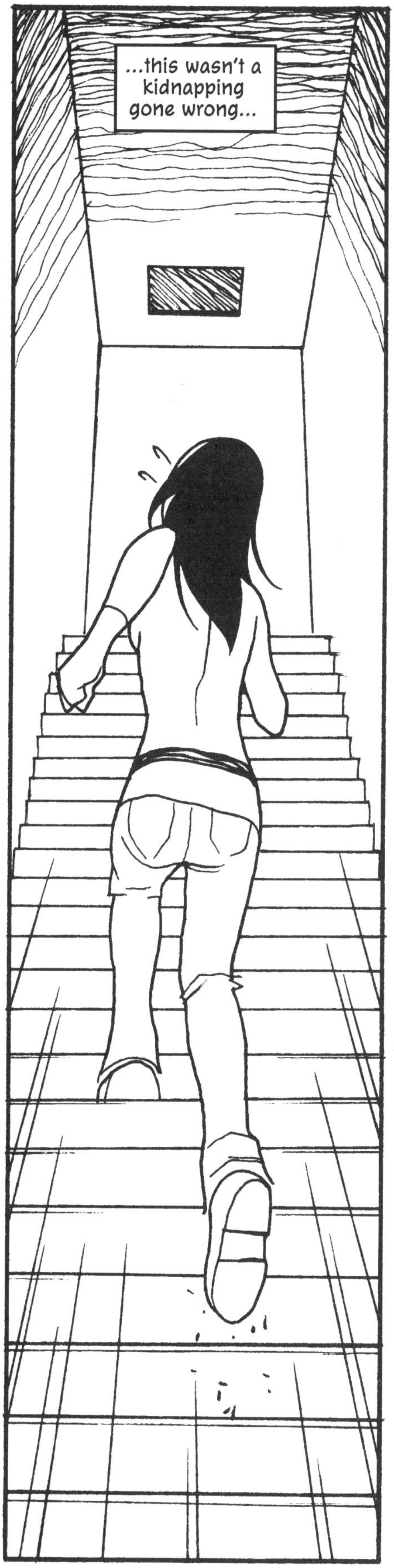
...this wasn't a kidnapping gone wrong...

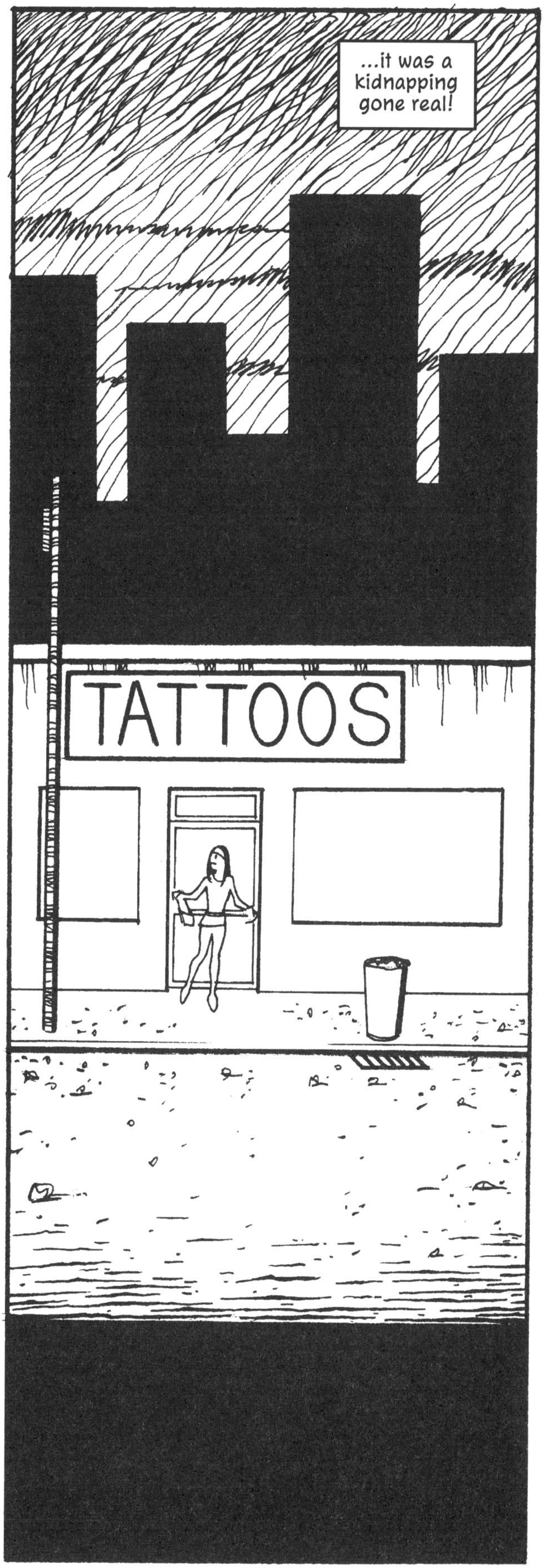
...it was a kidnapping gone real!
TATTOOS

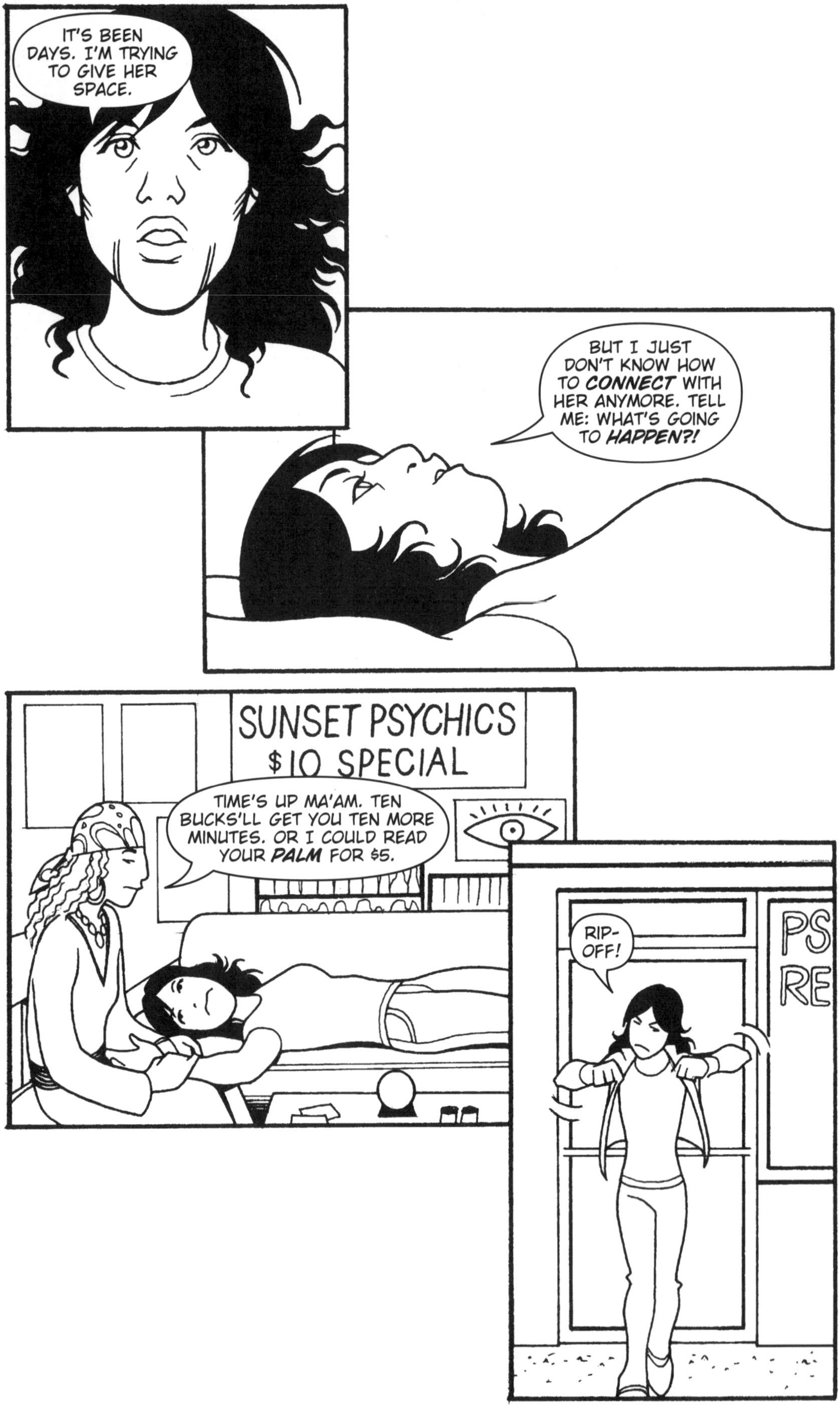
IT'S BEEN DAYS. I'M TRYING TO GIVE HER SPACE.
BUT I JUST DON'T KNOW HOW TO **CONNECT** WITH HER ANYMORE. TELL ME: WHAT'S GOING TO **HAPPEN?!**
SUNSET PSYCHICS
$10 SPECIAL
TIME'S UP MA'AM. TEN BUCKS'LL GET YOU TEN MORE MINUTES. OR I COULD READ YOUR **PALM** FOR $5.
RIP-OFF!
PS
RE

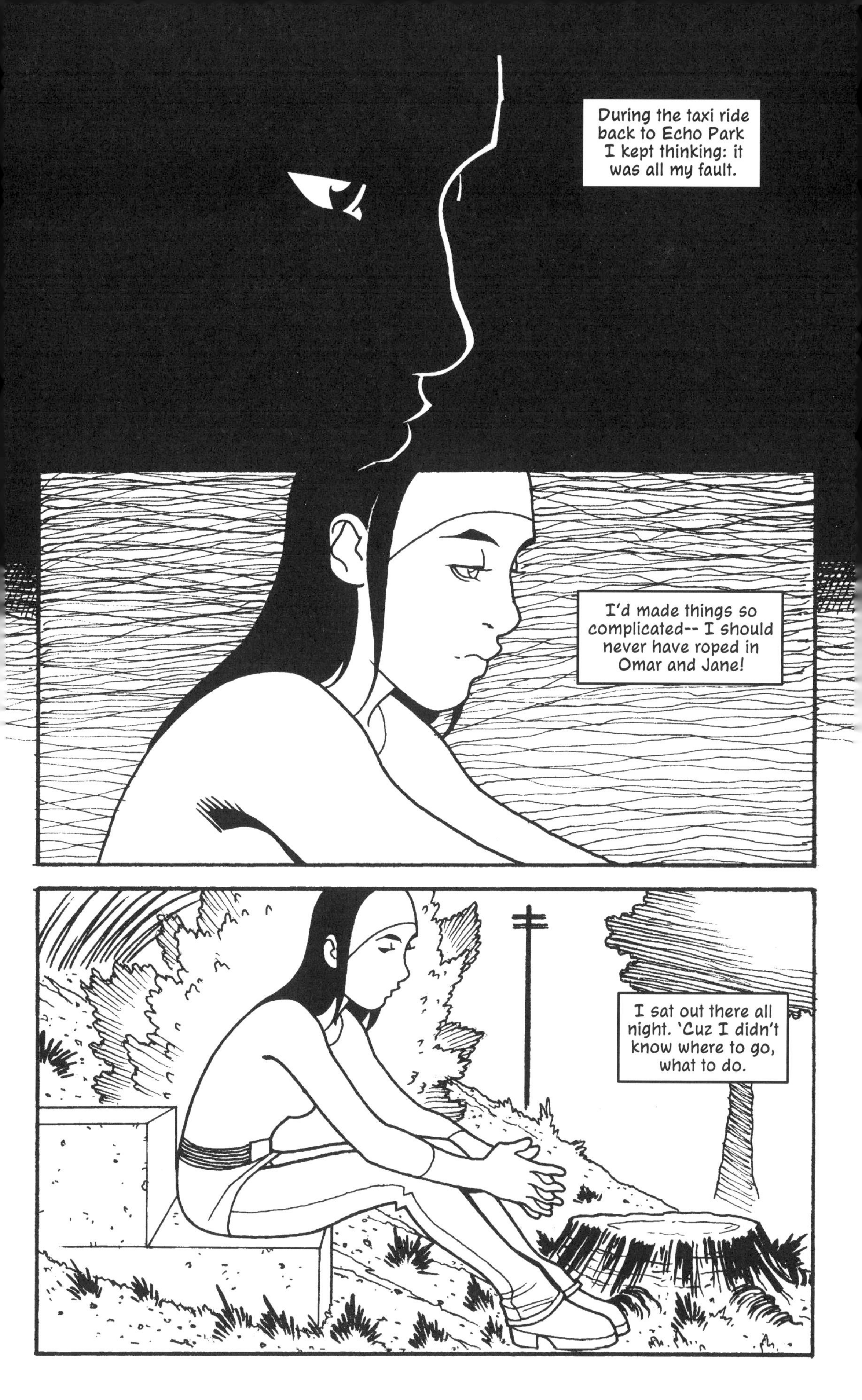
During the taxi ride back to Echo Park I kept thinking: it was all my fault.
I'd made things so complicated-- I should never have roped in Omar and Jane!
I sat out there all night. 'Cuz I didn't know where to go, what to do.

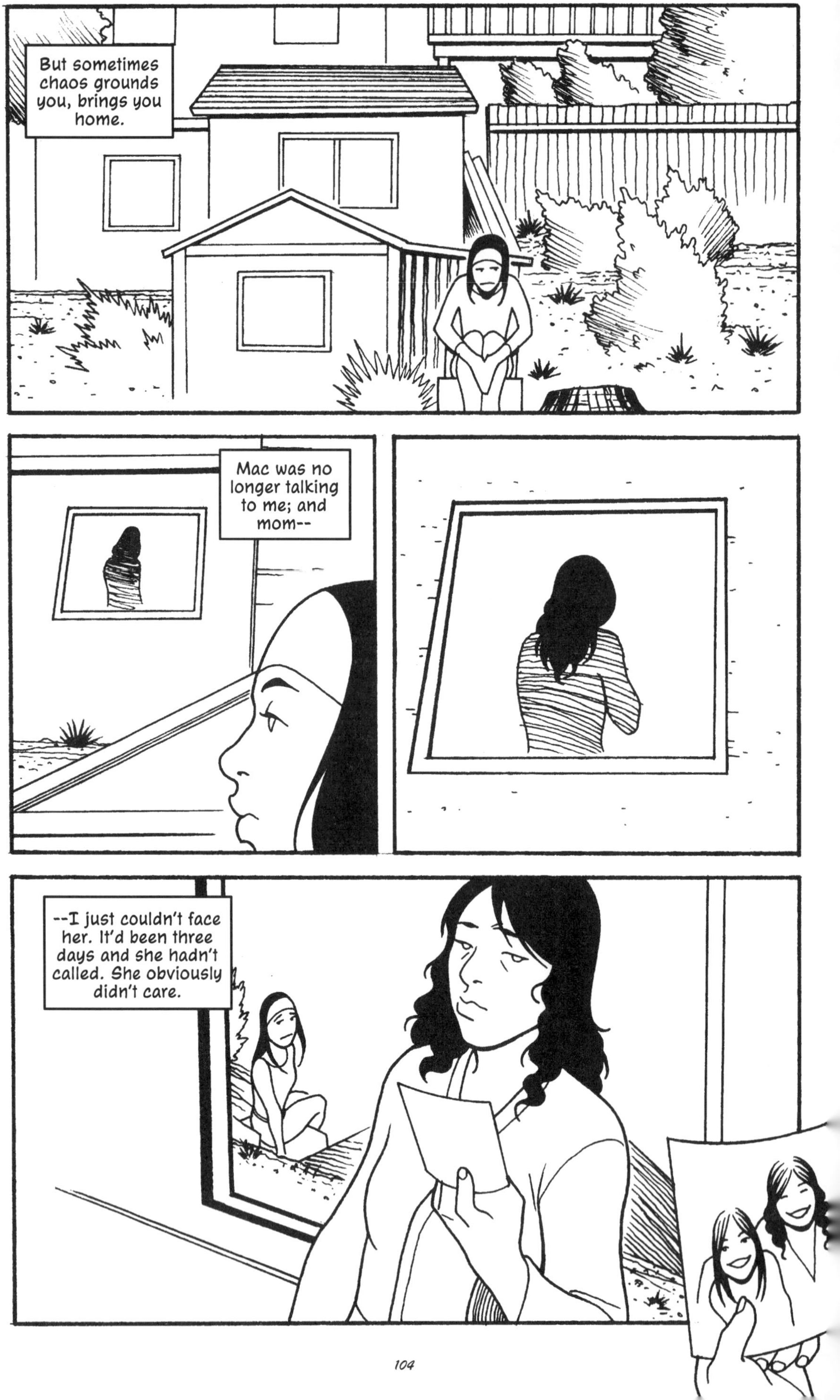

But sometimes chaos grounds you, brings you home.
Mac was no longer talking to me; and mom--
--I just couldn't face her. It'd been three days and she hadn't called. She obviously didn't care.

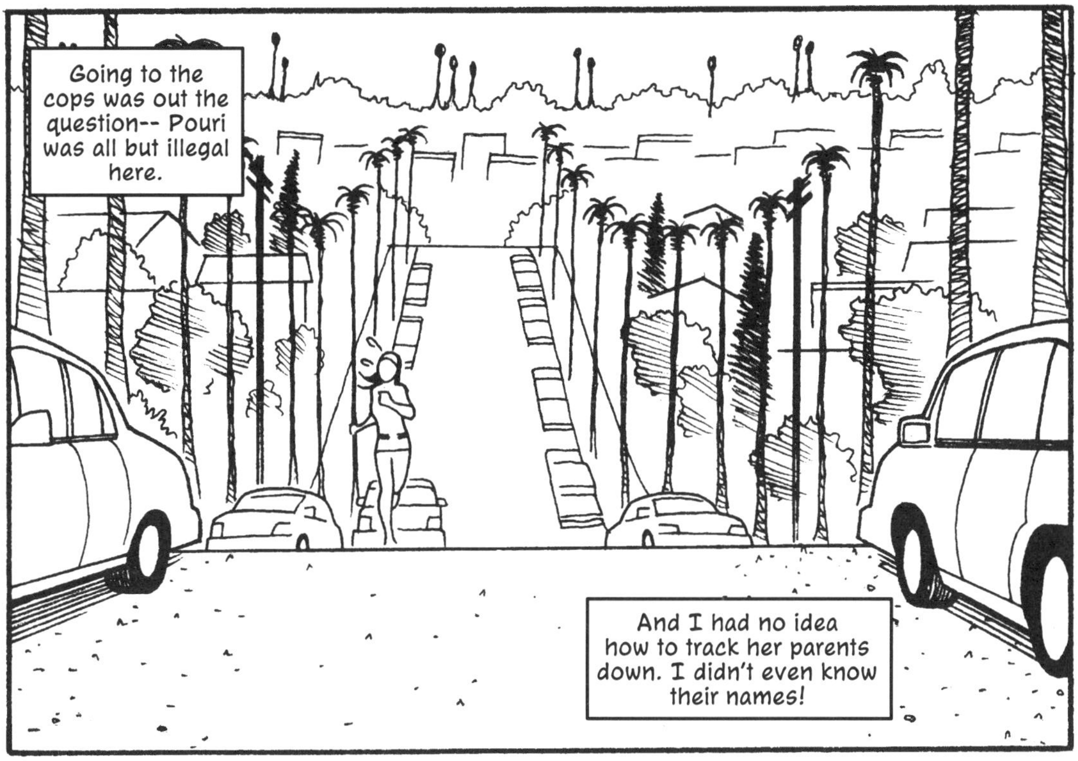
Going to the cops was out the question-- Pouri was all but illegal here.
And I had no idea how to track her parents down. I didn't even know their names!

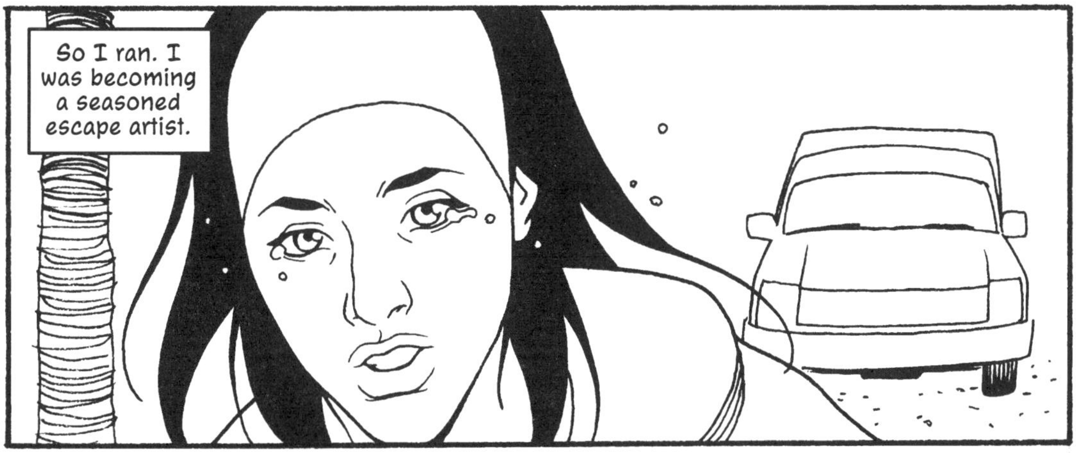
So I ran. I was becoming a seasoned escape artist.

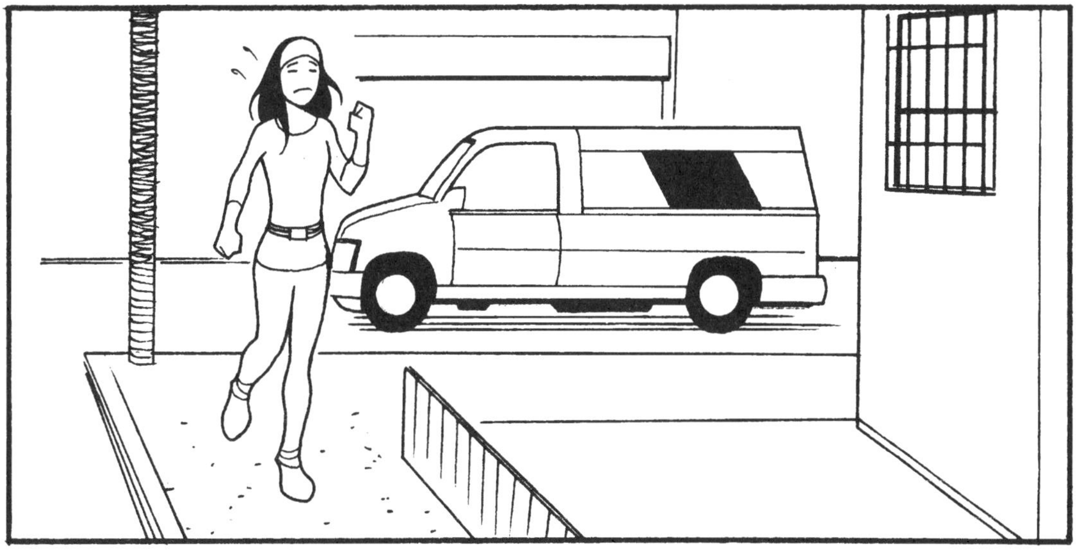

When
I finally
stopped...

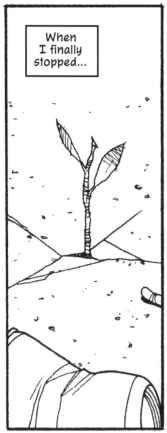

...it was at
the L.A. river.
Which was
bone *dry.*

Okay, so
it wasn't the
Charles.

Mom and I used to
come here on Rosh
Hashanah to "wash
away our sins."

Right. It was a
spiritual cleansing.
Like I said, no
water.

Hundreds of years ago,
there were Gabrieleno Indian
villages along the river.

I felt
clarity
here.

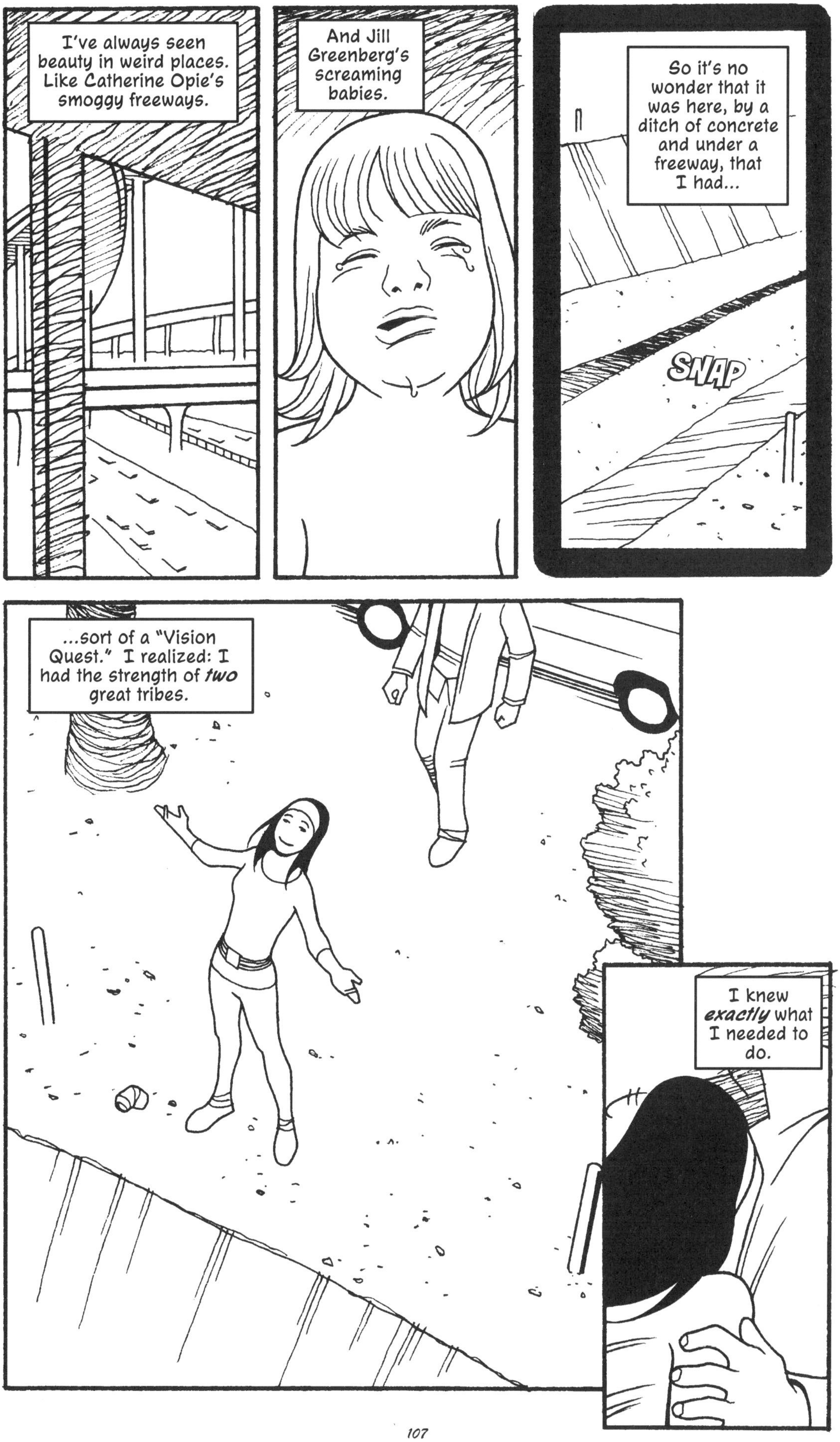
I've always seen beauty in weird places. Like Catherine Opie's smoggy freeways.
And Jill Greenberg's screaming babies.
So it's no wonder that it was here, by a ditch of concrete and under a freeway, that I had...
SNAP
...sort of a "Vision Quest." I realized: I had the strength of *two* great tribes.
I knew *exactly* what I needed to do.

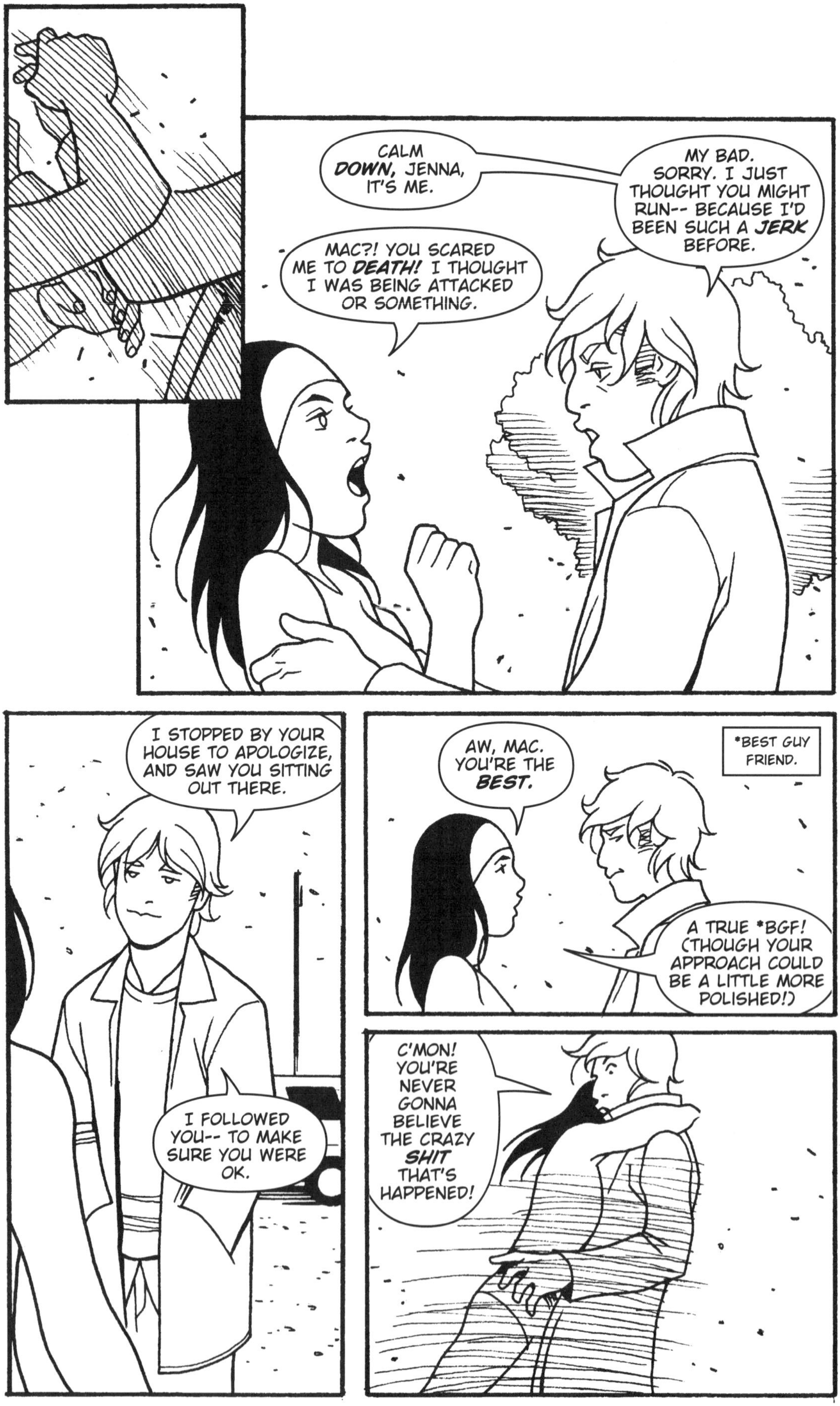
CALM DOWN, JENNA, IT'S ME.
MAC?! YOU SCARED ME TO DEATH! I THOUGHT I WAS BEING ATTACKED OR SOMETHING.
MY BAD. SORRY. I JUST THOUGHT YOU MIGHT RUN-- BECAUSE I'D BEEN SUCH A JERK BEFORE.
I STOPPED BY YOUR HOUSE TO APOLOGIZE, AND SAW YOU SITTING OUT THERE.
I FOLLOWED YOU-- TO MAKE SURE YOU WERE OK.
AW, MAC. YOU'RE THE BEST.
*BEST GUY FRIEND.
A TRUE *BGF! (THOUGH YOUR APPROACH COULD BE A LITTLE MORE POLISHED!)
C'MON! YOU'RE NEVER GONNA BELIEVE THE CRAZY SHIT THAT'S HAPPENED!

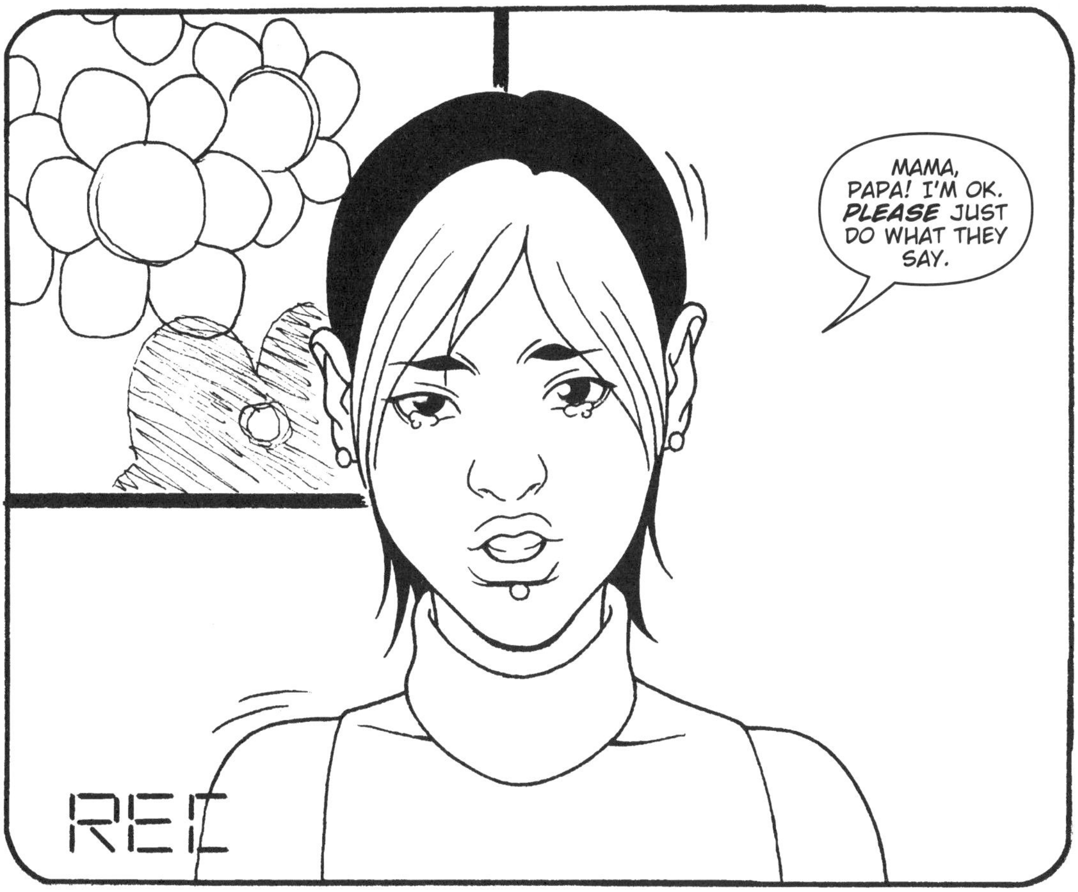
REC
MAMA, PAPA! I'M OK. **PLEASE** JUST DO WHAT THEY SAY.

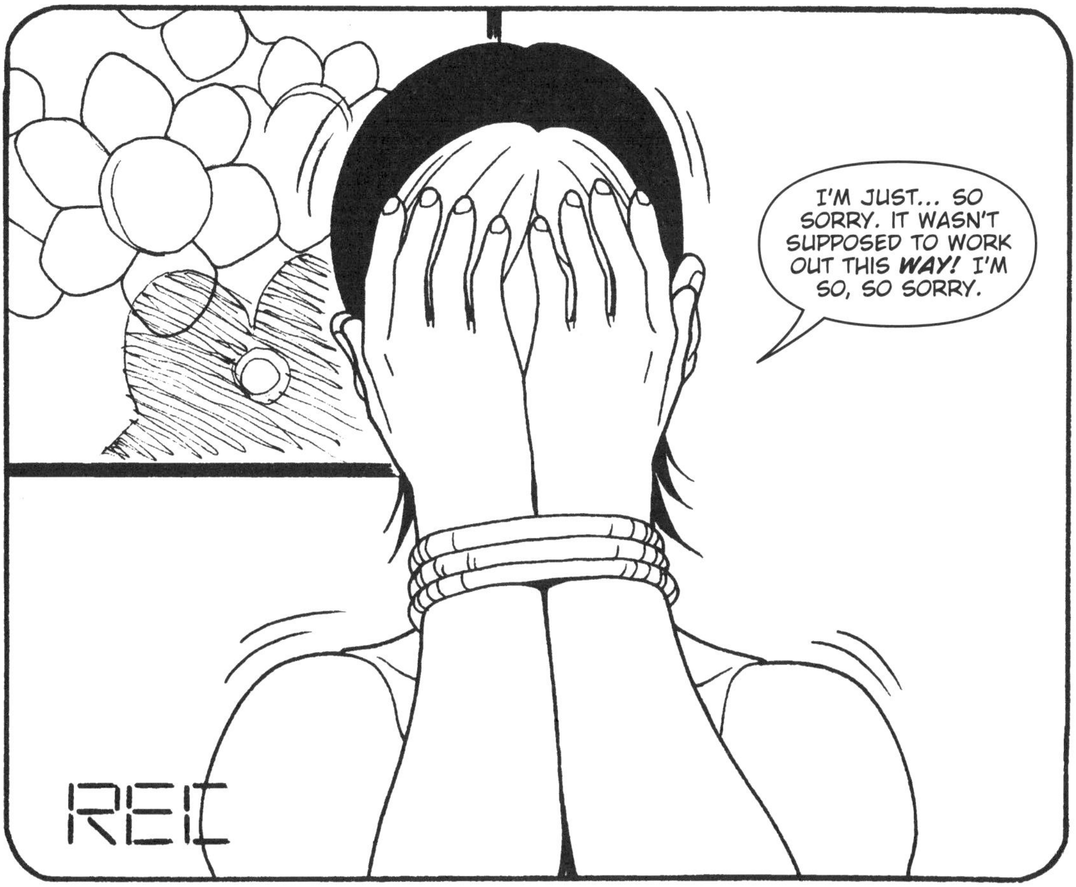
REC
I'M JUST... SO SORRY. IT WASN'T SUPPOSED TO WORK OUT THIS **WAY!** I'M SO, SO SORRY.

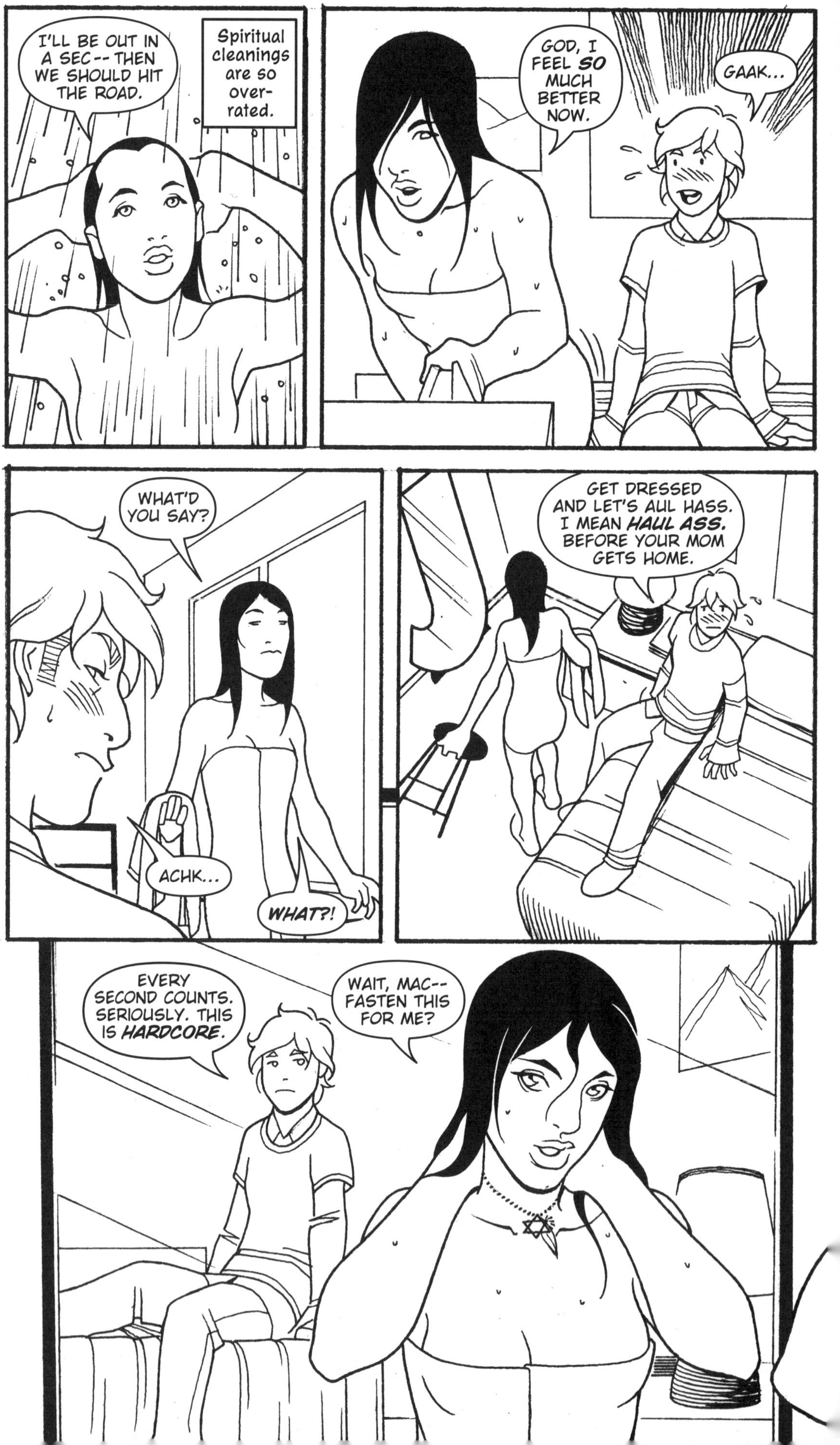
I'LL BE OUT IN A SEC-- THEN WE SHOULD HIT THE ROAD.
Spiritual cleanings are so over-rated.
GOD, I FEEL SO MUCH BETTER NOW.
GAAK...
WHAT'D YOU SAY?
ACHK...
WHAT?!
GET DRESSED AND LET'S AUL HASS. I MEAN HAUL ASS. BEFORE YOUR MOM GETS HOME.
EVERY SECOND COUNTS. SERIOUSLY. THIS IS HARDCORE.
WAIT, MAC-- FASTEN THIS FOR ME?

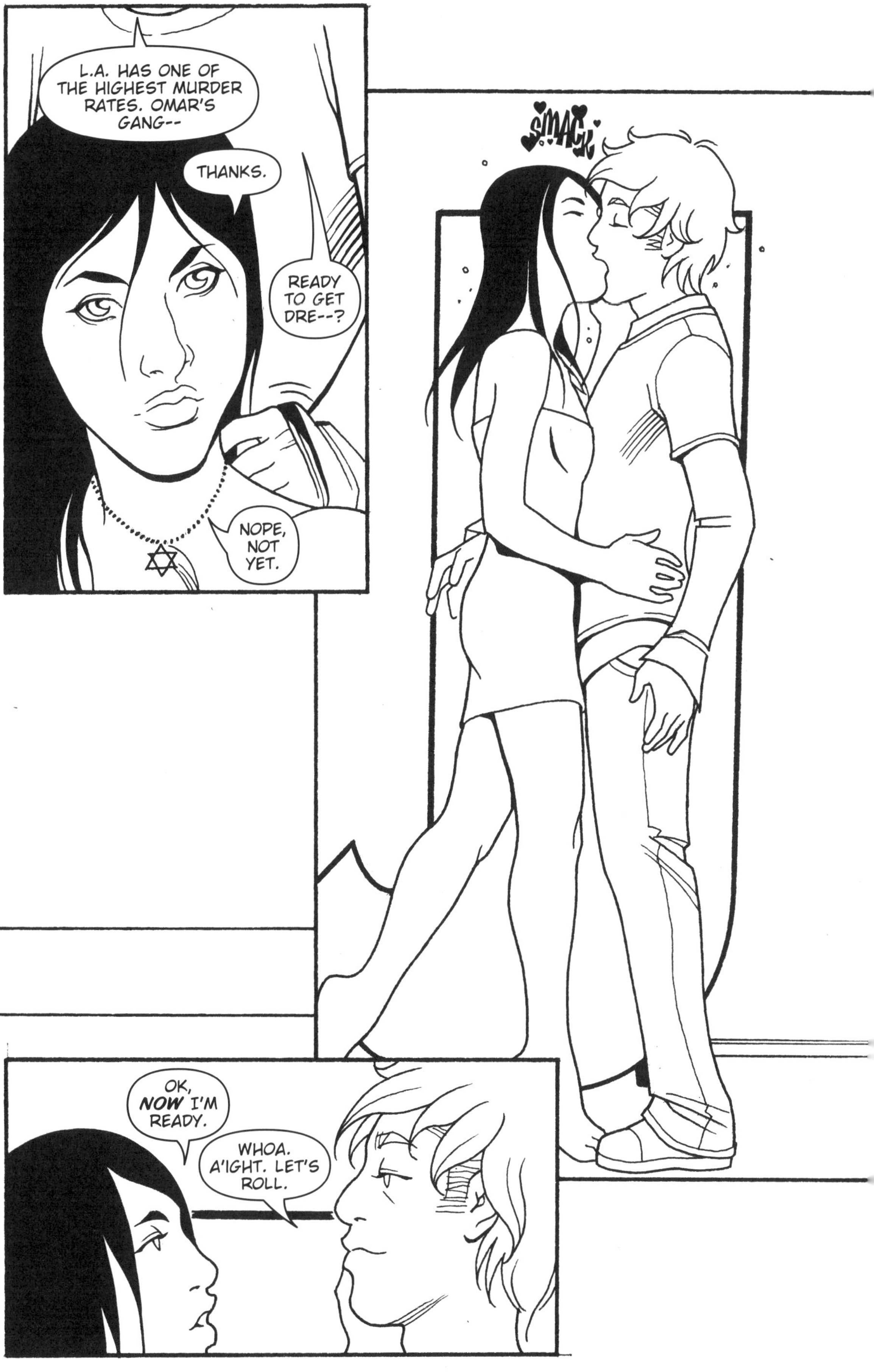
L.A. HAS ONE OF THE HIGHEST MURDER RATES. OMAR'S GANG--
THANKS.
READY TO GET DRE--?
NOPE, NOT YET.
SMACK
OK, **NOW** I'M READY.
WHOA. A'IGHT. LET'S ROLL.

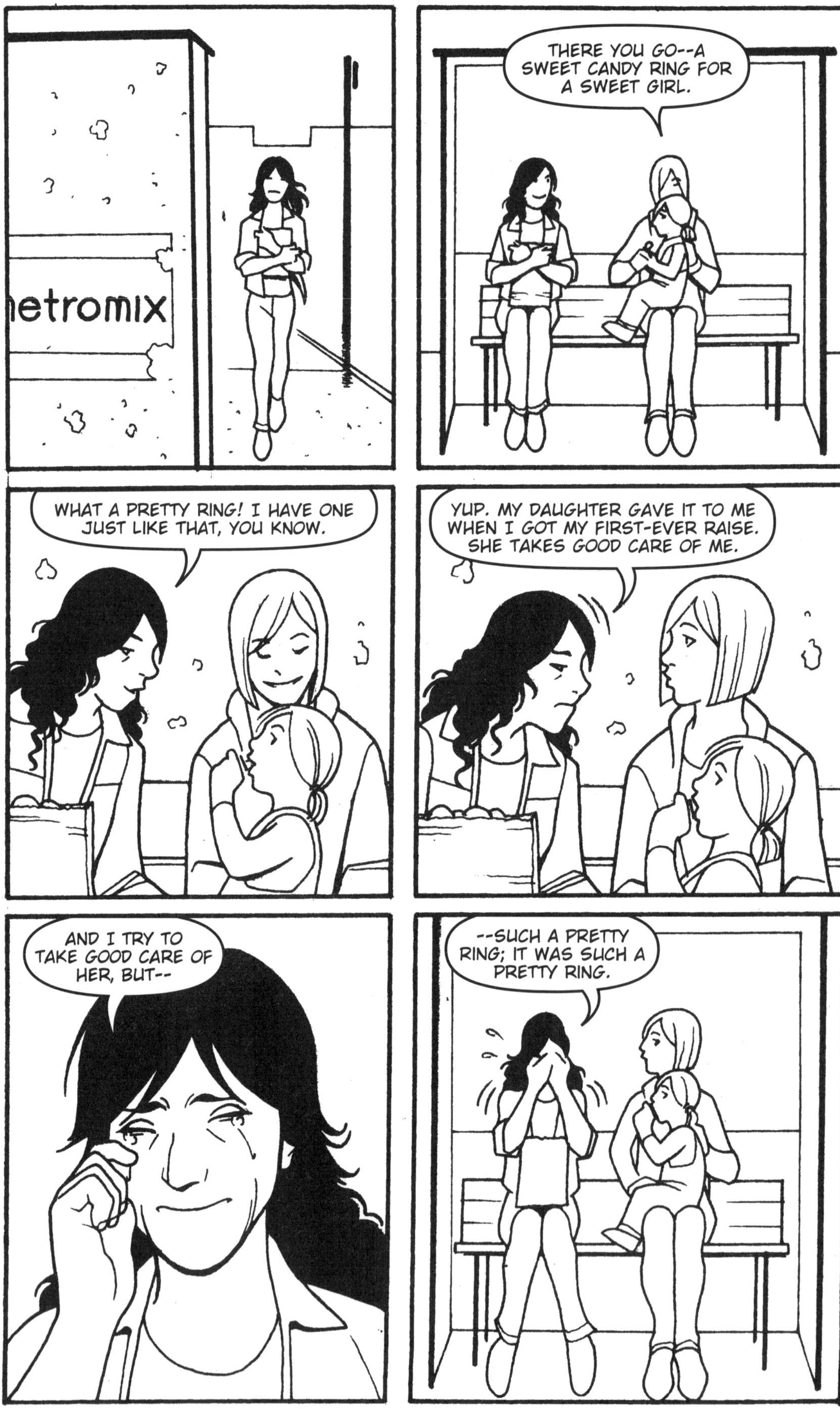

metromix
THERE YOU GO--A SWEET CANDY RING FOR A SWEET GIRL.
WHAT A PRETTY RING! I HAVE ONE JUST LIKE THAT, YOU KNOW.
YUP. MY DAUGHTER GAVE IT TO ME WHEN I GOT MY FIRST-EVER RAISE. SHE TAKES GOOD CARE OF ME.
AND I TRY TO TAKE GOOD CARE OF HER, BUT--
--SUCH A PRETTY RING; IT WAS SUCH A PRETTY RING.

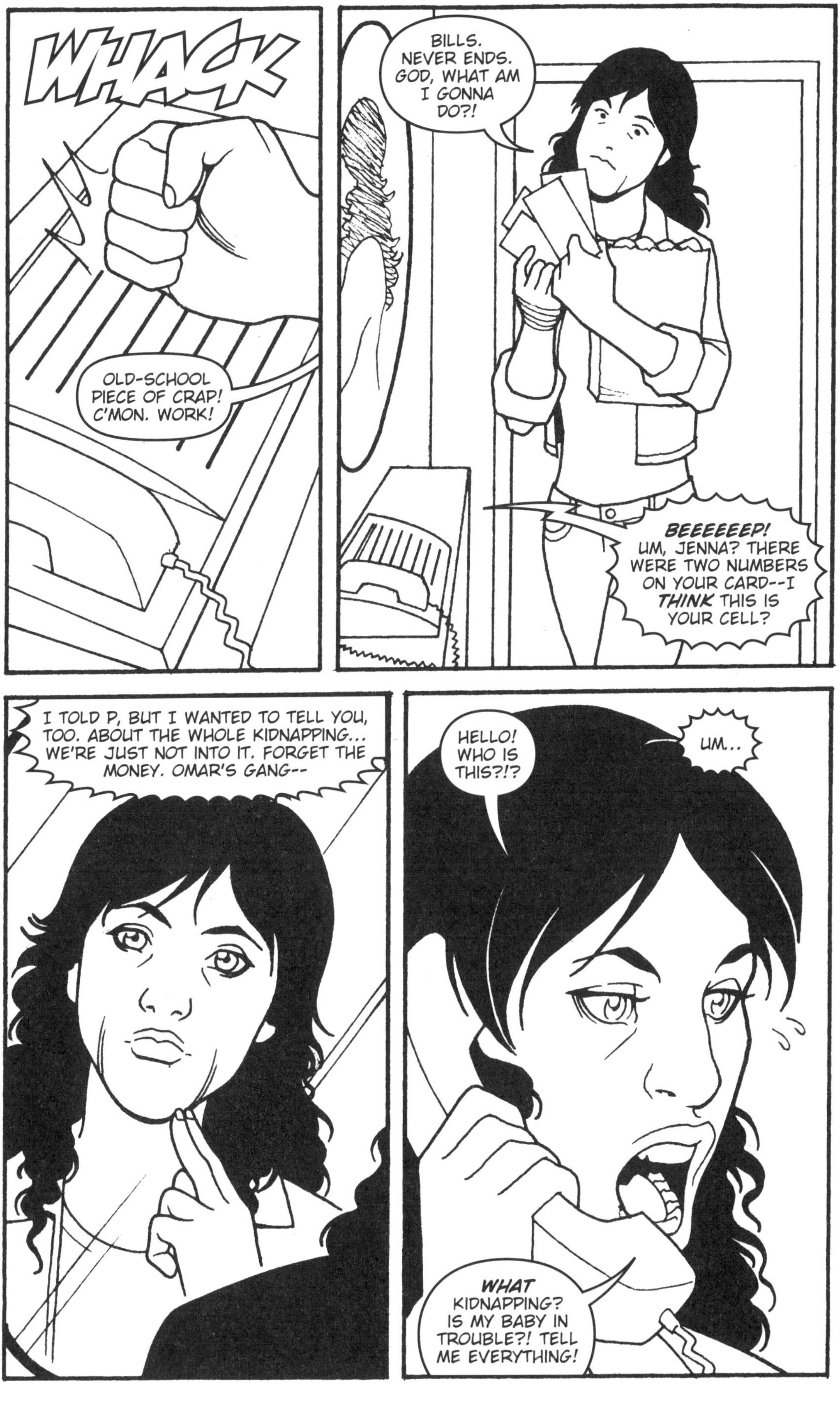
WHACK
OLD-SCHOOL PIECE OF CRAP! C'MON. WORK!
BILLS. NEVER ENDS. GOD, WHAT AM I GONNA DO?!
BEEEEEEP! UM, JENNA? THERE WERE TWO NUMBERS ON YOUR CARD--I THINK THIS IS YOUR CELL?
I TOLD P, BUT I WANTED TO TELL YOU, TOO. ABOUT THE WHOLE KIDNAPPING... WE'RE JUST NOT INTO IT. FORGET THE MONEY. OMAR'S GANG--
HELLO! WHO IS THIS?!?
UM...
WHAT KIDNAPPING? IS MY BABY IN TROUBLE?! TELL ME EVERYTHING!

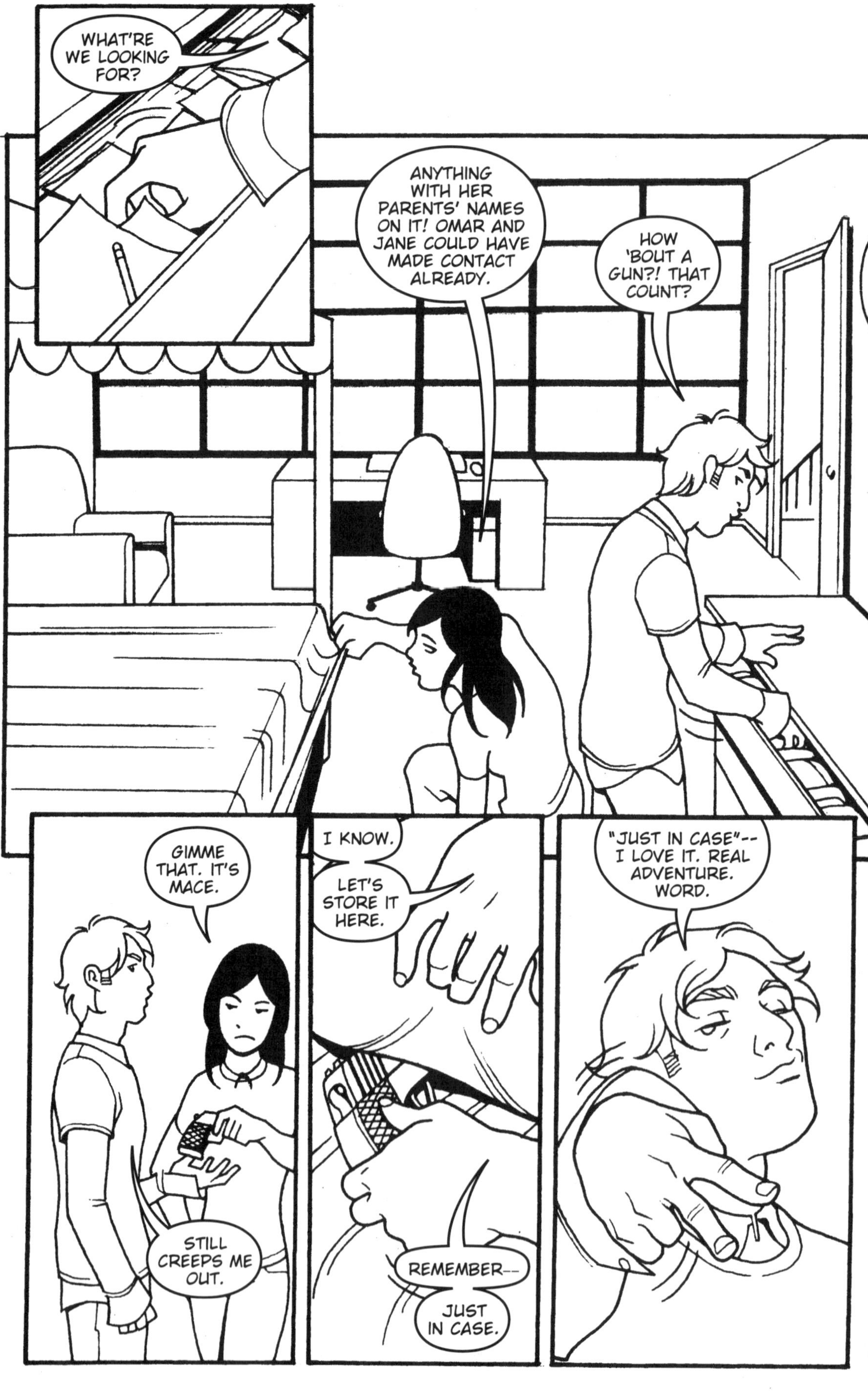
WHAT'RE WE LOOKING FOR?
ANYTHING WITH HER PARENTS' NAMES ON IT! OMAR AND JANE COULD HAVE MADE CONTACT ALREADY.
HOW 'BOUT A GUN?! THAT COUNT?
GIMME THAT. IT'S MACE.
STILL CREEPS ME OUT.
I KNOW.
LET'S STORE IT HERE.
REMEMBER--
JUST IN CASE.
"JUST IN CASE"-- I LOVE IT. REAL ADVENTURE. WORD.

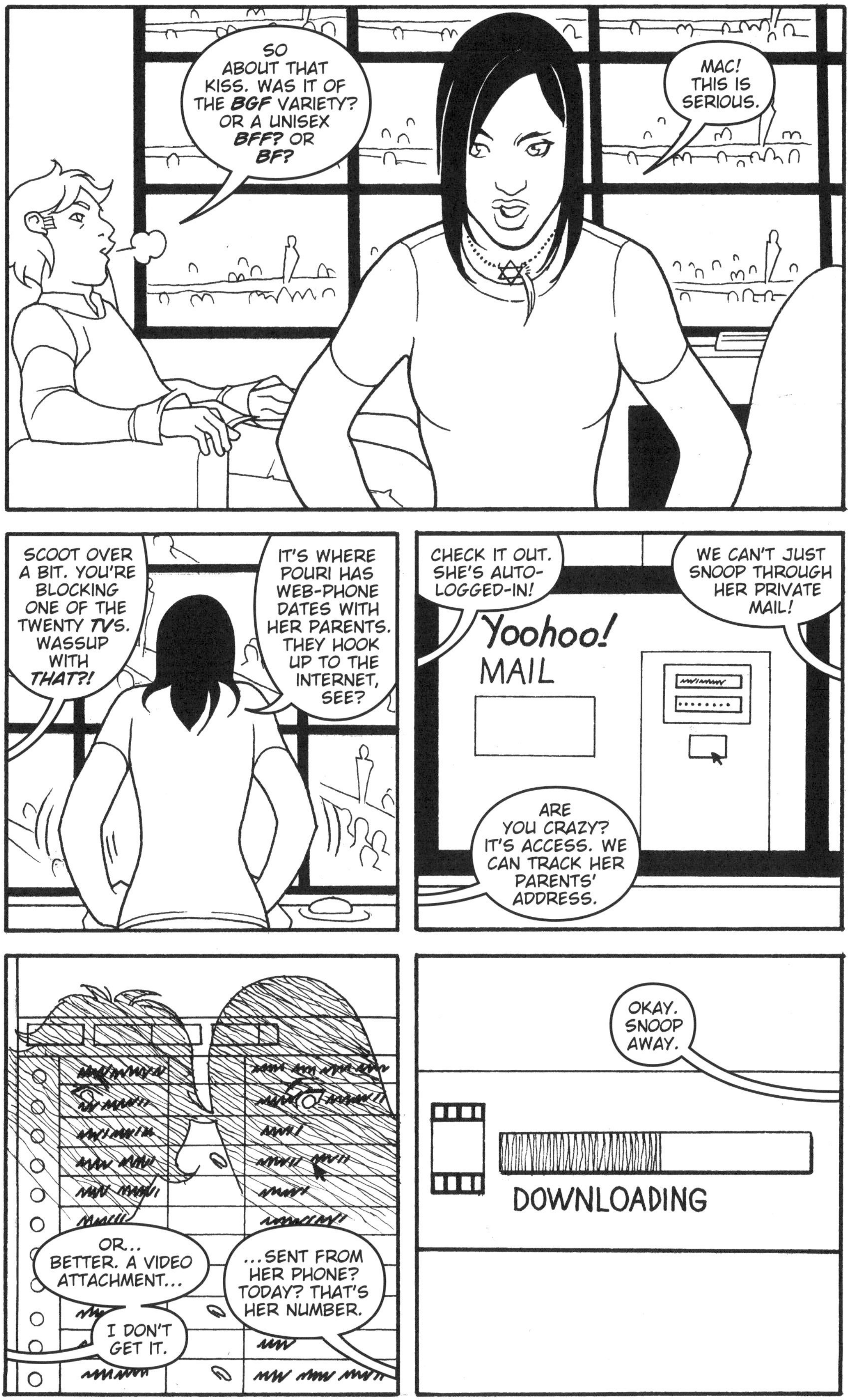
SO ABOUT THAT KISS. WAS IT OF THE BGF VARIETY? OR A UNISEX BFF? OR BF?
MAC! THIS IS SERIOUS.
SCOOT OVER A BIT. YOU'RE BLOCKING ONE OF THE TWENTY TVS. WASSUP WITH THAT?!
IT'S WHERE POURI HAS WEB-PHONE DATES WITH HER PARENTS. THEY HOOK UP TO THE INTERNET, SEE?
CHECK IT OUT. SHE'S AUTO-LOGGED-IN!
WE CAN'T JUST SNOOP THROUGH HER PRIVATE MAIL!
Yoohoo! MAIL
ARE YOU CRAZY? IT'S ACCESS. WE CAN TRACK HER PARENTS' ADDRESS.
OR... BETTER. A VIDEO ATTACHMENT...
...SENT FROM HER PHONE? TODAY? THAT'S HER NUMBER.
I DON'T GET IT.
OKAY. SNOOP AWAY.
DOWNLOADING

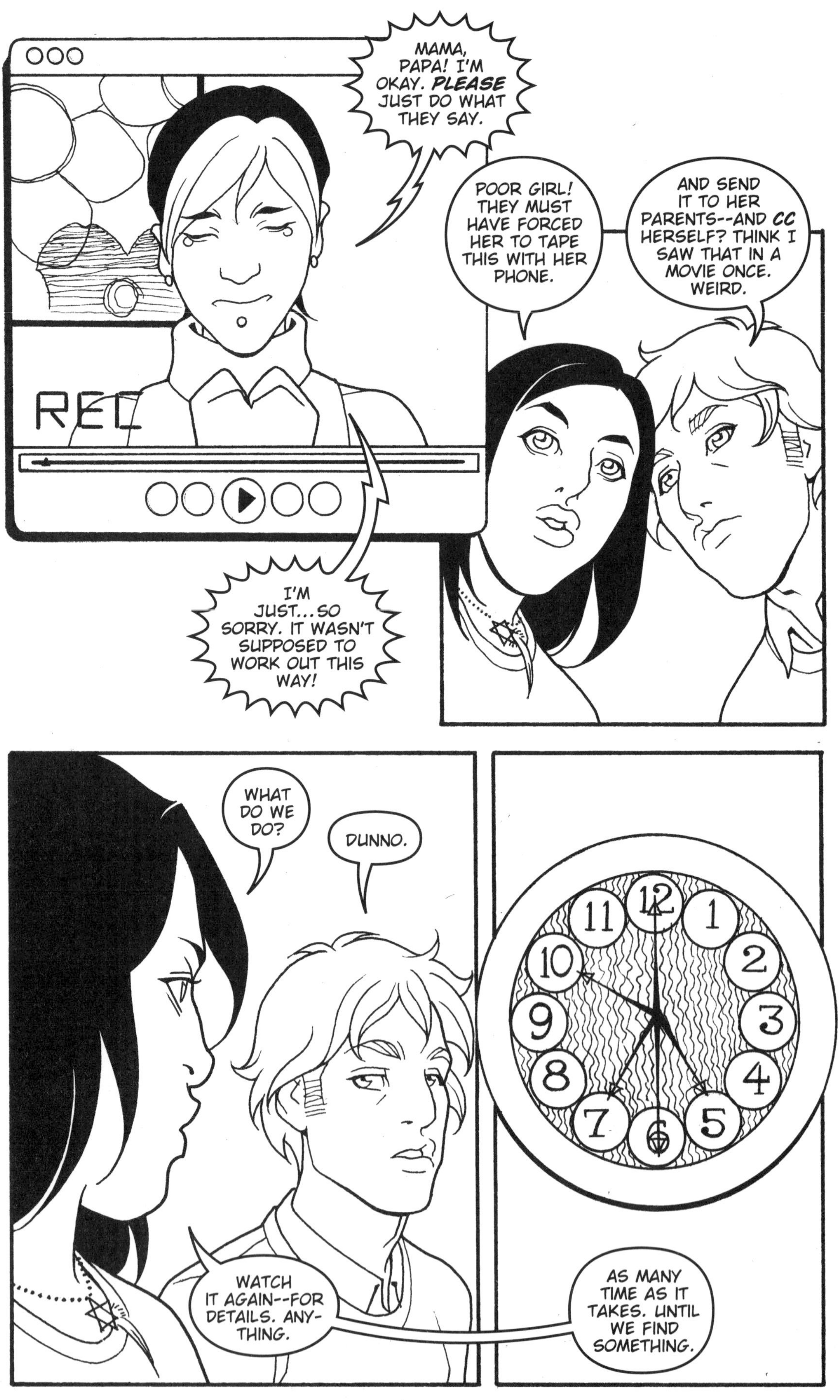

MAMA, PAPA! I'M OKAY. PLEASE JUST DO WHAT THEY SAY.
REC
I'M JUST...SO SORRY. IT WASN'T SUPPOSED TO WORK OUT THIS WAY!
POOR GIRL! THEY MUST HAVE FORCED HER TO TAPE THIS WITH HER PHONE.
AND SEND IT TO HER PARENTS--AND CC HERSELF? THINK I SAW THAT IN A MOVIE ONCE. WEIRD.
WHAT DO WE DO?
DUNNO.
WATCH IT AGAIN--FOR DETAILS. ANY-THING.
AS MANY TIME AS IT TAKES. UNTIL WE FIND SOMETHING.

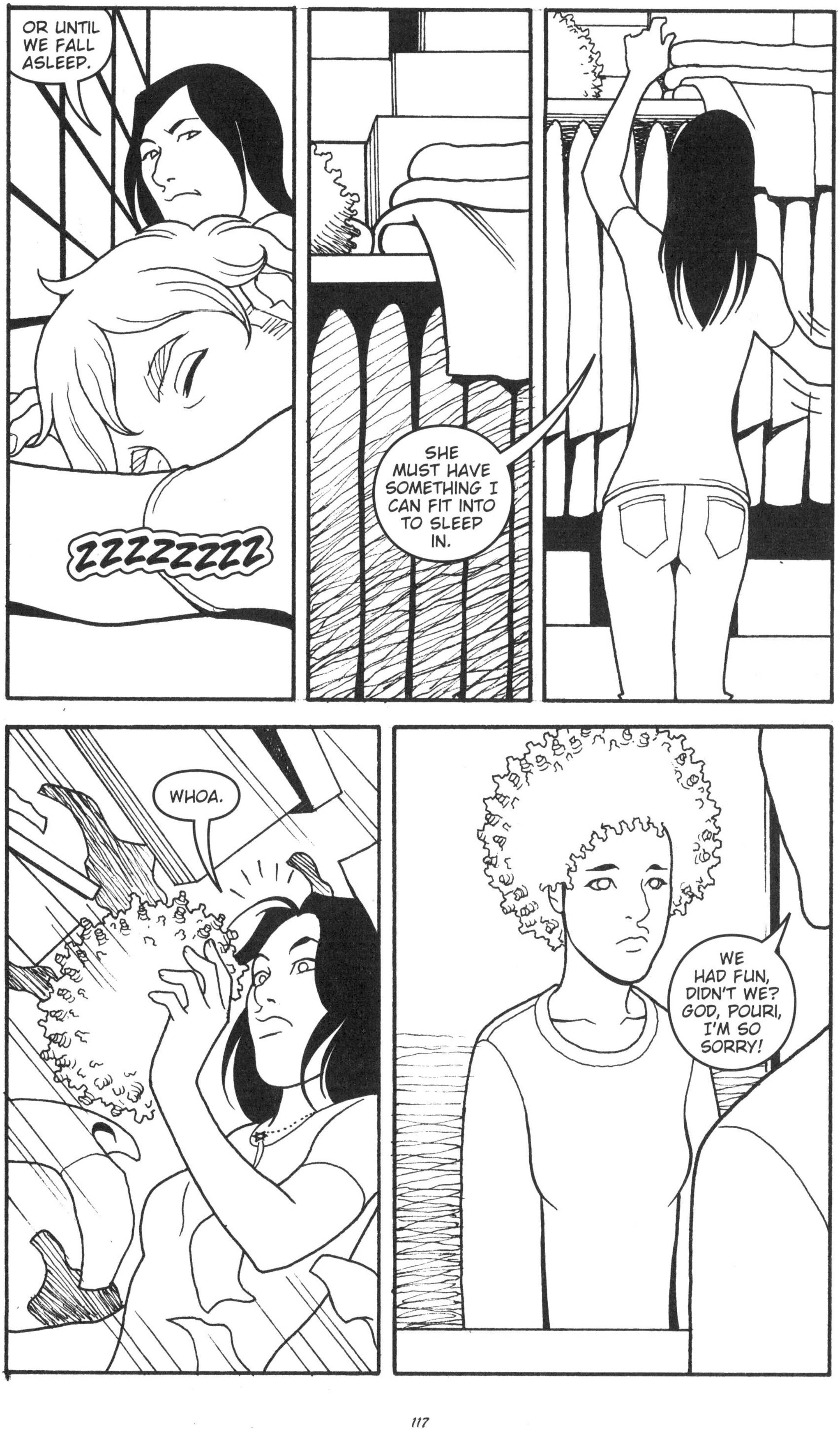
OR UNTIL WE FALL ASLEEP.
ZZZZZZZZ
SHE MUST HAVE SOMETHING I CAN FIT INTO TO SLEEP IN.
WHOA.
WE HAD FUN, DIDN'T WE? GOD, POURI, I'M SO SORRY!

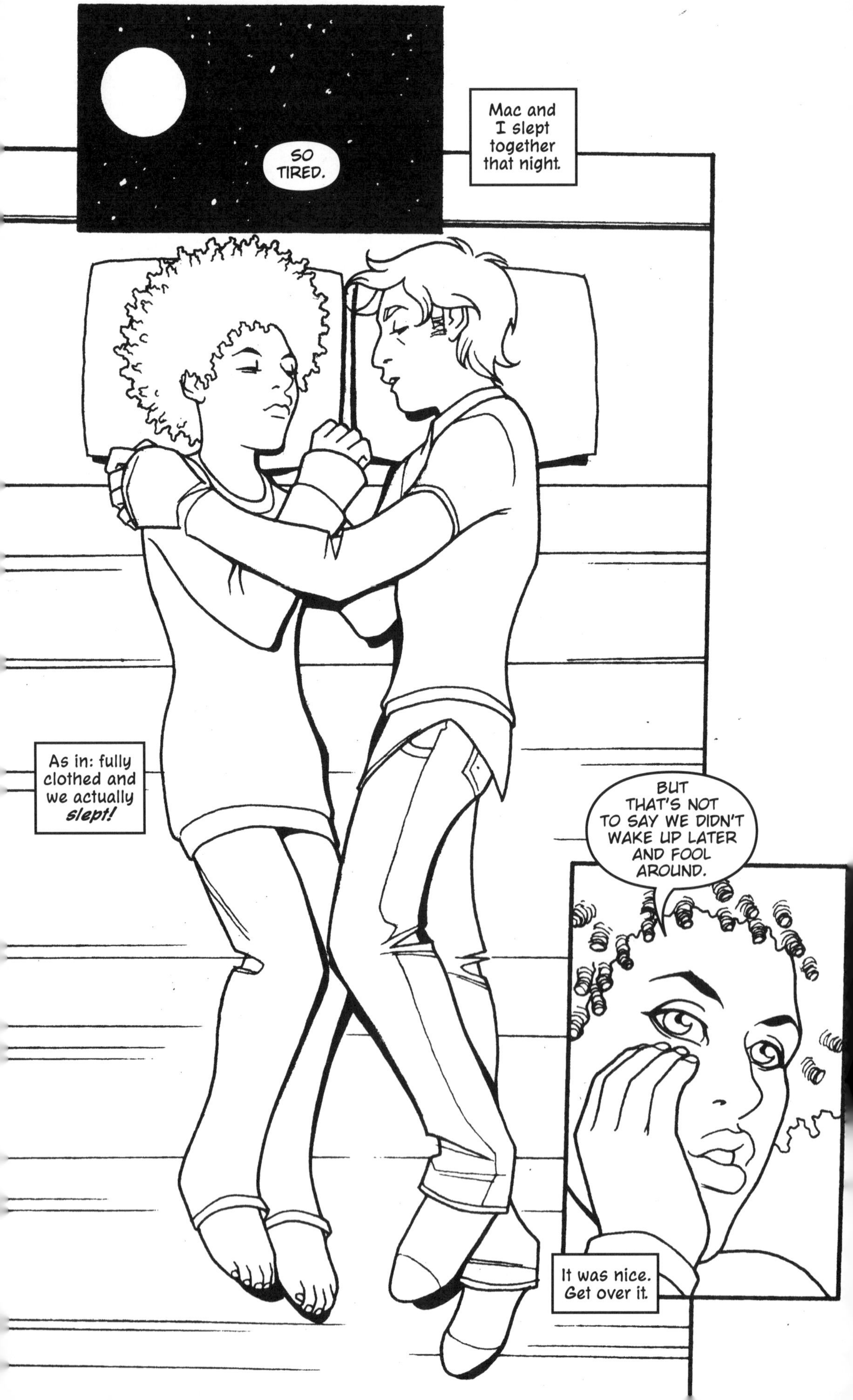
SO TIRED.
Mac and I slept together that night.
As in: fully clothed and we actually *slept!*
BUT THAT'S NOT TO SAY WE DIDN'T WAKE UP LATER AND FOOL AROUND.
It was nice. Get over it.

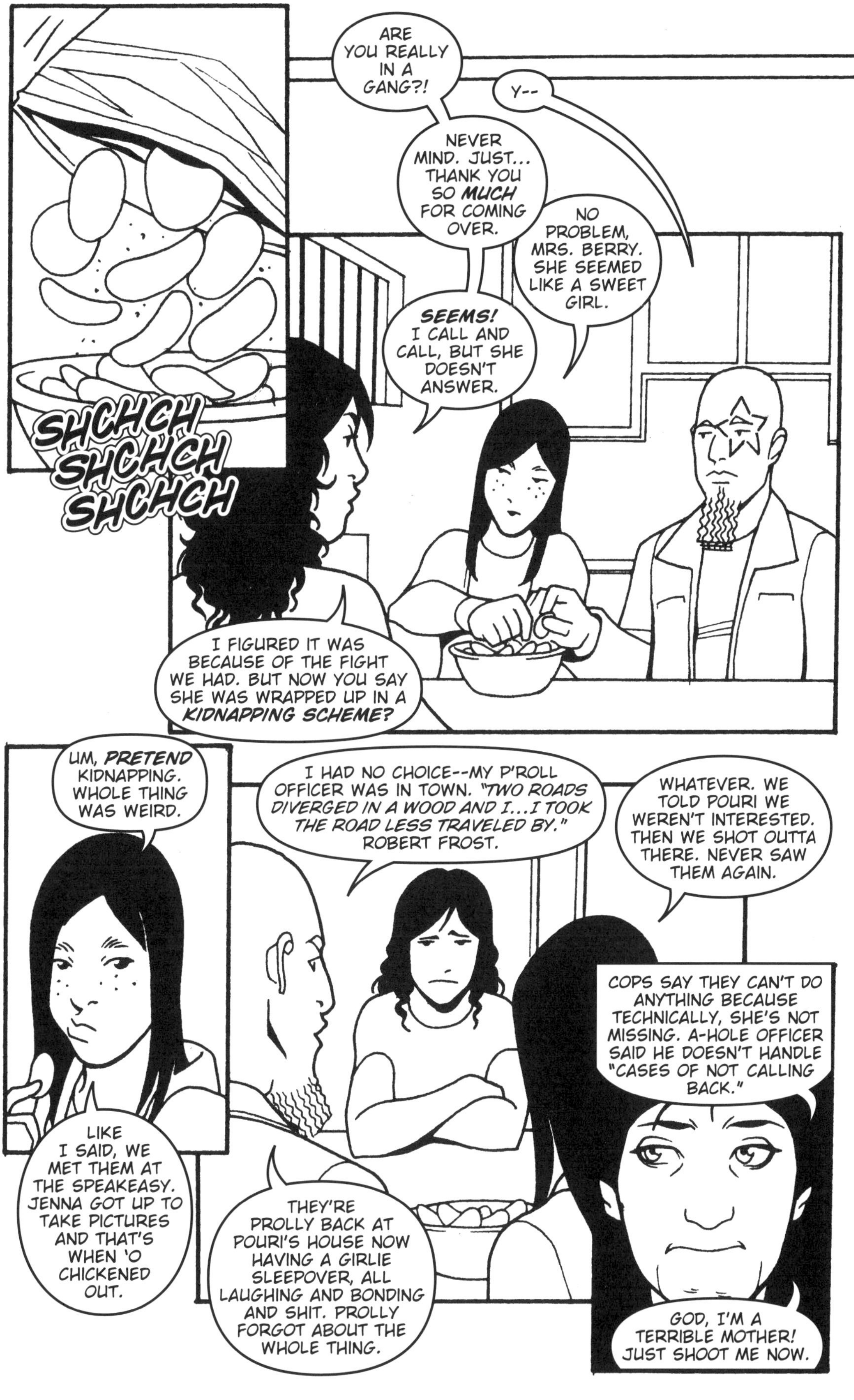

ARE YOU REALLY IN A GANG?!
Y--
NEVER MIND. JUST... THANK YOU SO MUCH FOR COMING OVER.
NO PROBLEM, MRS. BERRY. SHE SEEMED LIKE A SWEET GIRL.
SEEMS! I CALL AND CALL, BUT SHE DOESN'T ANSWER.
SHCHCH SHCHCH SHCHCH
I FIGURED IT WAS BECAUSE OF THE FIGHT WE HAD. BUT NOW YOU SAY SHE WAS WRAPPED UP IN A KIDNAPPING SCHEME?
UM, PRETEND KIDNAPPING. WHOLE THING WAS WEIRD.
LIKE I SAID, WE MET THEM AT THE SPEAKEASY. JENNA GOT UP TO TAKE PICTURES AND THAT'S WHEN 'O CHICKENED OUT.
I HAD NO CHOICE--MY P'ROLL OFFICER WAS IN TOWN. "TWO ROADS DIVERGED IN A WOOD AND I...I TOOK THE ROAD LESS TRAVELED BY." ROBERT FROST.
THEY'RE PROLLY BACK AT POURI'S HOUSE NOW HAVING A GIRLIE SLEEPOVER, ALL LAUGHING AND BONDING AND SHIT. PROLLY FORGOT ABOUT THE WHOLE THING.
WHATEVER. WE TOLD POURI WE WEREN'T INTERESTED. THEN WE SHOT OUTTA THERE. NEVER SAW THEM AGAIN.
COPS SAY THEY CAN'T DO ANYTHING BECAUSE TECHNICALLY, SHE'S NOT MISSING. A-HOLE OFFICER SAID HE DOESN'T HANDLE "CASES OF NOT CALLING BACK."
GOD, I'M A TERRIBLE MOTHER! JUST SHOOT ME NOW.

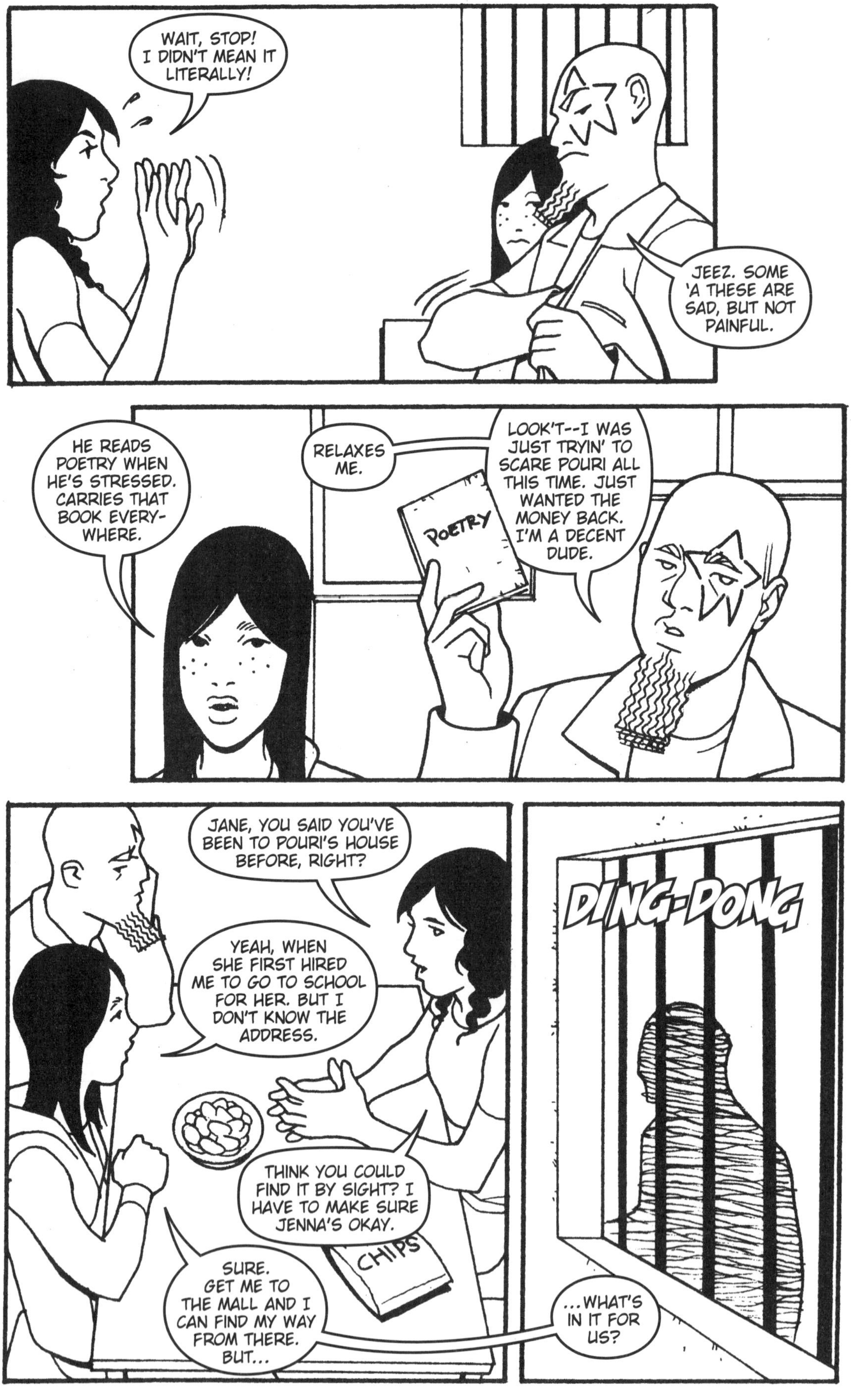
WAIT, STOP! I DIDN'T MEAN IT LITERALLY!
JEEZ. SOME 'A THESE ARE SAD, BUT NOT PAINFUL.
HE READS POETRY WHEN HE'S STRESSED. CARRIES THAT BOOK EVERY-WHERE.
RELAXES ME.
LOOK'T--I WAS JUST TRYIN' TO SCARE POURI ALL THIS TIME. JUST WANTED THE MONEY BACK. I'M A DECENT DUDE.
POETRY
JANE, YOU SAID YOU'VE BEEN TO POURI'S HOUSE BEFORE, RIGHT?
YEAH, WHEN SHE FIRST HIRED ME TO GO TO SCHOOL FOR HER. BUT I DON'T KNOW THE ADDRESS.
THINK YOU COULD FIND IT BY SIGHT? I HAVE TO MAKE SURE JENNA'S OKAY.
CHIPS
SURE. GET ME TO THE MALL AND I CAN FIND MY WAY FROM THERE. BUT...
...WHAT'S IN IT FOR US?
DING-DONG

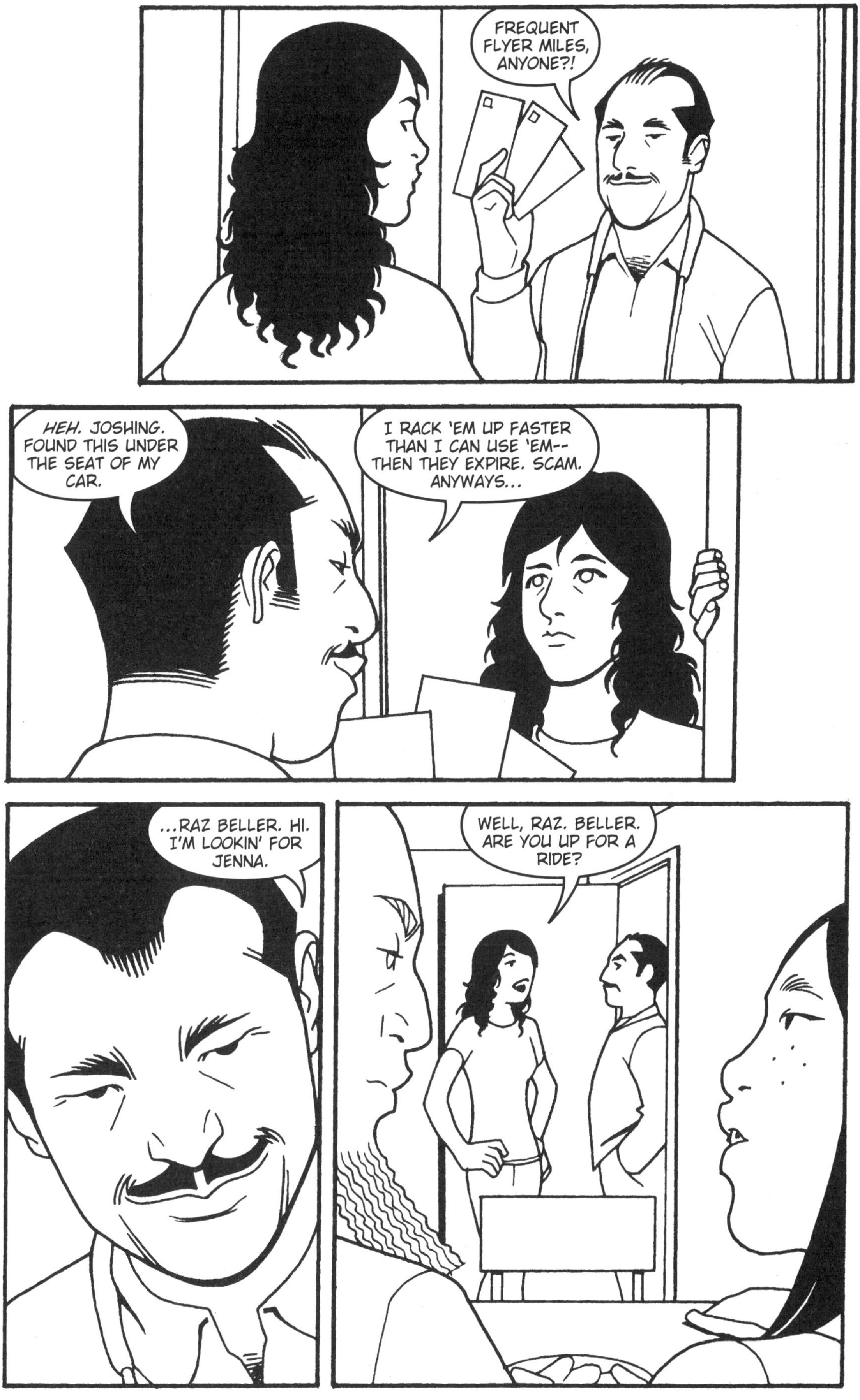
FREQUENT FLYER MILES, ANYONE?!
HEH. JOSHING. FOUND THIS UNDER THE SEAT OF MY CAR.
I RACK 'EM UP FASTER THAN I CAN USE 'EM-- THEN THEY EXPIRE. SCAM. ANYWAYS...
...RAZ BELLER. HI. I'M LOOKIN' FOR JENNA.
WELL, RAZ. BELLER. ARE YOU UP FOR A RIDE?

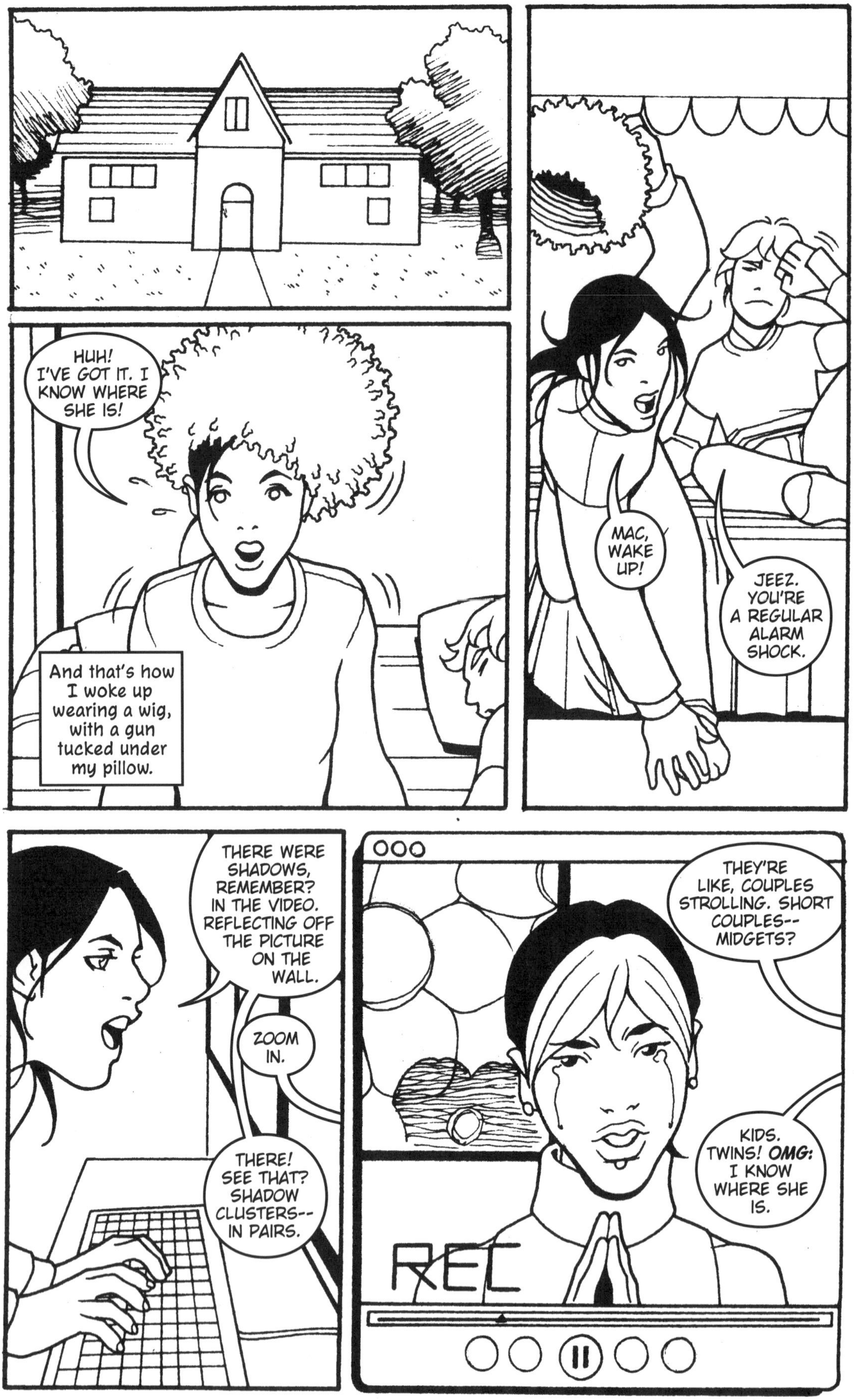
HUH! I'VE GOT IT. I KNOW WHERE SHE IS!
And that's how I woke up wearing a wig, with a gun tucked under my pillow.
MAC, WAKE UP!
JEEZ. YOU'RE A REGULAR ALARM SHOCK.
THERE WERE SHADOWS, REMEMBER? IN THE VIDEO. REFLECTING OFF THE PICTURE ON THE WALL.
ZOOM IN.
THERE! SEE THAT? SHADOW CLUSTERS--IN PAIRS.
THEY'RE LIKE, COUPLES STROLLING. SHORT COUPLES--MIDGETS?
KIDS. TWINS! OMG: I KNOW WHERE SHE IS.
REC

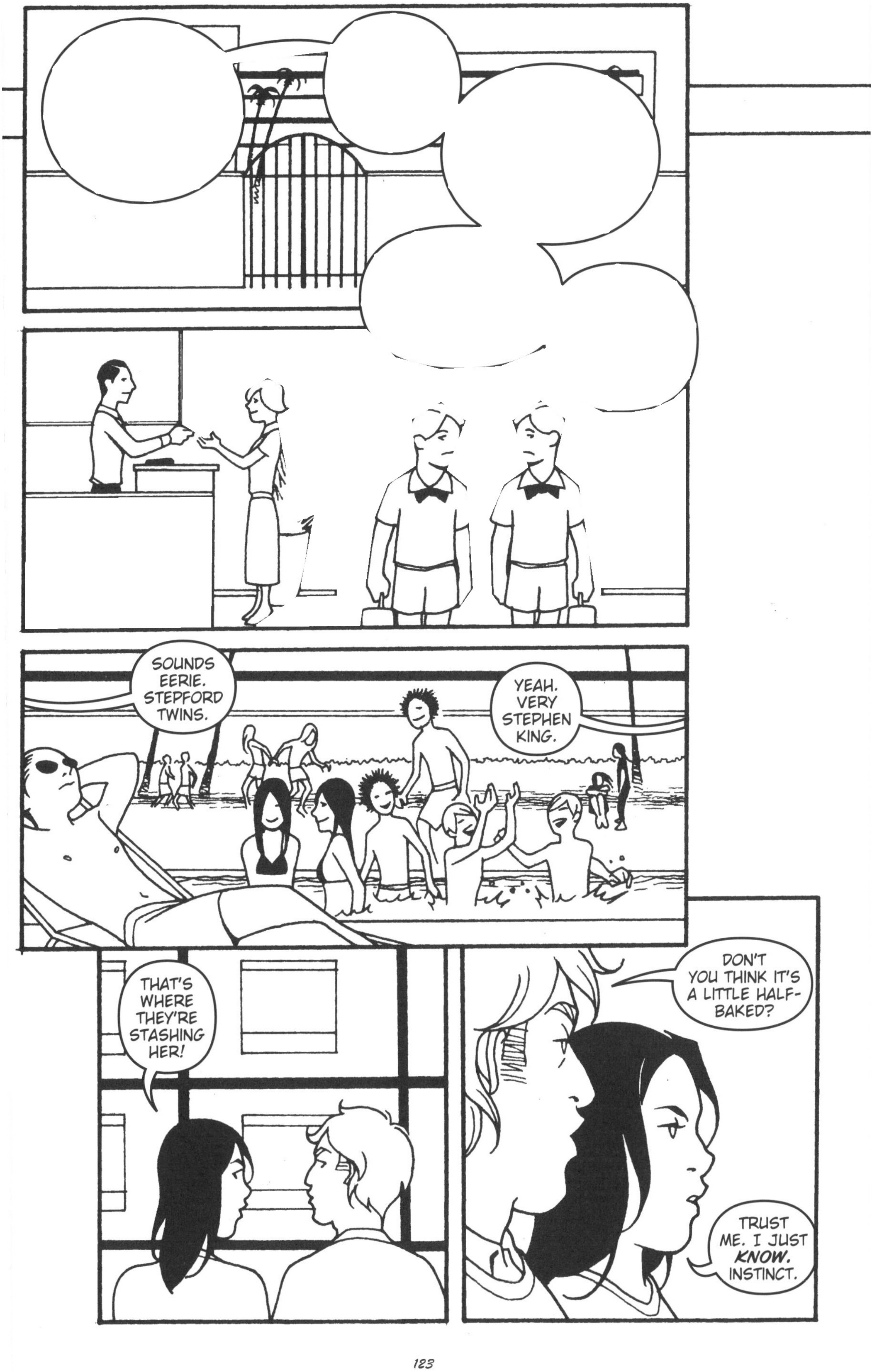
SOUNDS EERIE. STEPFORD TWINS.
YEAH. VERY STEPHEN KING.
THAT'S WHERE THEY'RE STASHING HER!
DON'T YOU THINK IT'S A LITTLE HALF-BAKED?
TRUST ME. I JUST ***KNOW.*** INSTINCT.

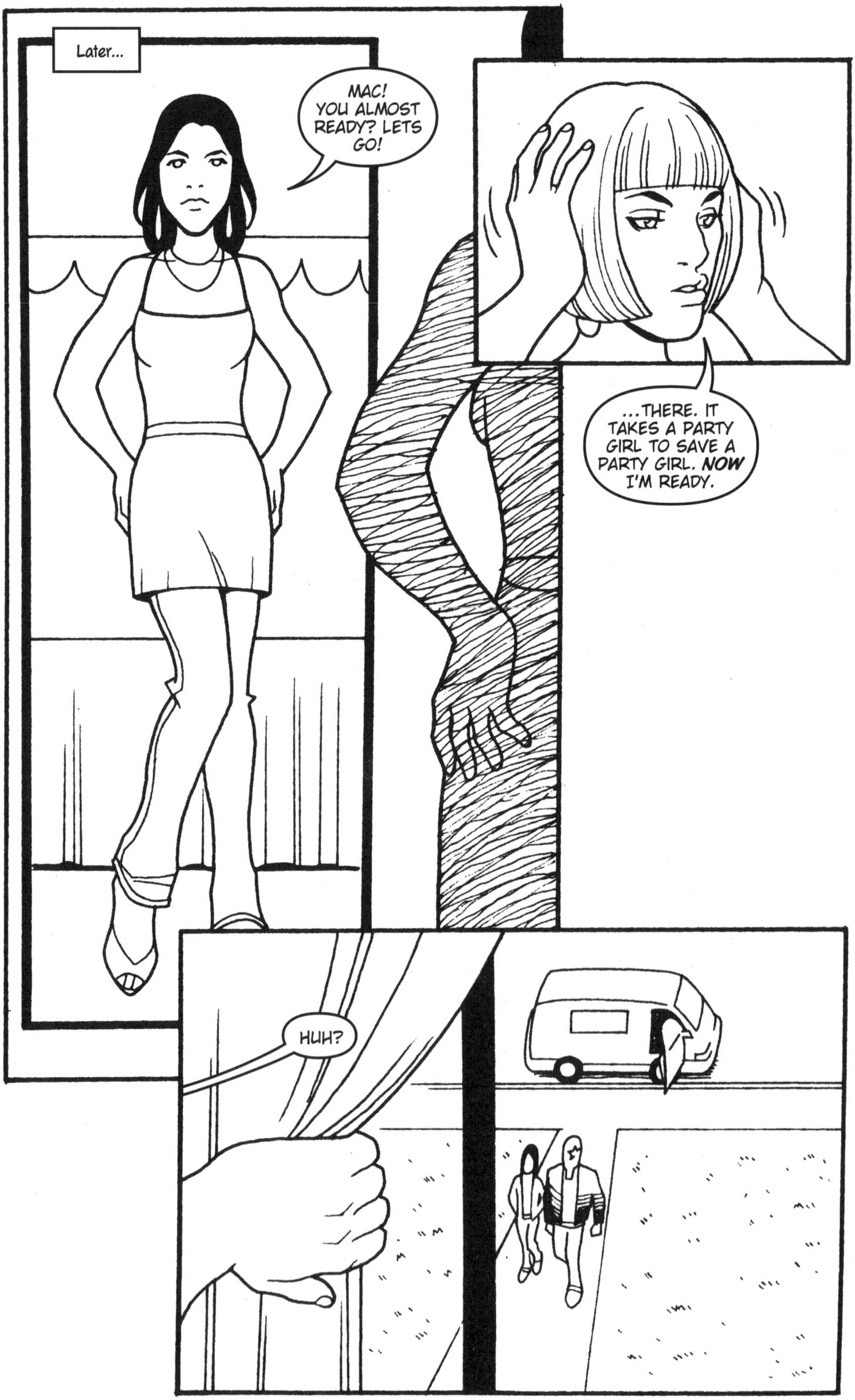
Later...
MAC! YOU ALMOST READY? LETS GO!
...THERE. IT TAKES A PARTY GIRL TO SAVE A PARTY GIRL. NOW I'M READY.
HUH?

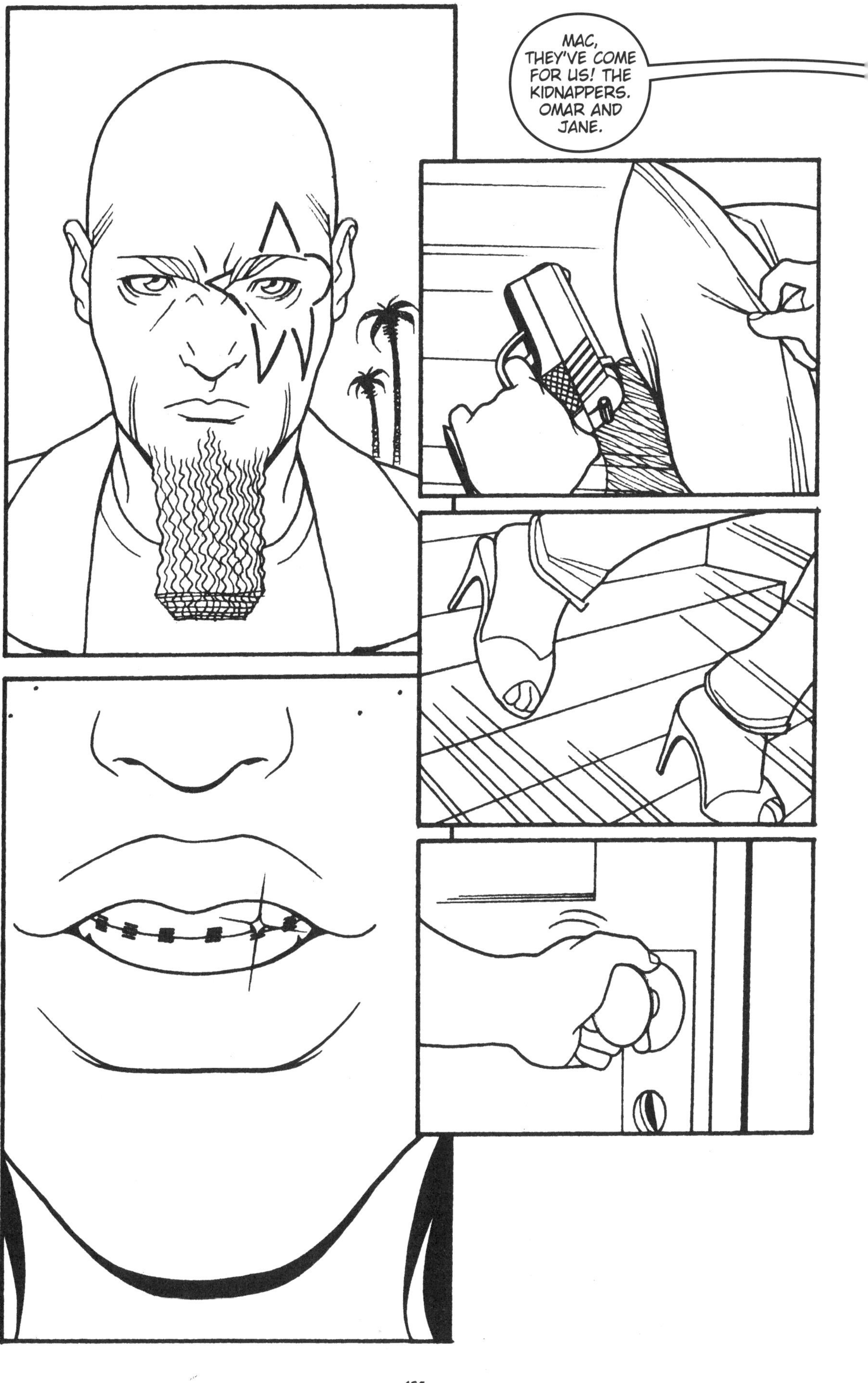
MAC, THEY'VE COME FOR US! THE KIDNAPPERS. OMAR AND JANE.

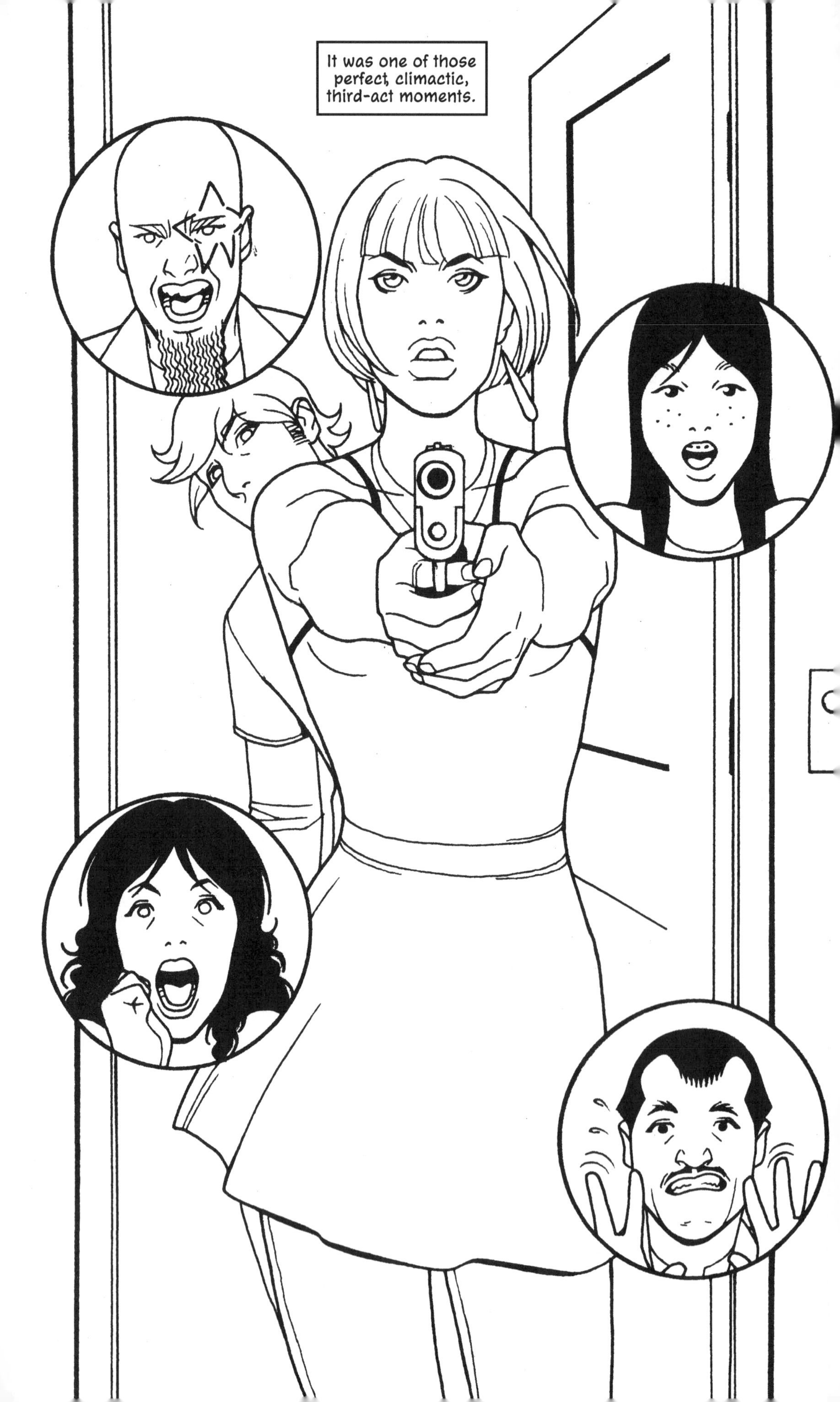
It was one of those perfect, climactic, third-act moments.

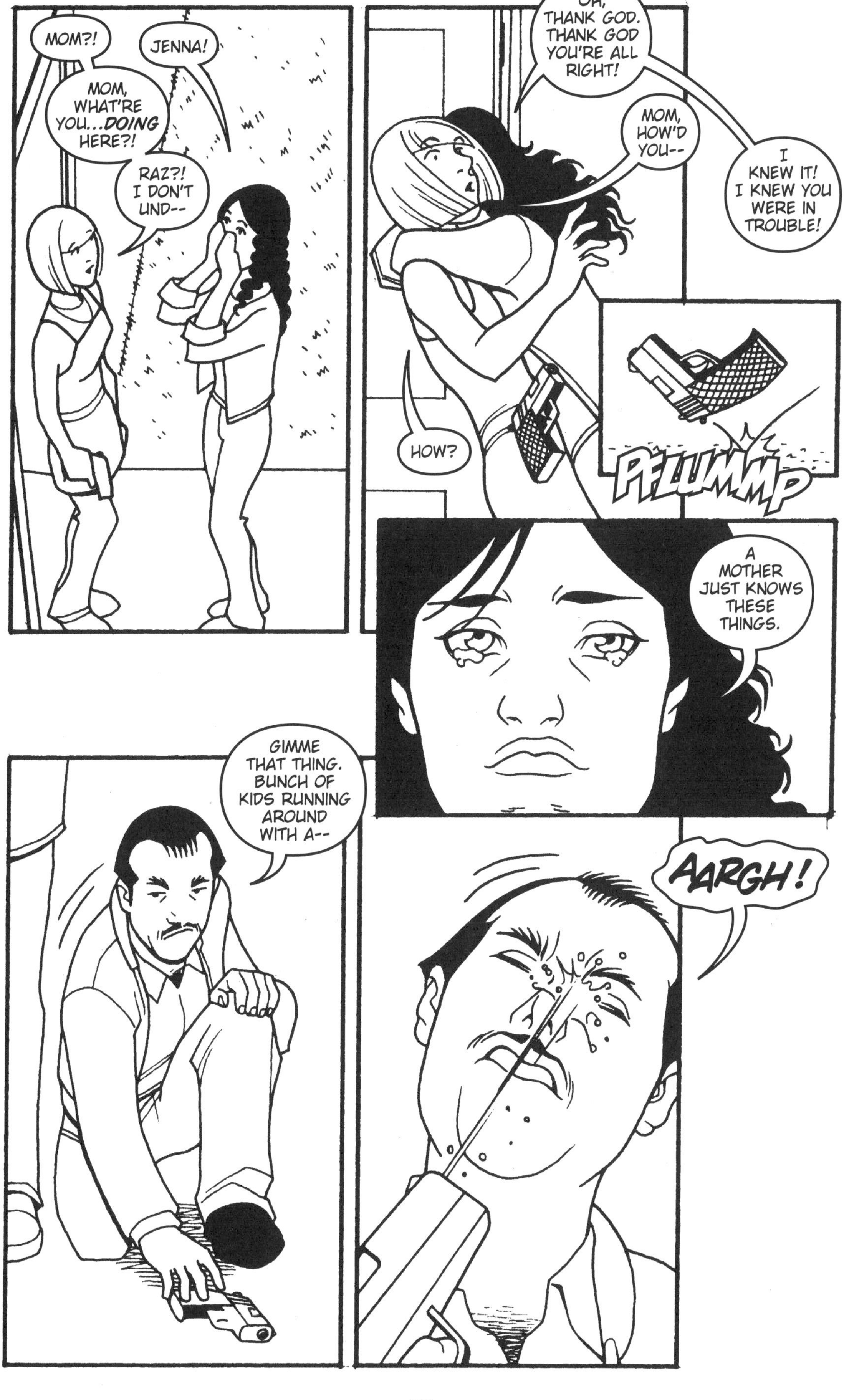
MOM?!
JENNA!
MOM, WHAT'RE YOU...DOING HERE?!
RAZ?! I DON'T UND--
OH, THANK GOD. THANK GOD YOU'RE ALL RIGHT!
MOM, HOW'D YOU--
I KNEW IT! I KNEW YOU WERE IN TROUBLE!
HOW?
PFLUMMP
A MOTHER JUST KNOWS THESE THINGS.
GIMME THAT THING. BUNCH OF KIDS RUNNING AROUND WITH A--
AARGH!

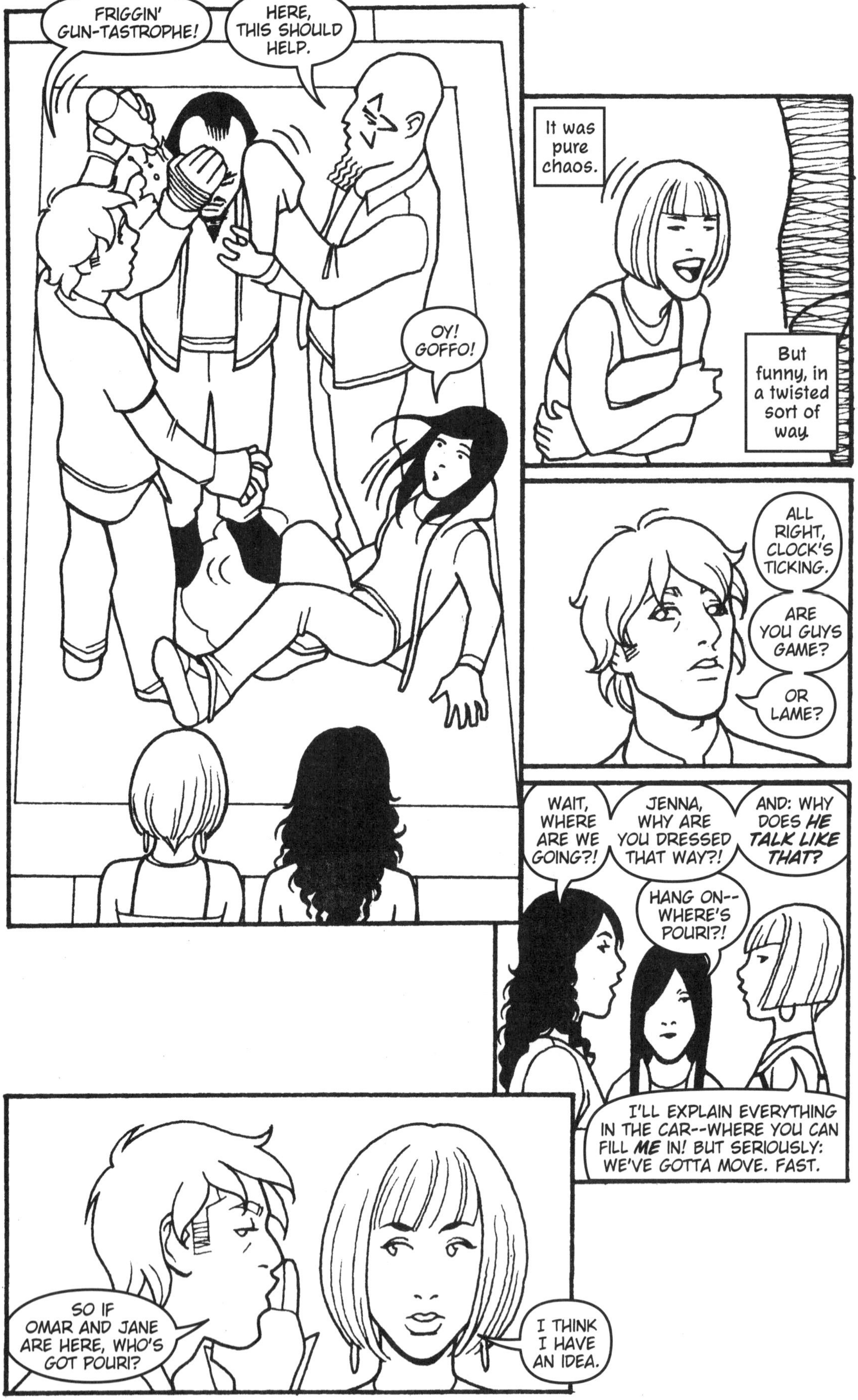
FRIGGIN' GUN-TASTROPHE!
HERE, THIS SHOULD HELP.
OY! GOFFO!
It was pure chaos.
But funny, in a twisted sort of way.
ALL RIGHT, CLOCK'S TICKING.
ARE YOU GUYS GAME?
OR LAME?
WAIT, WHERE ARE WE GOING?!
JENNA, WHY ARE YOU DRESSED THAT WAY?!
AND: WHY DOES **HE TALK LIKE THAT?**
HANG ON--WHERE'S POURI?!
I'LL EXPLAIN EVERYTHING IN THE CAR--WHERE YOU CAN FILL **ME** IN! BUT SERIOUSLY: WE'VE GOTTA MOVE. FAST.
SO IF OMAR AND JANE ARE HERE, WHO'S GOT POURI?
I THINK I HAVE AN IDEA.

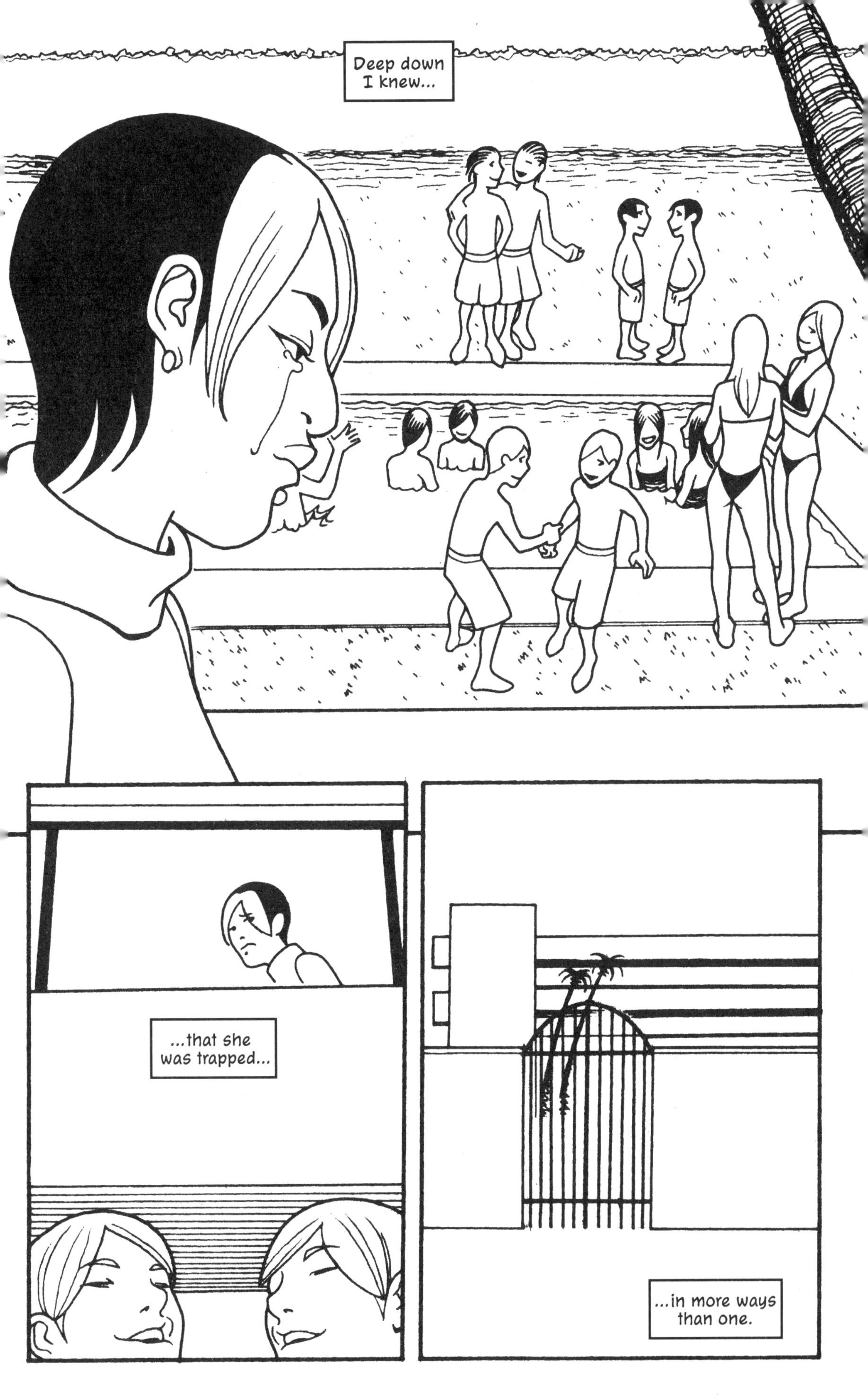
Deep down I knew...
...that she was trapped...
...in more ways than one.

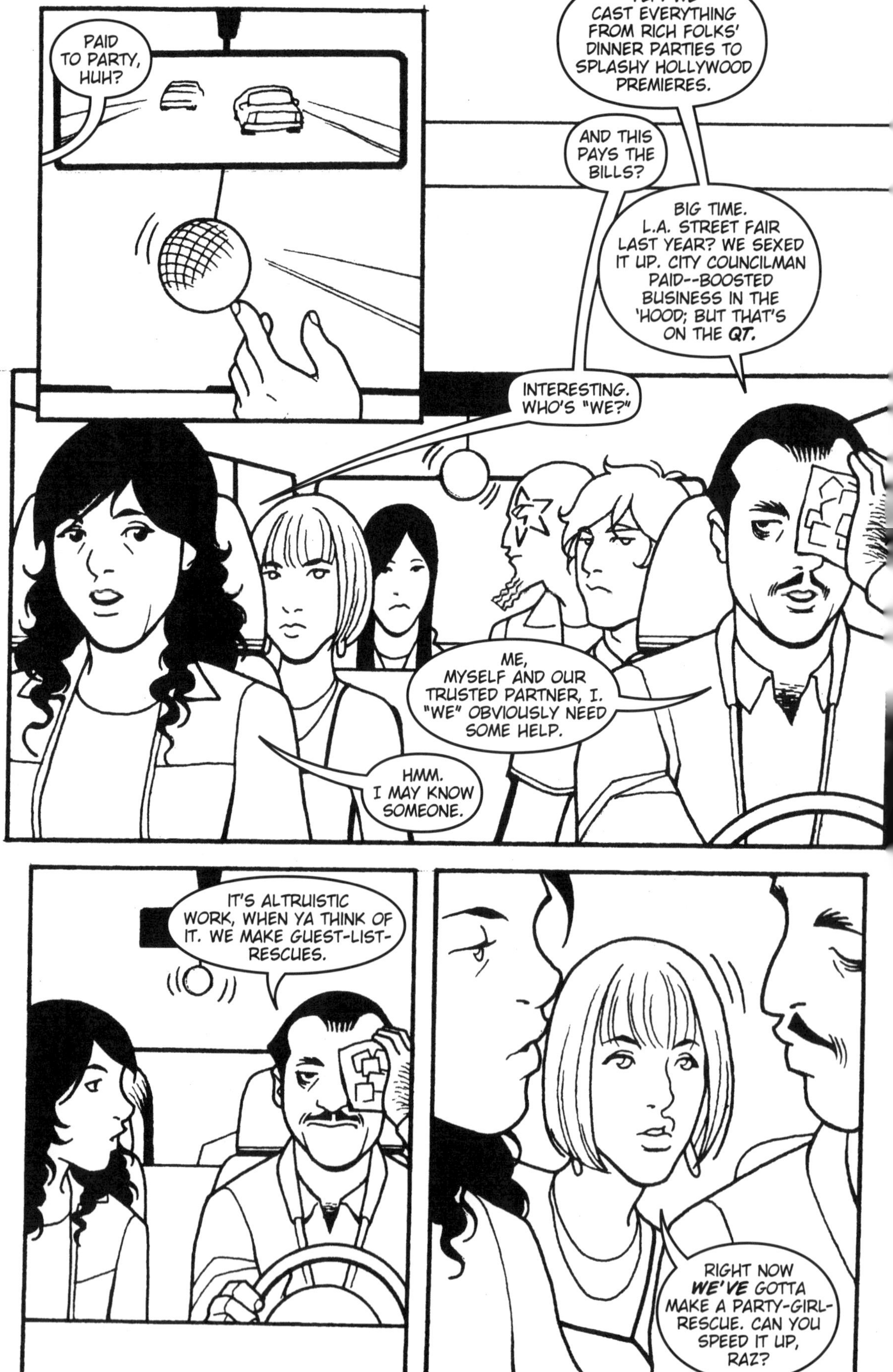
PAID TO PARTY, HUH?
YEP. WE CAST EVERYTHING FROM RICH FOLKS' DINNER PARTIES TO SPLASHY HOLLYWOOD PREMIERES.
AND THIS PAYS THE BILLS?
BIG TIME. L.A. STREET FAIR LAST YEAR? WE SEXED IT UP. CITY COUNCILMAN PAID--BOOSTED BUSINESS IN THE 'HOOD; BUT THAT'S ON THE **QT.**
INTERESTING. WHO'S "WE?"
ME, MYSELF AND OUR TRUSTED PARTNER, I. "WE" OBVIOUSLY NEED SOME HELP.
HMM. I MAY KNOW SOMEONE.
IT'S ALTRUISTIC WORK, WHEN YA THINK OF IT. WE MAKE GUEST-LIST-RESCUES.
RIGHT NOW ***WE'VE*** GOTTA MAKE A PARTY-GIRL-RESCUE. CAN YOU SPEED IT UP, RAZ?

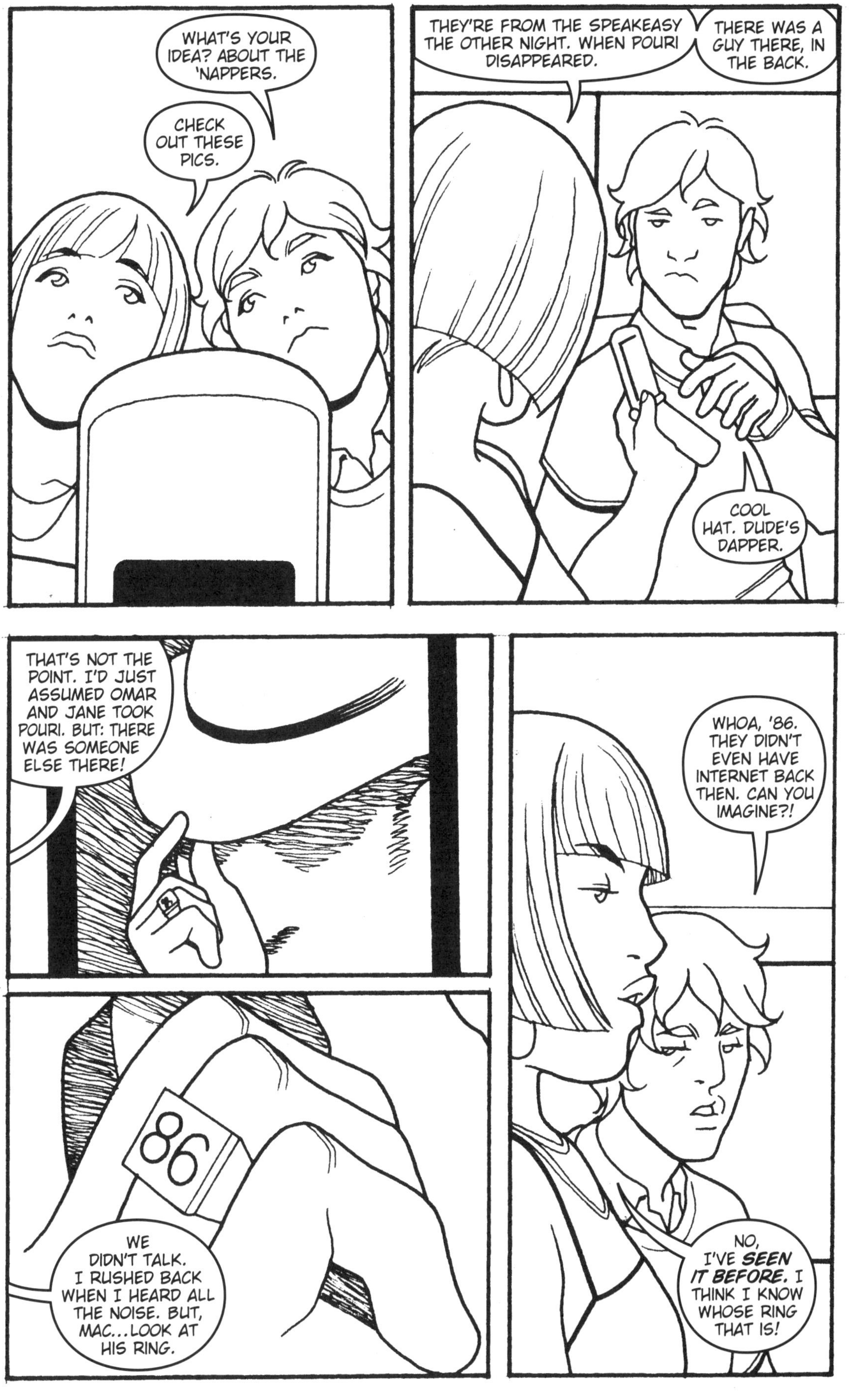

WHAT'S YOUR IDEA? ABOUT THE 'NAPPERS.
CHECK OUT THESE PICS.
THEY'RE FROM THE SPEAKEASY THE OTHER NIGHT. WHEN POURI DISAPPEARED.
THERE WAS A GUY THERE, IN THE BACK.
COOL HAT. DUDE'S DAPPER.
THAT'S NOT THE POINT. I'D JUST ASSUMED OMAR AND JANE TOOK POURI. BUT: THERE WAS SOMEONE ELSE THERE!
86
WE DIDN'T TALK. I RUSHED BACK WHEN I HEARD ALL THE NOISE. BUT, MAC...LOOK AT HIS RING.
WHOA, '86. THEY DIDN'T EVEN HAVE INTERNET BACK THEN. CAN YOU IMAGINE?!
NO, I'VE ***SEEN IT BEFORE.*** I THINK I KNOW WHOSE RING THAT IS!

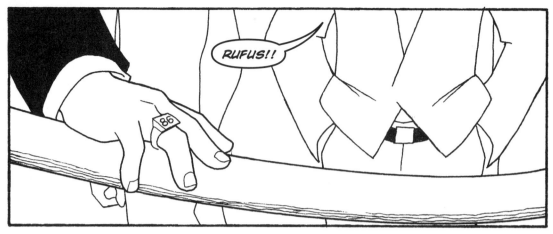

RUFUS!!

RUFUS, YOU'RE A PARTY PROMOTER. STOP STAR-F***ING AND PROMOTE!

YO, I'Z JUST TRYING T' GET AN AUTOGRAPH.

WELL, GET BACK TO WORK. SECURITY'S TIGHTER THAN--

BUT I WORKED ON THIS FILM!

SORRY, INVITES ONLY. WE'RE AT 1,000% CAPACITY.

BUT I WAS THE ASSISTANT! TO THE AGENT! WHO REPPED THE CATERER!

SORRY, MISS. YOU'RE NOT ON THE LIST, YOU DON'T EXIST.

DAMN. HARSH.

IT'S A-LIST-ONLY TONIGHT. LIKE, THOSE "PARTY TOURISTS" OVER THERE...?

...THEY DON'T STAND A CHANCE.

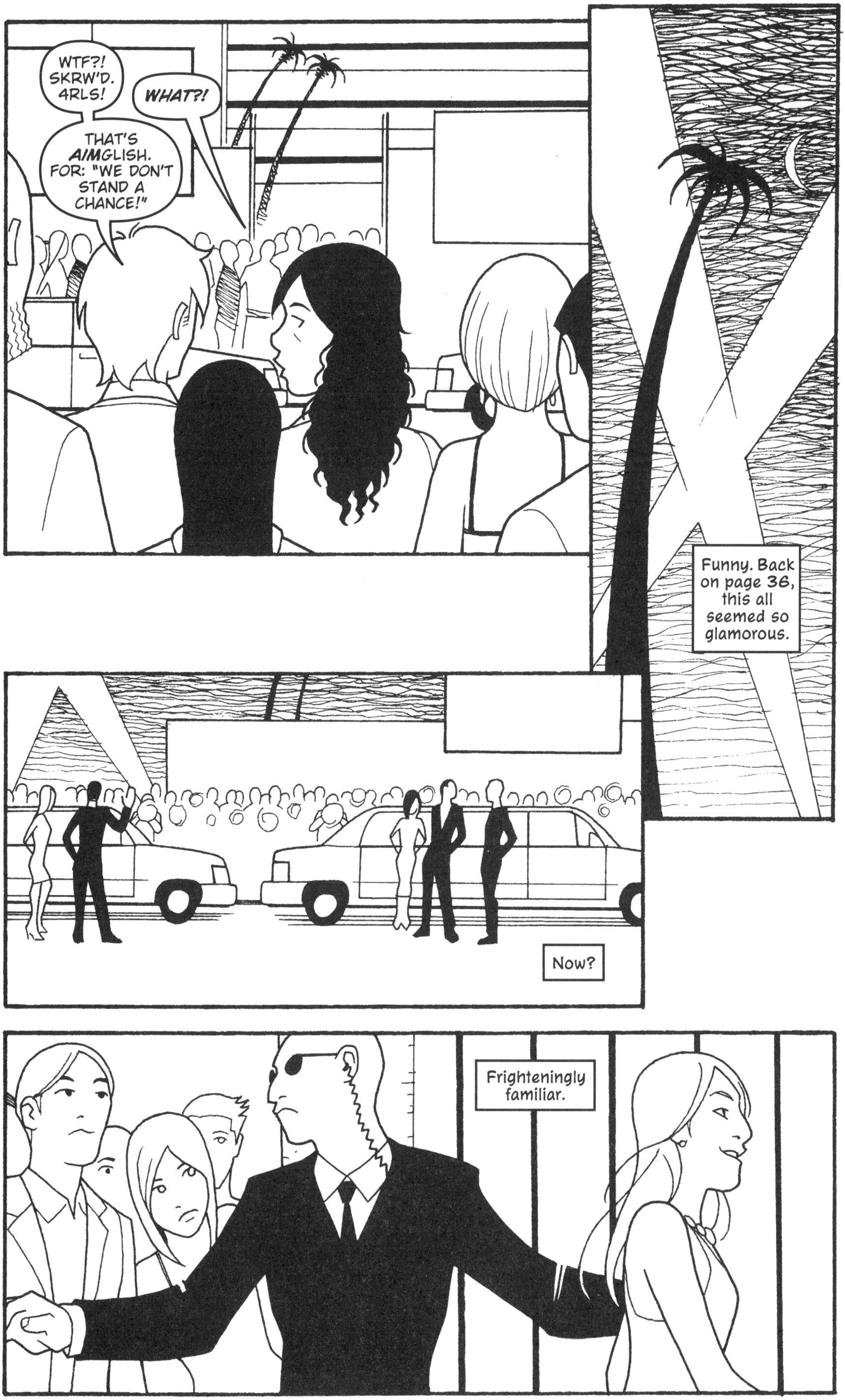
WTF?! SKRW'D. 4RLS!
WHAT?!
THAT'S AIMGLISH. FOR: "WE DON'T STAND A CHANCE!"
Funny. Back on page 36, this all seemed so glamorous.
Now?
Frighteningly familiar.

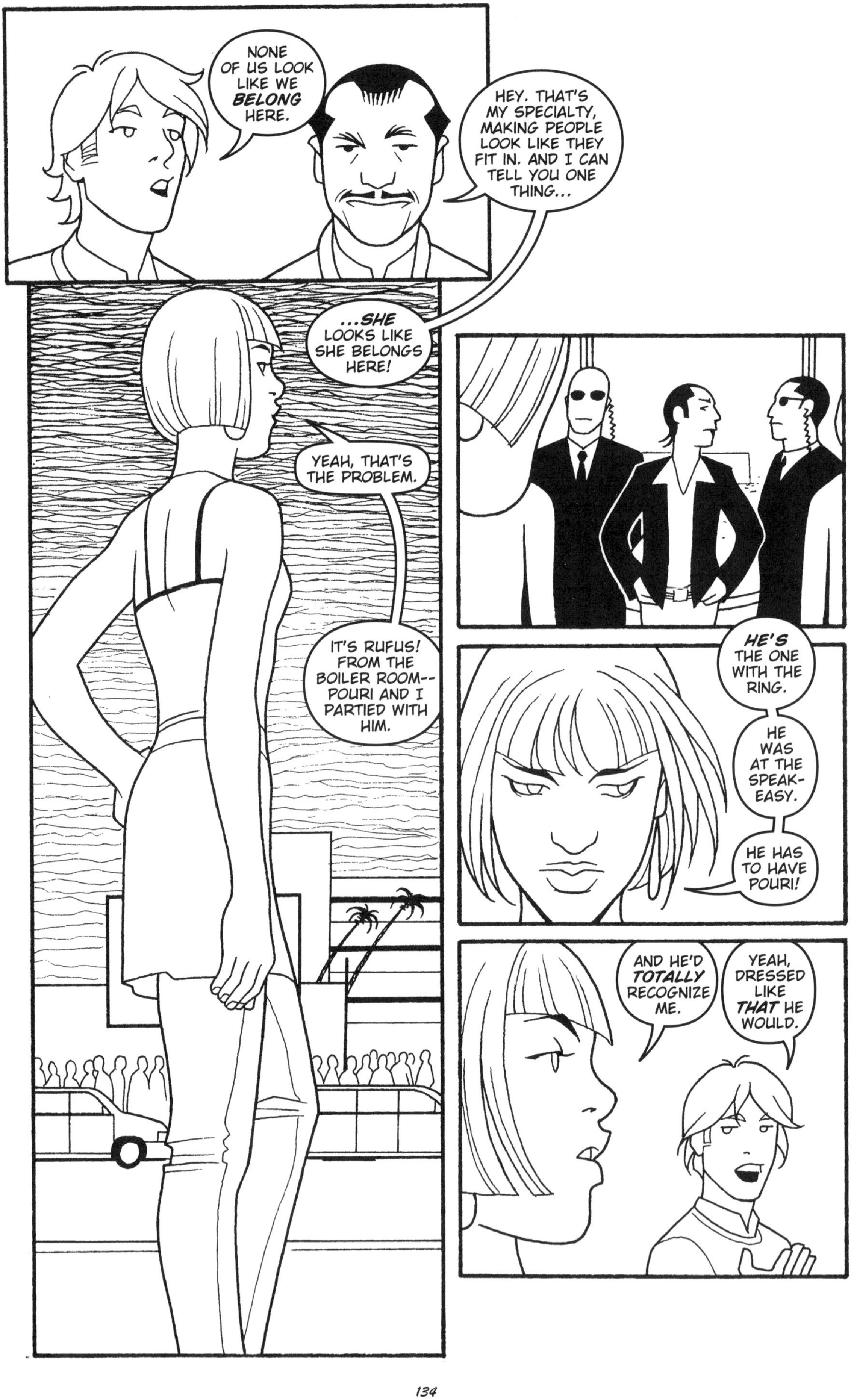
NONE OF US LOOK LIKE WE BELONG HERE.
HEY. THAT'S MY SPECIALTY, MAKING PEOPLE LOOK LIKE THEY FIT IN. AND I CAN TELL YOU ONE THING...
...SHE LOOKS LIKE SHE BELONGS HERE!
YEAH, THAT'S THE PROBLEM.
IT'S RUFUS! FROM THE BOILER ROOM-- POURI AND I PARTIED WITH HIM.
HE'S THE ONE WITH THE RING.
HE WAS AT THE SPEAK-EASY.
HE HAS TO HAVE POURI!
AND HE'D TOTALLY RECOGNIZE ME.
YEAH, DRESSED LIKE THAT HE WOULD.

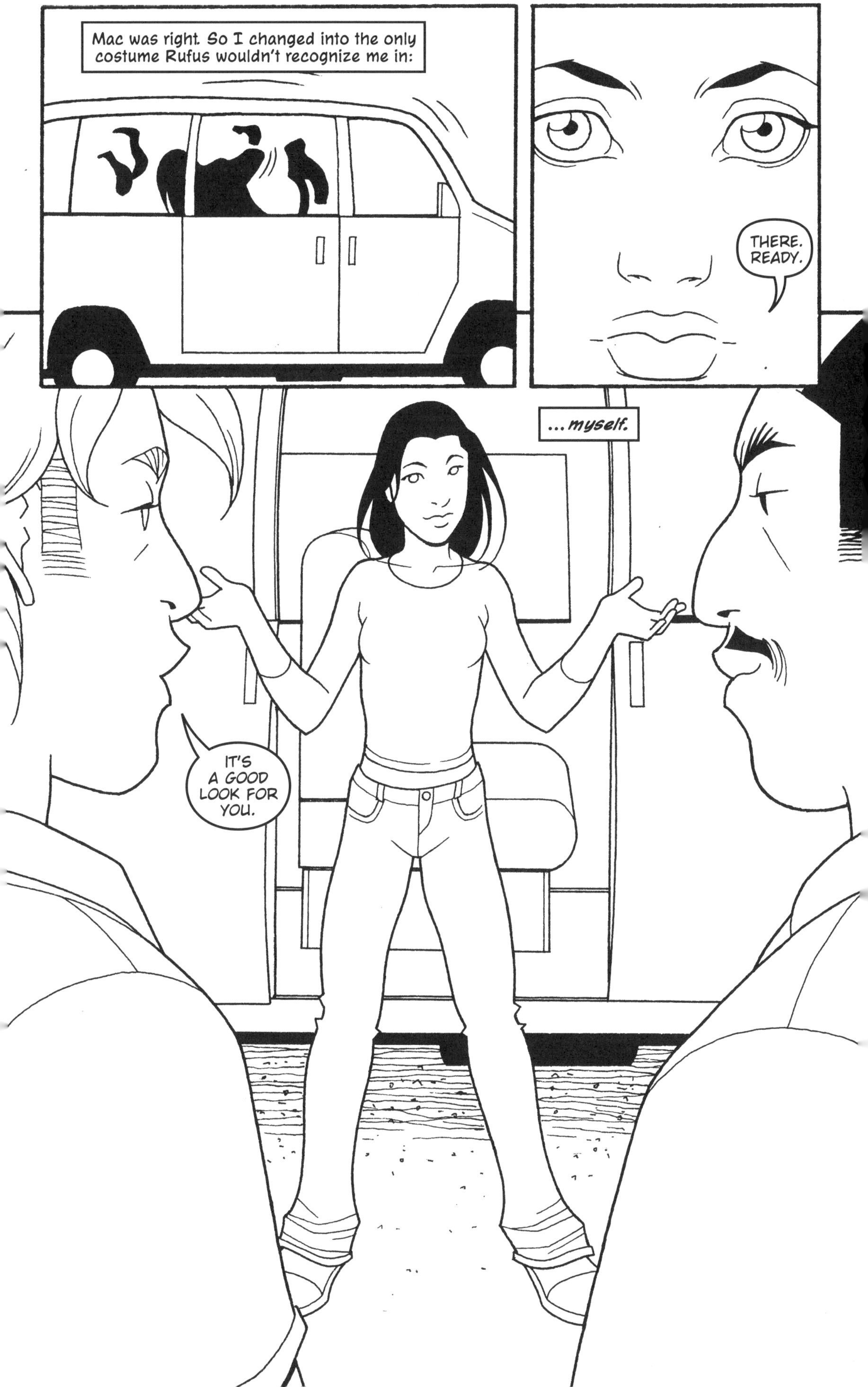

Mac was right. So I changed into the only costume Rufus wouldn't recognize me in:
THERE. READY.
...myself.
IT'S A GOOD LOOK FOR YOU.

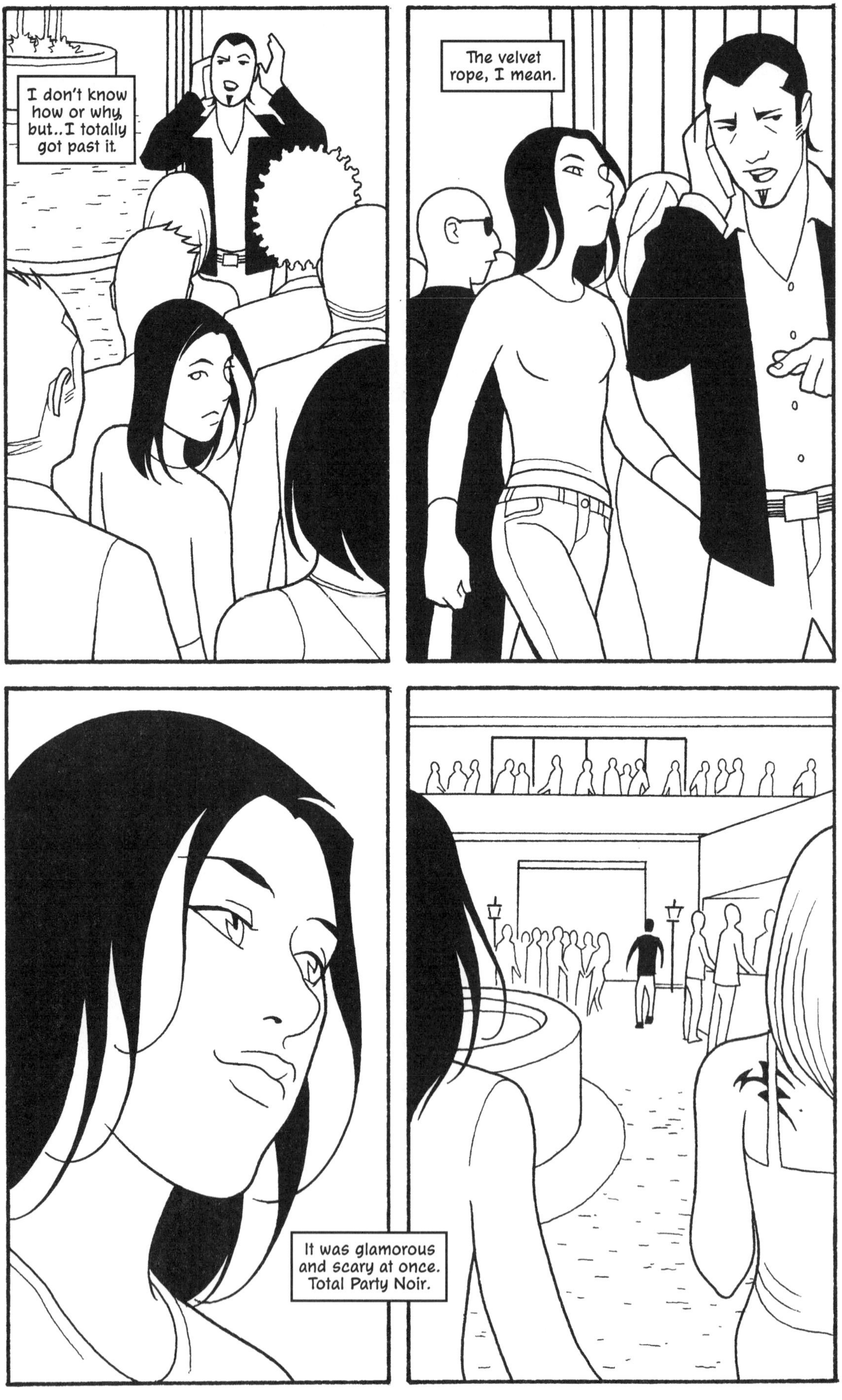
I don't know how or why, but..I totally got past it.
The velvet rope, I mean.
It was glamorous and scary at once. Total Party Noir.

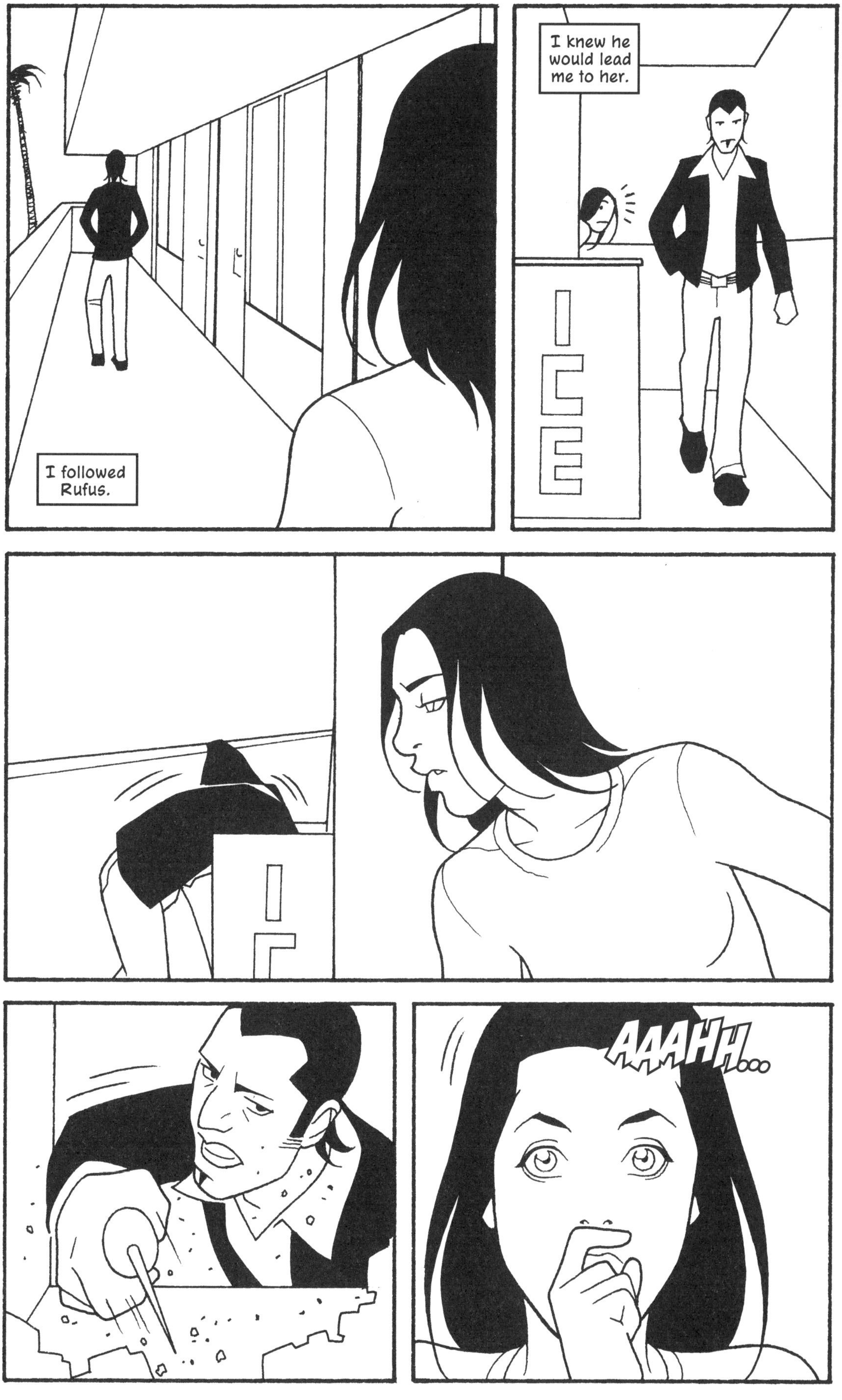

I followed Rufus.
I knew he would lead me to her.
ICE
AAAHH...

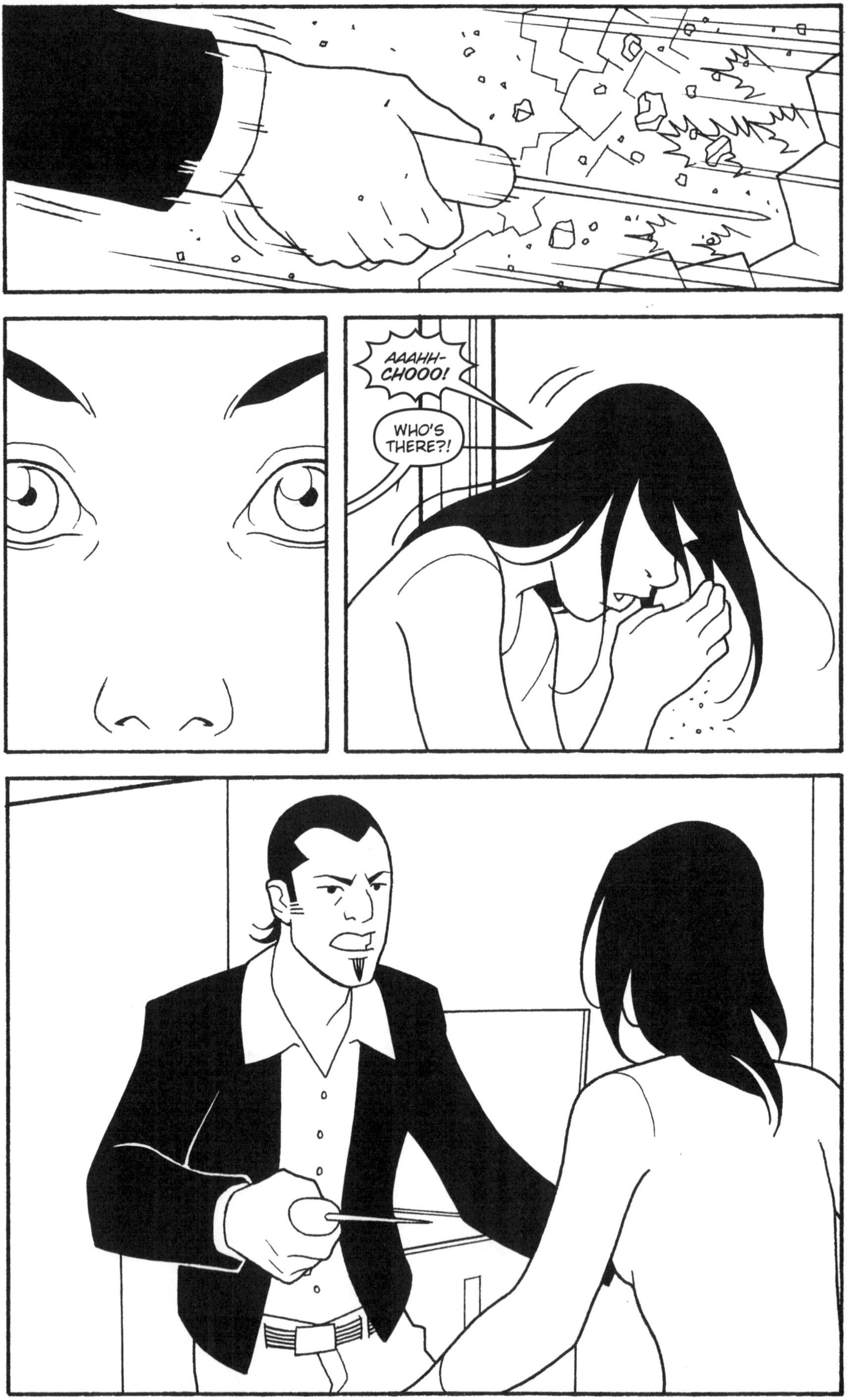
AAAHH-CHOOO!
WHO'S THERE?!

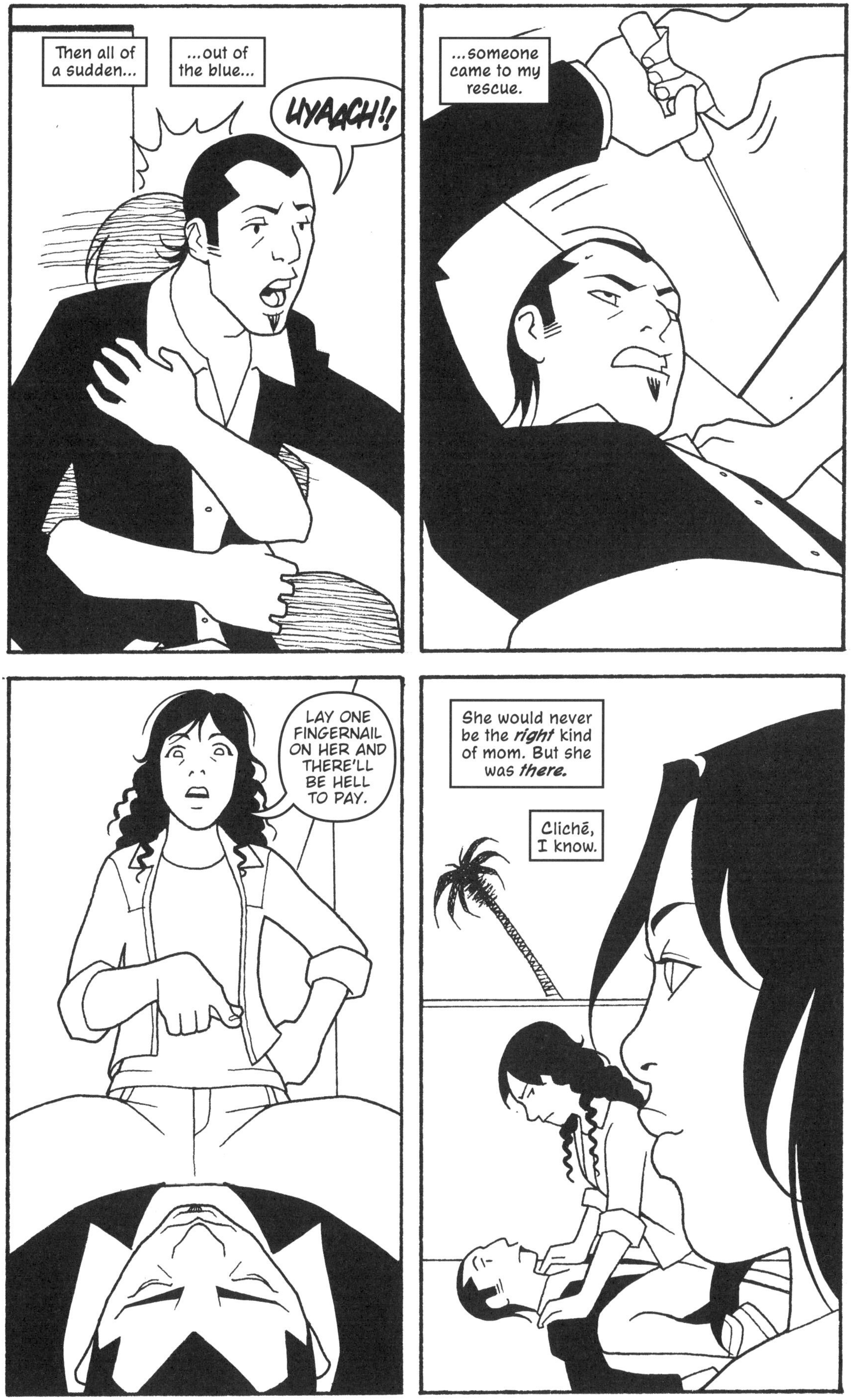
Then all of a sudden...
...out of the blue...
UYAACH!!
...someone came to my rescue.
LAY ONE FINGERNAIL ON HER AND THERE'LL BE HELL TO PAY.
She would never be the *right* kind of mom. But she was *there.*
Cliché, I know.

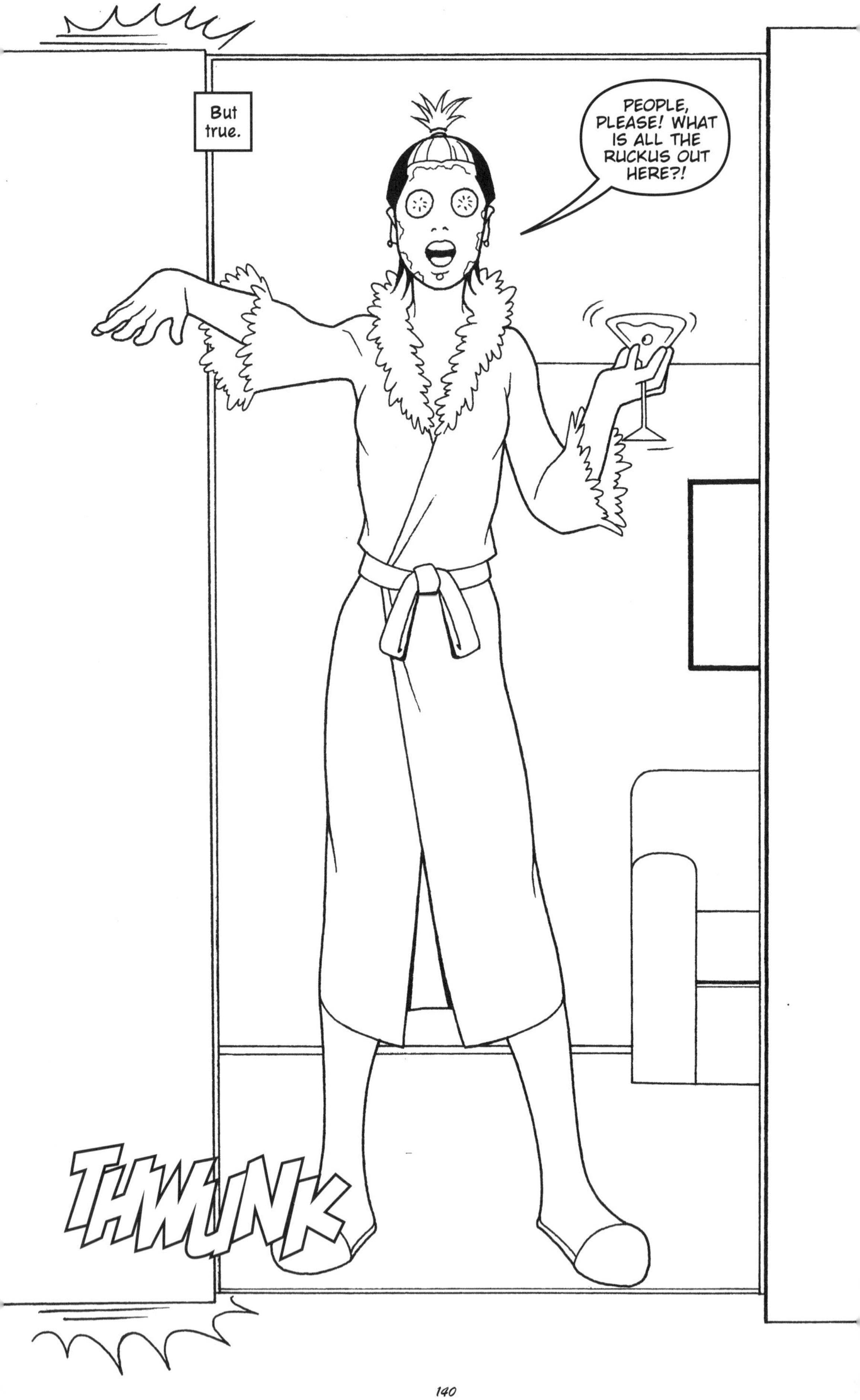
But true.
PEOPLE, PLEASE! WHAT IS ALL THE RUCKUS OUT HERE?!
THWUNK

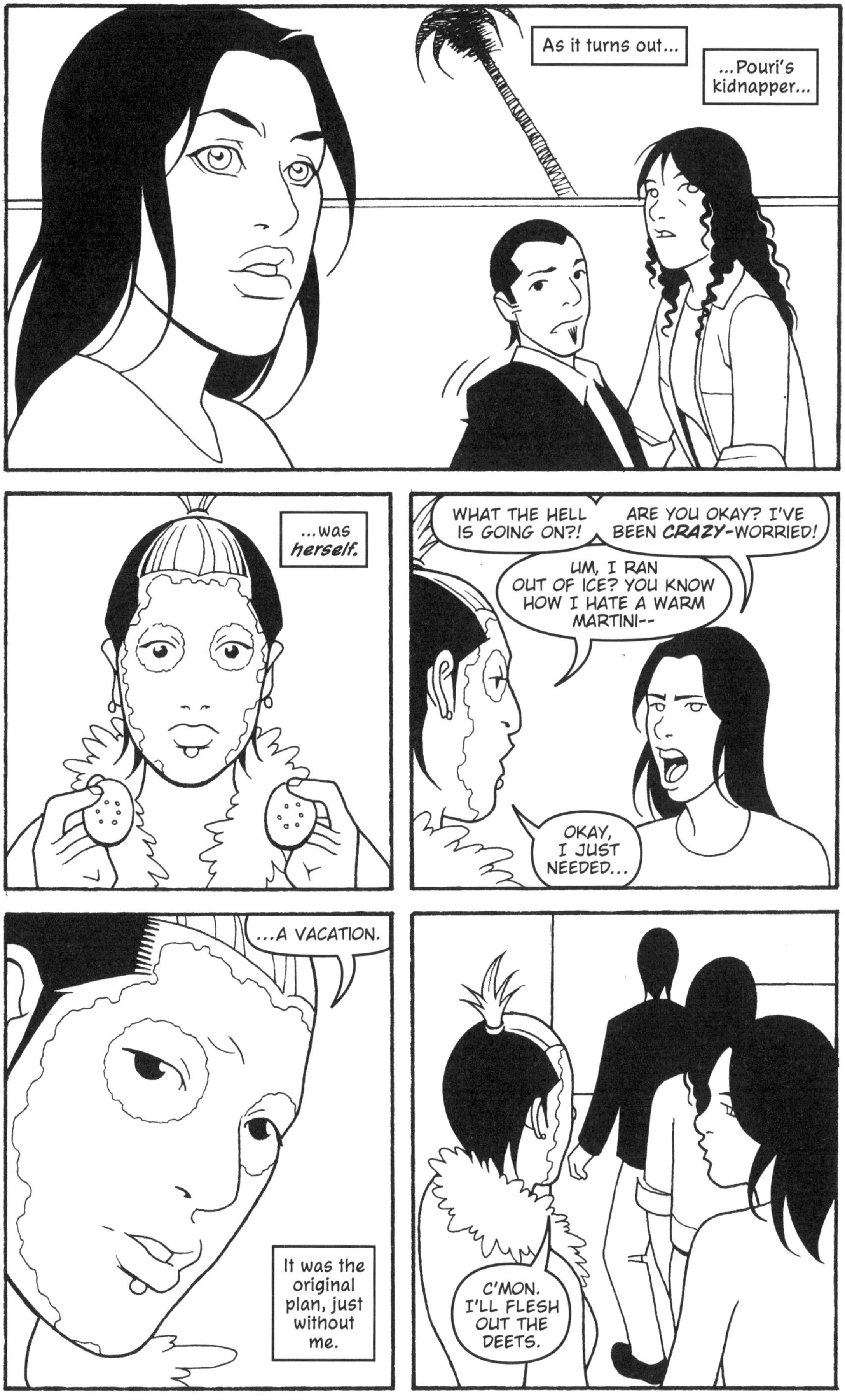
As it turns out...
...Pouri's kidnapper...
...was *herself.*
WHAT THE HELL IS GOING ON?!
ARE YOU OKAY? I'VE BEEN *CRAZY*-WORRIED!
UM, I RAN OUT OF ICE? YOU KNOW HOW I HATE A WARM MARTINI--
OKAY, I JUST NEEDED...
...A VACATION.
It was the original plan, just without me.
C'MON. I'LL FLESH OUT THE DEETS.

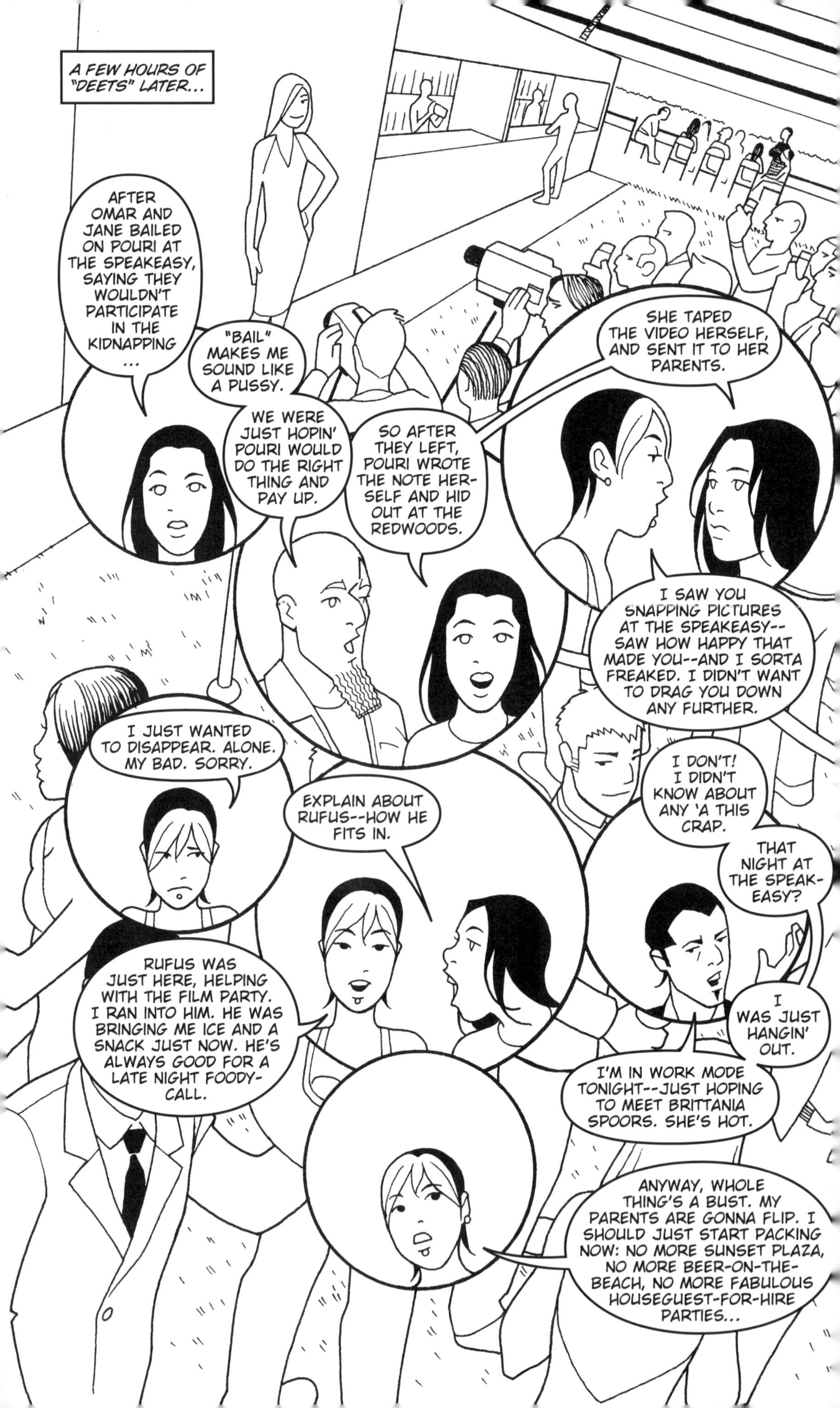
A FEW HOURS OF "DEETS" LATER...
AFTER OMAR AND JANE BAILED ON POURI AT THE SPEAKEASY, SAYING THEY WOULDN'T PARTICIPATE IN THE KIDNAPPING ...
"BAIL" MAKES ME SOUND LIKE A PUSSY.
WE WERE JUST HOPIN' POURI WOULD DO THE RIGHT THING AND PAY UP.
SO AFTER THEY LEFT, POURI WROTE THE NOTE HER-SELF AND HID OUT AT THE REDWOODS.
SHE TAPED THE VIDEO HERSELF, AND SENT IT TO HER PARENTS.
I SAW YOU SNAPPING PICTURES AT THE SPEAKEASY--SAW HOW HAPPY THAT MADE YOU--AND I SORTA FREAKED. I DIDN'T WANT TO DRAG YOU DOWN ANY FURTHER.
I JUST WANTED TO DISAPPEAR. ALONE. MY BAD. SORRY.
EXPLAIN ABOUT RUFUS--HOW HE FITS IN.
I DON'T! I DIDN'T KNOW ABOUT ANY 'A THIS CRAP.
THAT NIGHT AT THE SPEAK-EASY?
RUFUS WAS JUST HERE, HELPING WITH THE FILM PARTY. I RAN INTO HIM. HE WAS BRINGING ME ICE AND A SNACK JUST NOW. HE'S ALWAYS GOOD FOR A LATE NIGHT FOODY-CALL.
I WAS JUST HANGIN' OUT.
I'M IN WORK MODE TONIGHT--JUST HOPING TO MEET BRITTANIA SPOORS. SHE'S HOT.
ANYWAY, WHOLE THING'S A BUST. MY PARENTS ARE GONNA FLIP. I SHOULD JUST START PACKING NOW: NO MORE SUNSET PLAZA, NO MORE BEER-ON-THE-BEACH, NO MORE FABULOUS HOUSEGUEST-FOR-HIRE PARTIES...

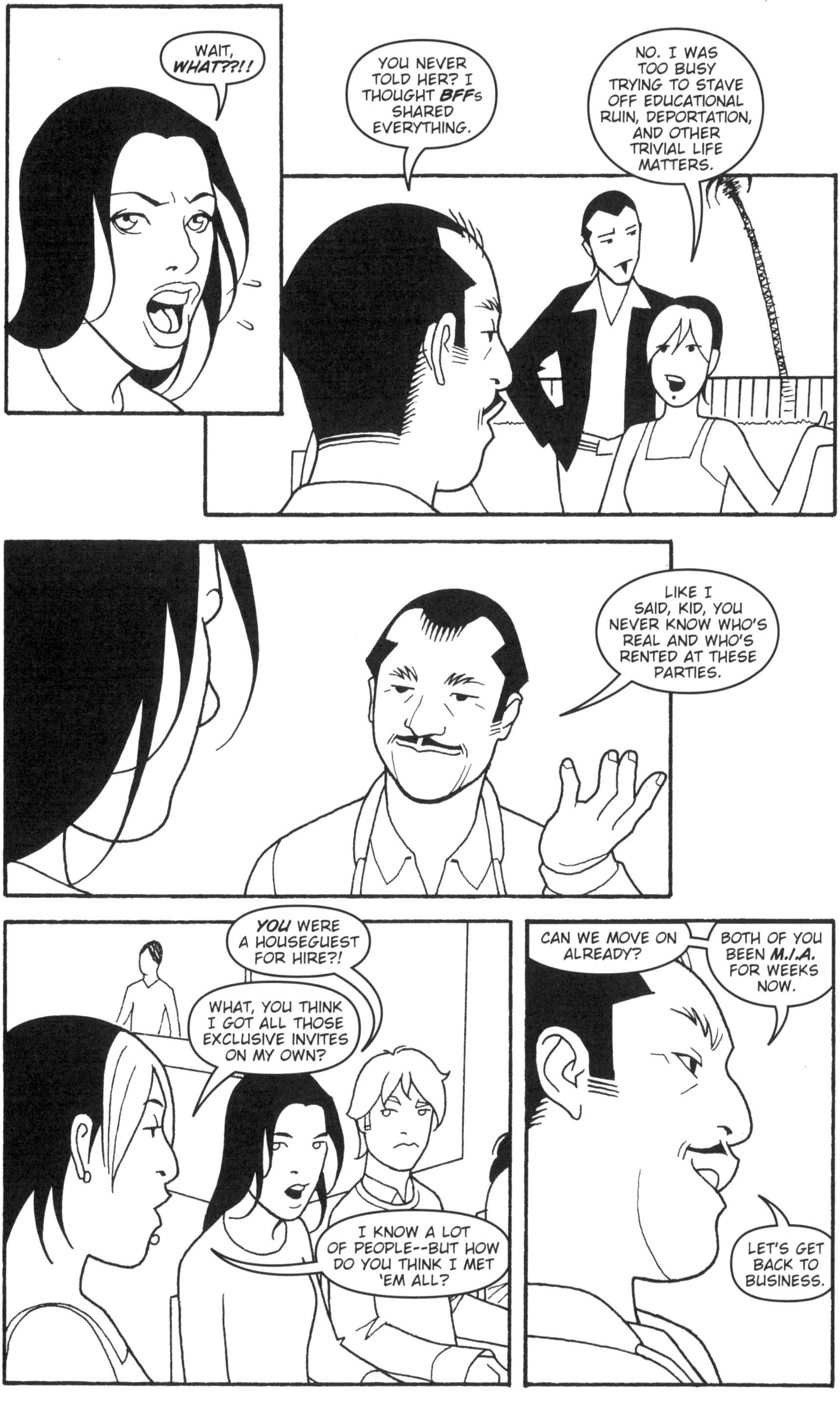
WAIT, WHAT??!!
YOU NEVER TOLD HER? I THOUGHT BFFs SHARED EVERYTHING.
NO. I WAS TOO BUSY TRYING TO STAVE OFF EDUCATIONAL RUIN, DEPORTATION, AND OTHER TRIVIAL LIFE MATTERS.
LIKE I SAID, KID, YOU NEVER KNOW WHO'S REAL AND WHO'S RENTED AT THESE PARTIES.
YOU WERE A HOUSEGUEST FOR HIRE?!
WHAT, YOU THINK I GOT ALL THOSE EXCLUSIVE INVITES ON MY OWN?
I KNOW A LOT OF PEOPLE--BUT HOW DO YOU THINK I MET 'EM ALL?
CAN WE MOVE ON ALREADY?
BOTH OF YOU BEEN M.I.A. FOR WEEKS NOW.
LET'S GET BACK TO BUSINESS.

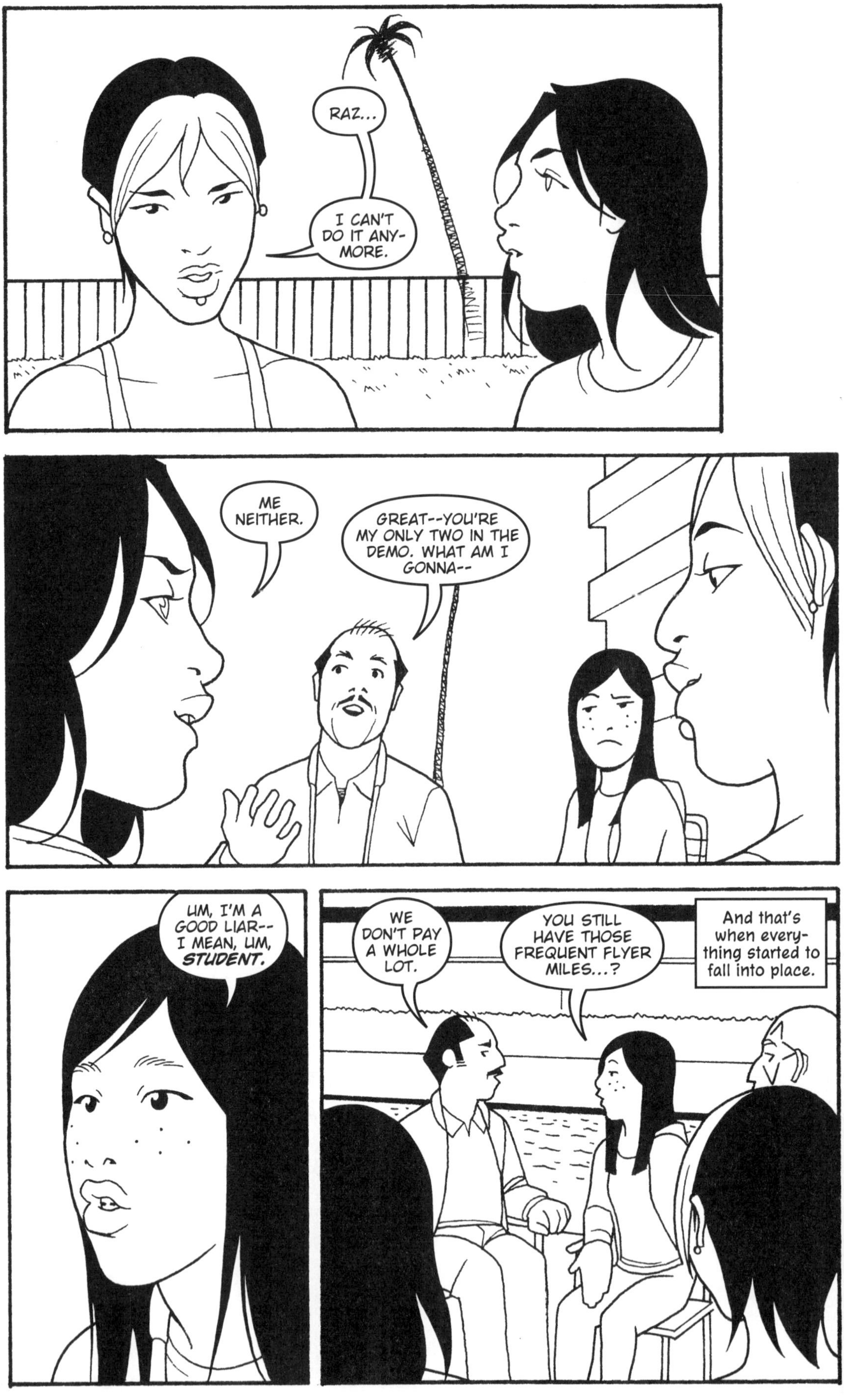
RAZ...
I CAN'T DO IT ANY-MORE.
ME NEITHER.
GREAT--YOU'RE MY ONLY TWO IN THE DEMO. WHAT AM I GONNA--
UM, I'M A GOOD LIAR-- I MEAN, UM, *STUDENT.*
WE DON'T PAY A WHOLE LOT.
YOU STILL HAVE THOSE FREQUENT FLYER MILES...?
And that's when every-thing started to fall into place.

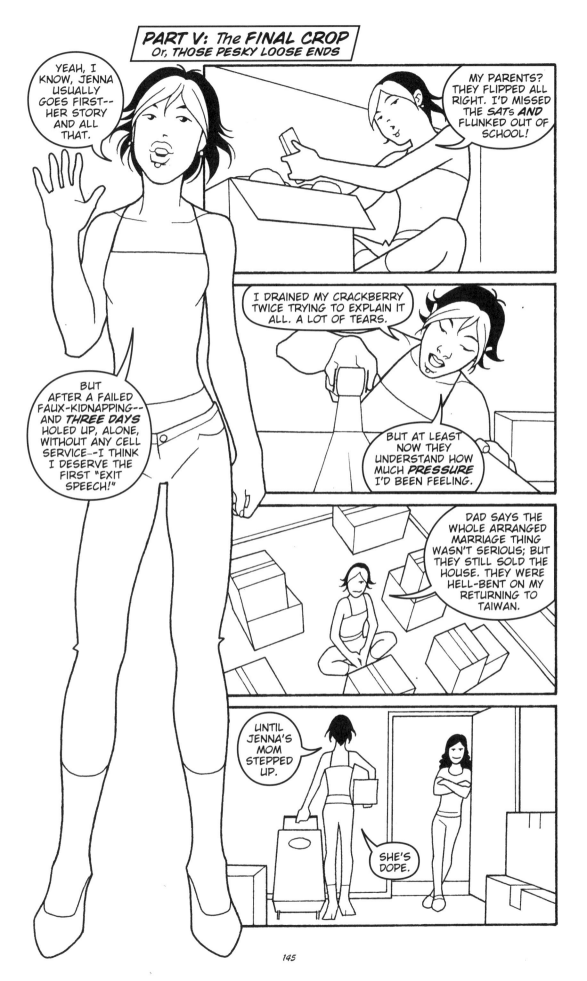

PART V: The FINAL CROP
Or, THOSE PESKY LOOSE ENDS

YEAH, I KNOW, JENNA USUALLY GOES FIRST-- HER STORY AND ALL THAT.

MY PARENTS? THEY FLIPPED ALL RIGHT. I'D MISSED THE SATs AND FLUNKED OUT OF SCHOOL!

I DRAINED MY CRACKBERRY TWICE TRYING TO EXPLAIN IT ALL. A LOT OF TEARS.

BUT AFTER A FAILED FAUX-KIDNAPPING-- AND THREE DAYS HOLED UP, ALONE, WITHOUT ANY CELL SERVICE--I THINK I DESERVE THE FIRST "EXIT SPEECH!"

BUT AT LEAST NOW THEY UNDERSTAND HOW MUCH PRESSURE I'D BEEN FEELING.

DAD SAYS THE WHOLE ARRANGED MARRIAGE THING WASN'T SERIOUS; BUT THEY STILL SOLD THE HOUSE. THEY WERE HELL-BENT ON MY RETURNING TO TAIWAN.

UNTIL JENNA'S MOM STEPPED UP.

SHE'S DOPE.

145

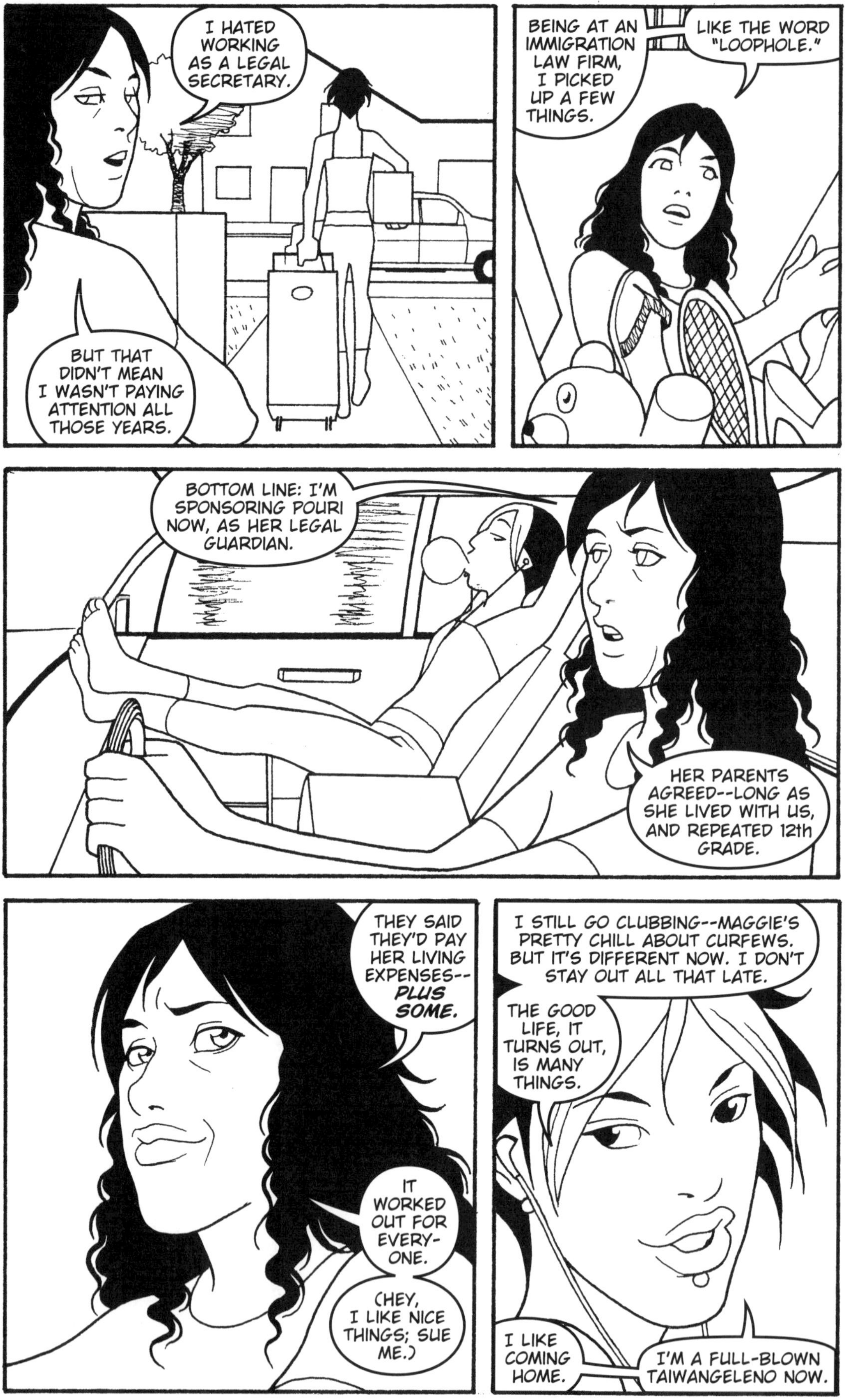
I HATED WORKING AS A LEGAL SECRETARY.
BUT THAT DIDN'T MEAN I WASN'T PAYING ATTENTION ALL THOSE YEARS.
BEING AT AN IMMIGRATION LAW FIRM, I PICKED UP A FEW THINGS.
LIKE THE WORD "LOOPHOLE."
BOTTOM LINE: I'M SPONSORING POURI NOW, AS HER LEGAL GUARDIAN.
HER PARENTS AGREED--LONG AS SHE LIVED WITH US, AND REPEATED 12th GRADE.
THEY SAID THEY'D PAY HER LIVING EXPENSES-- ***PLUS SOME.***
IT WORKED OUT FOR EVERY-ONE.
(HEY, I LIKE NICE THINGS; SUE ME.)
I STILL GO CLUBBING--MAGGIE'S PRETTY CHILL ABOUT CURFEWS. BUT IT'S DIFFERENT NOW. I DON'T STAY OUT ALL THAT LATE.
THE GOOD LIFE, IT TURNS OUT, IS MANY THINGS.
I LIKE COMING HOME.
I'M A FULL-BLOWN TAIWANGELENO NOW.

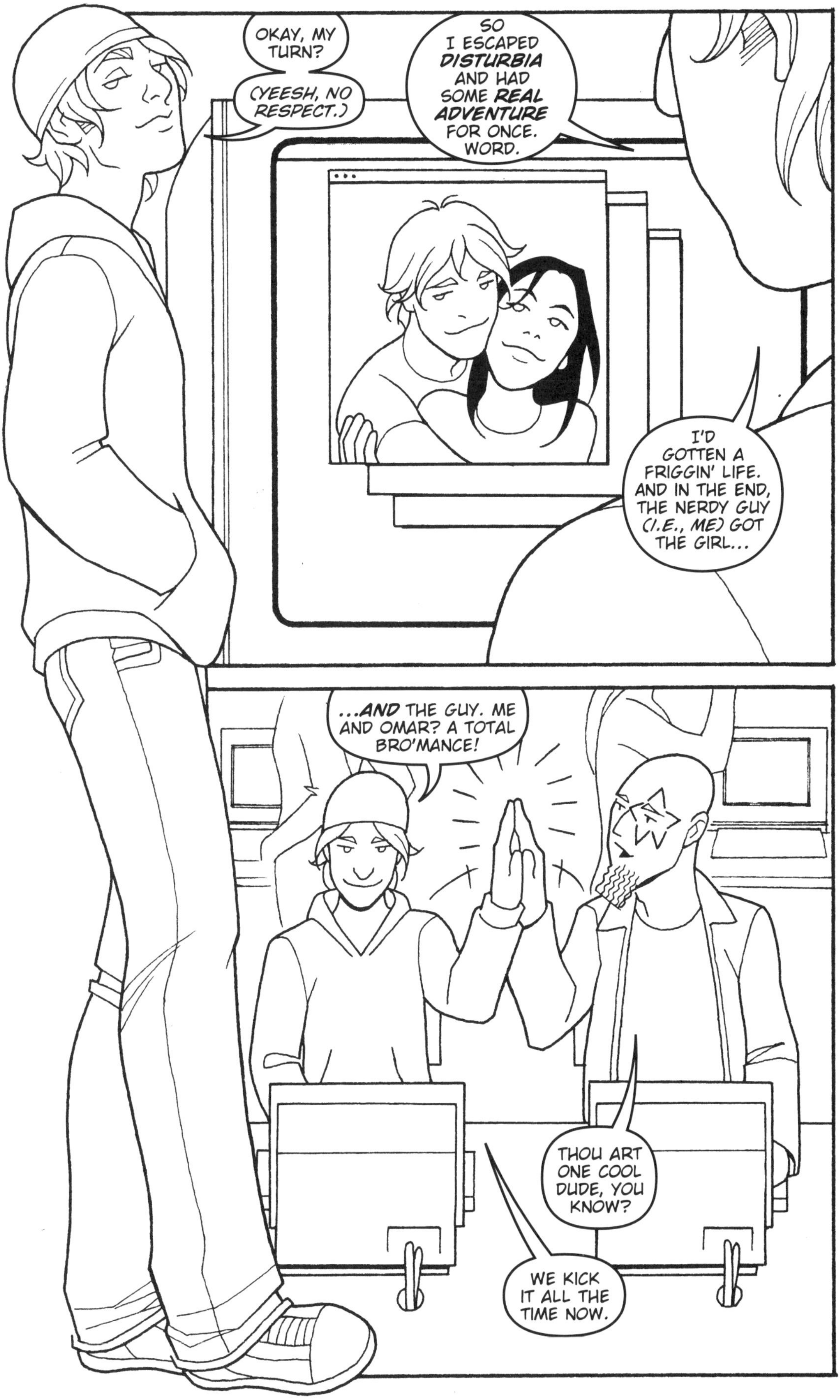
OKAY, MY TURN?
(YEESH, NO RESPECT.)
SO I ESCAPED **DISTURBIA** AND HAD SOME **REAL ADVENTURE** FOR ONCE. WORD.
I'D GOTTEN A FRIGGIN' LIFE. AND IN THE END, THE NERDY GUY (I.E., ME) GOT THE GIRL...
...**AND** THE GUY. ME AND OMAR? A TOTAL BRO'MANCE!
THOU ART ONE COOL DUDE, YOU KNOW?
WE KICK IT ALL THE TIME NOW.

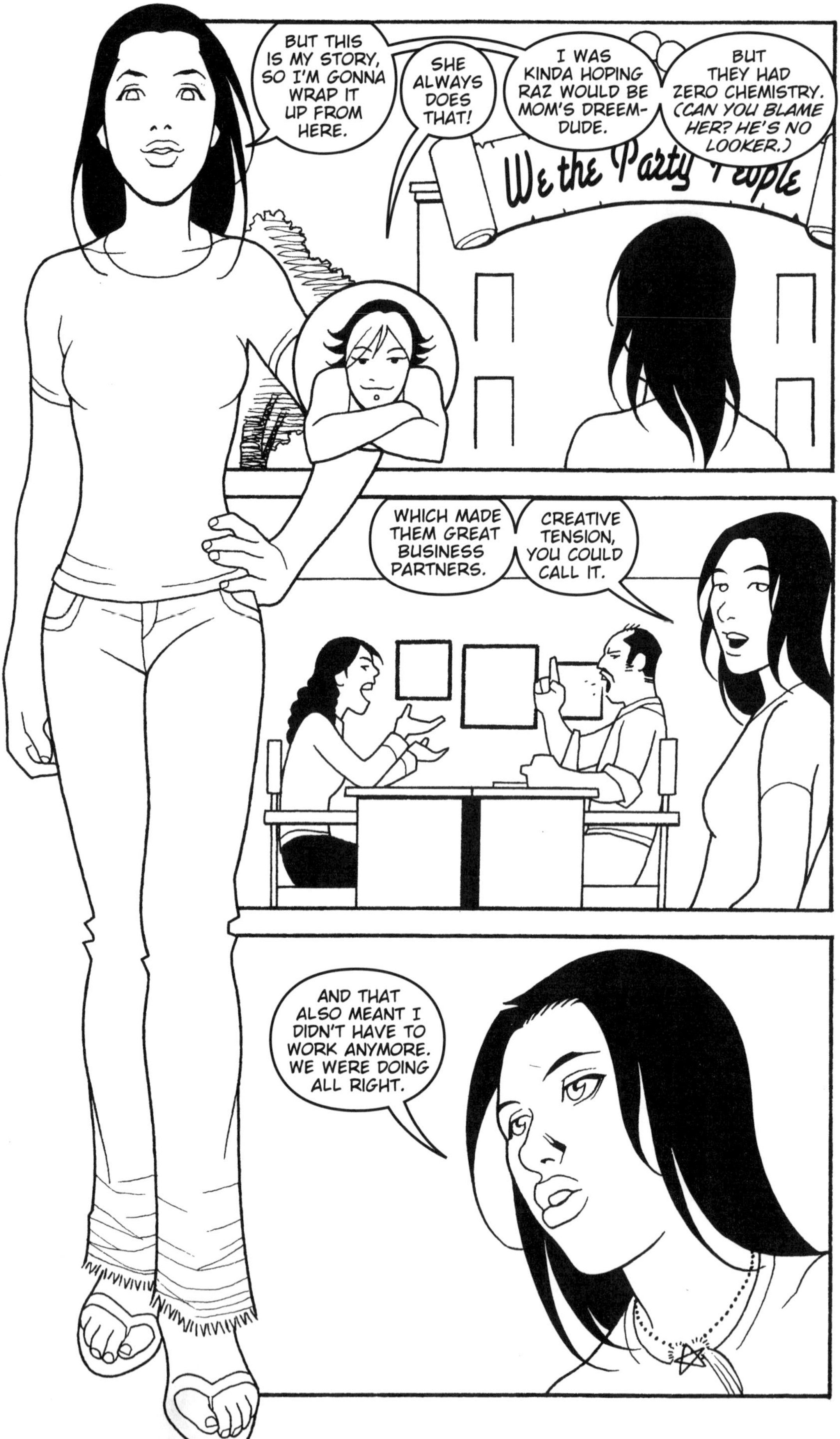
BUT THIS IS MY STORY, SO I'M GONNA WRAP IT UP FROM HERE.
SHE ALWAYS DOES THAT!
I WAS KINDA HOPING RAZ WOULD BE MOM'S DREEM-DUDE.
BUT THEY HAD ZERO CHEMISTRY. (CAN YOU BLAME HER? HE'S NO LOOKER.)
WHICH MADE THEM GREAT BUSINESS PARTNERS.
CREATIVE TENSION, YOU COULD CALL IT.
AND THAT ALSO MEANT I DIDN'T HAVE TO WORK ANYMORE. WE WERE DOING ALL RIGHT.

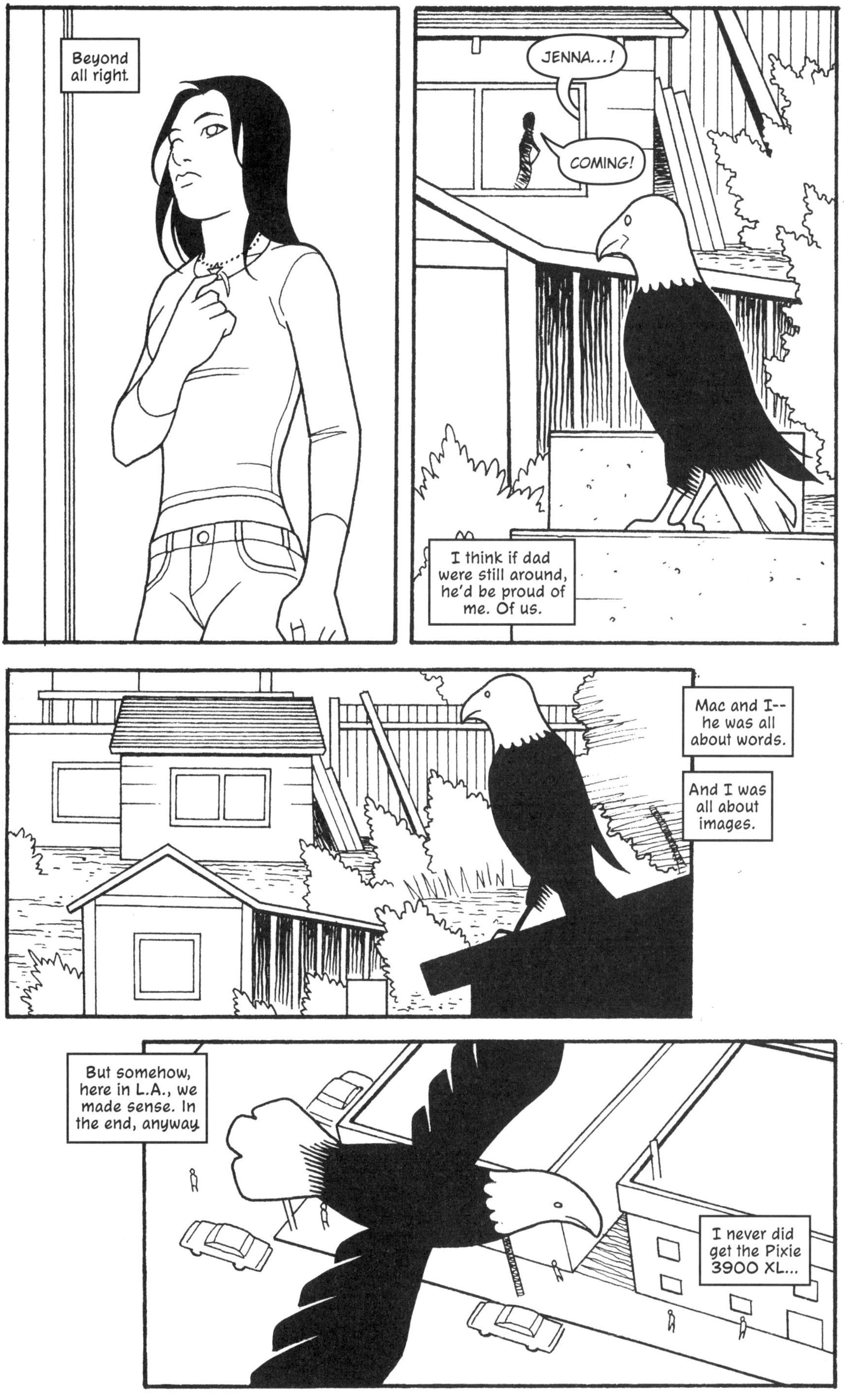

Beyond all right.
JENNA...!
COMING!
I think if dad were still around, he'd be proud of me. Of us.
Mac and I-- he was all about words.
And I was all about images.
But somehow, here in L.A., we made sense. In the end, anyway.
I never did get the Pixie 3900 XL...

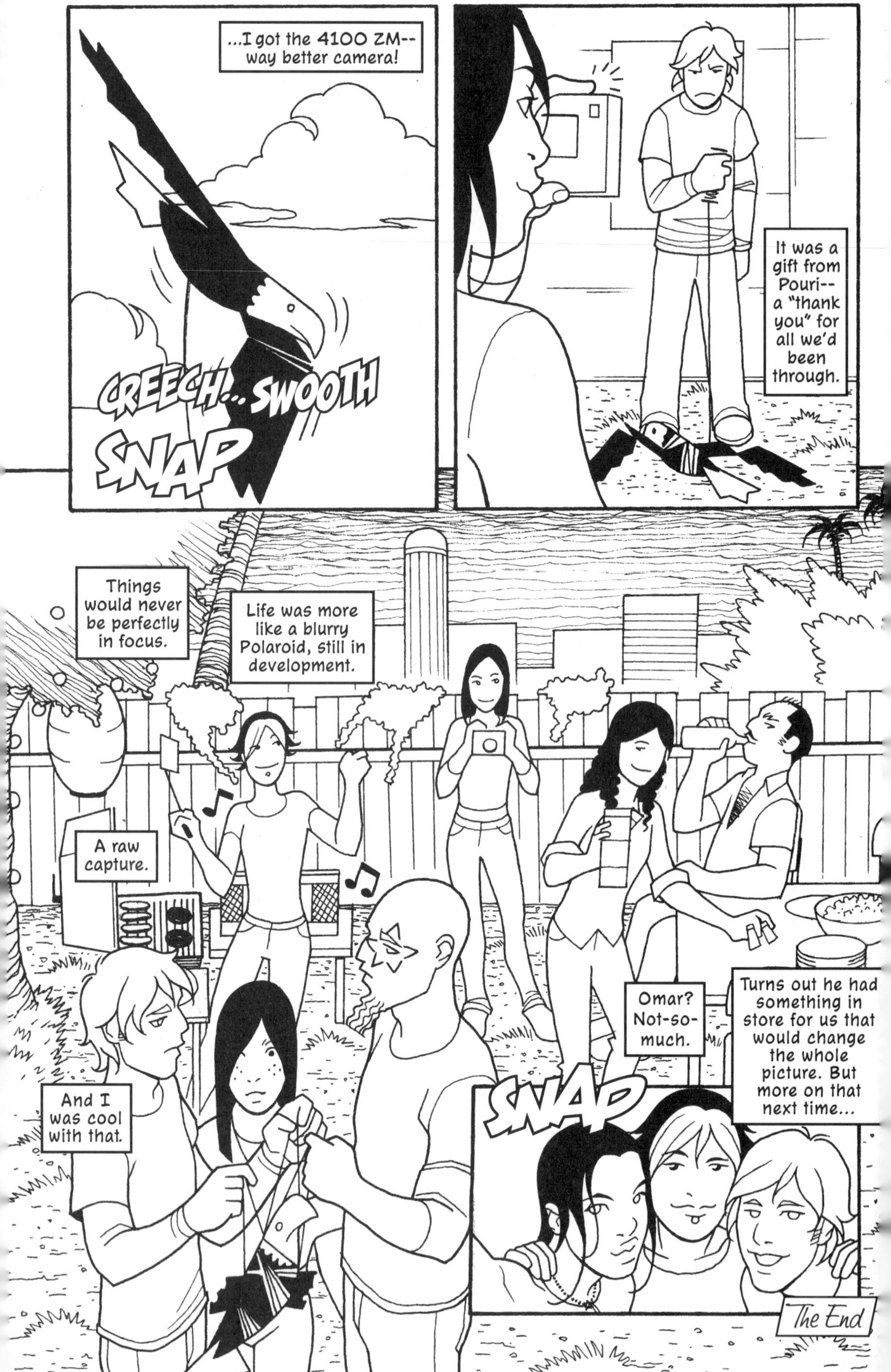
...I got the 4100 ZM--
way better camera!
CREECH... SWOOTH
SNAP
It was a gift from Pouri-- a "thank you" for all we'd been through.
Things would never be perfectly in focus.
Life was more like a blurry Polaroid, still in development.
A raw capture.
Omar? Not-so-much.
Turns out he had something in store for us that would change the whole picture. But more on that next time...
SNAP
And I was cool with that.
The End